TI

THE WAY THAIS LEAD
Face as Social Capital

Larry S. Persons

Silkworm Books

ISBN: 978-616-215-116-3

First published in 2016 by
Silkworm Books
430/58 Soi Ratchaphruek, M. 7, T. Mae Hia, A. Mueang Chiang Mai, Thailand 50100
info@silkwormbooks.com
www.silkwormbooks.com

Typeset in Minion Pro 10 pt. by Silk Type

Printed in Thailand by O.S. Printing House, Bangkok

5 4 3 2

CONTENTS

PART 3: REIMAGINING FACE

ACKNOWLEDGMENTS

DECADES OF SOAKING IN a Thai worldview have granted me many treasures, but none so precious as the lesson of gratitude. I have learned that nothing valuable or praiseworthy is ever achieved alone, and many of my debts, happily, will endure for a lifetime.

One of my greatest debts is to the dozens of Thai informants whose words gave birth and shape to the findings in this book. You taught me more than I ever imagined I could learn. I am delighted to give you voice.

I thank Dr. Sherwood Lingenfelter for guiding my doctoral research with uncanny wisdom and unflagging rigor. You were wonderfully honest, accessible, creative, and encouraging. I thank Dr. Amara Pongsapich for supervising my exploration of Thai face and helping me to gather an impressive sample of informants. I thank Dr. Stella Ting-Toomey for her invaluable critiques of my research and writing, always wrapped in gracious words of encouragement. I thank Dr. Christopher Flanders, my fellow face scholar, for generously sharing resources, insights, and encouragement as we pondered the riddles of Thai face. I honor these superb scholars.

I thank Dr. Thira Janepiriyaprayoon for his example of virtuous leadership, his longtime friendship, and his kind assistance in recruiting distinguished informants. I thank Khru Suntaree Maneenop for her incomparable ability to teach the Thai language and her dignified example of excellence, humility, and true kindness.

I thank my father and mother, Wayne and Minnie Persons, for their honorable examples of love and respect for the Thai people. I thank Naree Phuphanphet, my childhood nanny, who took me by the hand and led me into the Thai world. I thank Ed and Claire Miner, mentors since primary school, for loving me and believing in my intellect.

I am grateful to Dr. Marjie Persons and Robert Lewis for their vital feedback in proofreading this manuscript. I am especially indebted to my editor, Susan Offner, who patiently immersed herself in this project and brightly enhanced my message with her excellent suggestions.

Words cannot fully express my endless appreciation for Ginny Persons, my wife, who set me free to complete this project, believing with fierce determination that my discoveries deserve a wide hearing. You, my love, are the quiet and kind presence who made this achievement possible.

My greatest debt is to the only Face with whom all human facework is delightfully pointless. Full of grace and truth, you are the ultimate exemplar of honorable leadership.

INTRODUCTION

THIS BOOK PRESENTS a fresh and provocative analysis of how Thais lead. New insights will challenge your assumptions and help you grasp how power flows in Thai society.

You don't have to be a scholar to read on. This book is for everyone—foreigners living and working in Thailand, Thai leaders and intellectuals, researchers, and journalists. If you are a scholar or academic, please don't be fooled by the conversational style. Keep in mind that the statements and claims you are about to read are based on trustworthy anthropological research.

Have you ever been perplexed by the leadership scene in Thailand? What motivates Thai leaders? How do they win the cooperation of their followers? How do they gain and use power? What do they fear and how do those fears affect their decisions? How do they expect to be treated? How do they respond if others miss those cues? Where are the portals for new leaders to emerge? How do virtuous leaders behave? The questions are many.

These are uncharted waters, but respectable social research offers some intriguing answers. I have spent seven years researching and writing about Thai leaders and their use of cultural and social capital in getting things done.[1]

I was born and raised in Thailand. I look *farang* (foreign), but my primary socialization was through holistic submersion in Thai culture from preverbal days onward. I grew up speaking the central dialect and I have worked in Thailand for over twenty years.

Even so, I would not dare to trust intuition or mere conjecture to explain complex processes of leadership. For my PhD research, I conducted thirty-eight long interviews and eleven focus groups with a diverse sample of seventy-seven leaders and followers in Thai society. The youngest was nineteen years old, the oldest ninety-six. Of this selection, 64 percent were male and 36 percent female. They were born in twenty-six provinces of the kingdom and represented many walks of life: an author, a banker, a beautician, bookkeepers, educators, farmers, former prime ministers, government workers, a judge, managing directors of large companies, office workers, police, politicians, a privy councilor, religious leaders, small business owners, and university students. Some had just a fourth grade education; others had doctorates. I logged hundreds of hours listening to and dissecting seventy-five hours of digitally recorded interviews in Thai. Then I wrote about the things I was hearing.[2]

My point? If you catch yourself shaking your head at something I say, remember that I'm not making this up. The gems in this book were cut by a rich and diverse sample of Thai people who know well how their leaders wield power in society.

But every scholar dons a certain lens and writes from a certain point of view. My analyses and findings are guided by my keen interest in an abstract notion called "face."

What is "face?" If the question were, "What is *a* face?" we would do better in answering it. Isn't it the front part of the head from forehead to chin and from ear to ear? Yes, but it's a lot more.

The human face is an extraordinary symbol, a tangible representation of invisible things hidden deep in the sacred labyrinths of personhood. It both manifests and hides baffling mysteries that lie within each of us: emotions, thoughts, values, proclivities, and passions. Our faces mediate between our internal worlds and the external world. We use them to put on poses, to present ourselves in social space, and to manage the impressions of others. And all along we are very aware that there are dire consequences to our "facework."

Asians from many different cultures refer to this social phenomenon as "face." As far back as the fourth century BC, the Chinese were using this term to describe dimensions of worth and personal power in interpersonal dynamics (Hu 1944, 44).

To capture the essence of face, envision an encounter between any two people. Beginning the instant they engage one another in social space, whether for the first time or the thousandth time, each gives verbal and nonverbal signals to the other—perhaps eye contact, a smile, a handshake, a bow, or a verbal greeting. These signals help define the status of the relationship for that particular encounter. As they begin to converse, it may appear that their purpose in verbal exchange is largely instrumental—each is simply striving for a certain goal or outcome. One wants to sell a ticket and the other wants to buy it. One requests a favor and the other agrees to help. One invites the other to dine at her house and the other accepts or declines.

In each of these encounters, what is going on? It might look like nothing more and nothing less than basic communication. But beneath the rather inane verbal give and take, something else is happening. Each is saying something about who he thinks he is in relation to the other, and each is communicating what he thinks about the other. These two people are not just interested in exchanging information; they are *making value judgments about their worth and significance as human beings.* They are testing issues of autonomy and acceptance. Ultimately, they want to know, "What do you think of me, and where do I fit?"

People inherently have value and they know it. They determine that value by comparing it to some standard. When two people share the same social space they cannot resist a subtle (or perhaps not so subtle) urge to calibrate the level of worth each holds in the other's eyes. This calculus occurs in relational encounters in every culture, not just Thai culture, but it carries profound weight for those of us who develop and maintain relationships in Thailand.

Scholars have written curiously little about this pervasive and potent part of Thai culture. Face behavior to Thais is like water to fish—it is part of the environment where they live and move and have their being, yet they feel no inclination to analyze or dissect what is so thoroughly familiar to them. Thai face values are obscure because they are tacit: Thais do not study or discuss them—they simply live them out.

So to study face is to be drawn into a riddle:

> Face cannot be translated or defined. It is like honor and is not honor. It cannot be purchased with money, and gives a man or a woman a material pride. It is hollow and yet is what men fight for and what many women die for. It is invisible and yet by definition exists by being shown to the public. It exists in the ether and yet cannot be heard, and sounds eminently respectable and solid. (Lin 1939, 199–200).

That is the mystery. In short, I am inviting you into fresh anthropological waters. You may or may not be fluent in the Thai language, but even if your language skills are weak you can learn the meaning of five absolutely pivotal terms that will open a world of understanding about Thai face. These words are: *nata* (หน้าตา), *kiat* (เกียรติ), *chuesiang* (ชื่อเสียง), *barami* (บารมี), and *saksi* (ศักดิ์ศรี). I have found that when I engage a Thai in conversation about maintaining face, losing face, redeeming face, or gaining face, he or she will use every one of these foundational words within a span of fifteen minutes.

If you are Thai, try to define these very familiar words. Stretch their meanings apart. Explain each abstract notion so it's distinct from the other notions. It's difficult, isn't it? In the minds of most Thais, these words go together. They are so entangled they seem inseparable.

Keep at it. Ask yourself, "Do these words, then, carry the same meaning?" Are *nata* and *barami* the same thing? If someone has *chuesiang*, does he or she automatically have *kiat*?

Now you hesitate. The meanings are not identical. Where can we turn to find greater clarity?

Not to a dictionary. One government dictionary, for example, says that *kiat* means *chuesiang* and *chuesiang* means *kiatiyot*, a derivative of *kiat*. Face means *kiat* and *saksi*. *Saksi* means *kiatisak*, another derivative of *kiat* (Dictionary of the Royal Institute 2003).

If this is bewildering to a Thai, consider how much more baffling it is to foreigners living in Thailand! But let's take heart. We will find greater clarity.

All we need to note at this point is that face—stripped down to its bare essence—is about the human desires for *acceptance* and *significance*. We reach out to others seeking confirmation for what we hope is true: that we are lovable enough to be included and dignified enough to be respected.

These desires drive us to stake a certain claim-right to worth in public space, but that's only half the story.[3] Other members of society must weigh our self-presentations and award actual value for them. That's what face is all about: claims to worth and judgments of worth.

This evaluative undercurrent—the weighing of human worth—is always present in communication between Thai leaders and followers. In fact, face dynamics are preeminent in all arenas of leadership in Thailand.

Often the reasons behind a leader's choices "remain hidden, assumed, implicit, and unexamined" (Johnson 2007, 217). But I have discovered that if we use the lens of face to analyze them, we can gain extraordinary insights into relationships and the flow of power in Thai society. Simply put, leaders use the rules of face interaction to rally followers to accomplish their objectives. They use the very same rules to suppress or empower subordinates who are rising.

Face dynamics constitute a powerful heuristic—an aid to discovery—that lends meaning to many leadership behaviors. In fact, if we want to understand Thai leaders we must have a basic understanding of Thai face: its anatomy, its context of clientelism, its relationship to power, and its profoundly moral dimensions.

The face needs of leaders exercise substantive control over most of their leadership behaviors, shaping decisions in the course of leadership and generating their strategies for gaining power. That is why I am writing this book. The dynamics and principles I have uncovered are simply too valuable to ignore.

If you, the reader, are originally from the West, let me be clear so that all will go well. It is possible that you have embraced certain "pop" understandings of face behaviors in Thai society. You see the notorious penchant to save face as a matter of silly pride, something that could be shed effortlessly if people were not so enamored with themselves. You equate a loss of face with harmless feelings of mild embarrassment. You believe that social actors often manipulate rules of face interaction for the sole purpose of avoiding personal responsibility. You see face as a mask to hide behind, something that frustrates good communication and inhibits the expression of a person's true self.

But this topic is much more intricate than meets the eye and far too important to brush aside with disdain. We will be rewarded if we forgo our own frames of reference long enough to learn how Thais interpret face behaviors. If we will do that with genuine curiosity and a generous spirit, we will learn how things really work relationally, and we will do better at building healthy and lasting relationships with all Thais. We will also acquire a more precise understanding of Thai leaders and how we should relate to them.

Suntaree Komin (1990, 16), an eminent social psychologist, argues that modern studies of Thai behavior and social systems are too speculative, generating a host of claims that lack empirical support. Alan Johnson (2006) questions the value of research that attempts to verify Western leadership theories among Thai leaders. Both scholars are spot on: we need books on Thai leadership that are based on scrupulous ethnographic data.

The book you hold in your hands is exactly that. I drew my conceptual framework from social anthropology. I immersed myself in Thai culture to discover the social nature of face, the social values of face, the social dimensions of leadership, and the social context of power. My data reflect what Thai social actors feel and think about facework in the leadership process—specifically, how *they* frame the issues.

I explain my research findings in simple language, suggesting ways you can be more culturally appropriate in your business transactions and friendships. I avoid academic prose and offer compelling anecdotes that illustrate Thai leadership dynamics.

If you are an expat—perhaps a foreign diplomat, a member of the Peace Corps, a business executive working with Thais on a daily basis, an English teacher, or even someone married to a Thai—let me be forthright. This book will add value to your life. It is very readable, but it is also a serious academic work, thorough and thick with nuanced descriptions. It's not a "quick read" because there is nothing instant when it comes to learning a new worldview. Out of respect for my Thai friends, I would not offer anything so superficial. If you press into these pages, you will be rewarded with priceless insights that will help you adjust and thrive in your daily living.

To all readers, I offer a crucial disclaimer. This book is apolitical. I am not a political scientist and I am as overwhelmed as you by the complexity and volatility of the present political landscape. I do not align myself with any political party, and it is not my intent to join the host of pundits already critiquing the frightening partisan crevasses that separate Thais from Thais.

I offer something different. I present a neutral, prototypical view of what motivates leaders, how they explore paths to power, and how they treat others.

As you read along, I will give voice to Thai leaders and followers who have taught me so much. I ask you to welcome them as captivating guests who slip in and out of the narrative to offer timely insights. Here is the first of many.

"If a leader wants others to trust him and show him respect," says a Thai leader, "he must develop his face." The word he uses for face is *nata*.

This man is stating something many other Thais resoundingly confirm: when a leader accumulates face it constitutes valuable social capital that wins the cooperation of followers, and it gives him considerable prestige. In other words, if we want to understand how Thais lead, we must be watchful and wise about face dynamics that prevail in their society.

Our ultimate quest is to gain a sharper understanding of indigenous beliefs about face and leadership. Those discoveries will grace us with profound insights for building strategic relationships, training emerging leaders, and using power for the good of society.

Part 1

UNDERSTANDING THAI FACE

1
FACE IS EVERYWHERE

FACE IS ALL AROUND US. Sometimes we see it. Sometimes we don't. But it's there, right before our eyes. Very shortly we will be unpacking some abstract cultural values, but first, let's bring this topic to life. It's good to remind ourselves how *present* face is, especially for leaders.

Envision a simple scene. Two leaders are greeting one another. They smile, perhaps widely, perhaps modestly, as they press their palms together in front of their chests. Their fingers graciously extend upward to form the traditional greeting, the *wai*.[1] But subtle cues—body posture, the height of the hands, the angle of the face, whether or not the nose touches the fingertips—these things tell us a lot about which person has more face.

Meet a retired municipal officer from a district in Bangkok. He is nicely dressed as he graciously welcomes me into his home. He ushers me to see the official family portrait in the living room—resplendent, perfect poses casting an eternal aura of status and honor. He takes great care to show me each of his children's university diplomas. He proudly expounds on their collective success in the excellent jobs they have secured.

When it is time to have lunch together at a local restaurant, he excuses himself for a few minutes. He returns looking impeccable in a new outfit. Peering into a mirror in the family room, he meticulously combs every last hair into place. He adjusts his collar. He gives one final glance. Only then is he ready for the stroll down the lane in front of his house. All of this tells me that here is a man with face.

Join me on another day. I've been invited to accompany a district police chief for a day of participant observation. He is my friend. In fact, we used to be neighbors.

I arrive at his home promptly at eight thirty in the morning. The front gate is open, which I interpret to mean that he's been expecting me. His yard is faultlessly manicured, alive with splendor—healthy green grass, multicolored orchids, diverse tropical flora, and the soothing trickle of water in a small fountain. Stepping onto his front patio, I call out to him using an honorific pronoun. I approach the open doorway to his home, but then I hesitate. He is still dressing himself at the breakfast table. He warmly greets me, reassuring me that it's perfectly fine to enter.

The top of his uniform dangles on a nearby hanger—neatly pressed, laden with decorations and symbols of rank. His undershirt is the backdrop to a stunning display of gold necklaces. Five exotic amulets rest against his chest. One, he mentions, is very old, circa 1867. "When these are chipped or fragmented they are worth ten million baht," he says. "This one is whole."

I ask him why he wears them.

"I have confidence in them. They protect me. They give me inner energy. We believe that people who own important sacred amulets are people with 'face-eyes.' They're wealthy. They own things of value."

As he buttons up his uniform, we discuss the day ahead. We will be traveling to a nearby district where he was recently appointed as chief of police. This morning I will be attending a rare "town meeting" between top district police officers and prominent local leaders. In the afternoon I will be conducting a focus group with lower-ranking police.

He explains to me that these high-profile gatherings offer plentiful opportunities to gain face. As host of the event he stands to gain the most face. His face will be enhanced by the presence of a local representative of the national parliament who will be making an appearance. The chief is optimistic. "With face gain, the sky's the limit!" he bellows.

I find myself riding in the back seat of a brown and white double-cab police pickup. The chief's cell phones ring incessantly. At times he has a phone to each ear as he holds simultaneous conversations. His driver answers his own cell phone and chats as he speeds down the provincial road, often riding the dotted line between lanes. Neither man is wearing a seatbelt.

We arrive at the district police station. The chief and I enter a large air-conditioned conference room on the third floor. In the center of the room is a configuration of tables in the shape of an elongated O. The chief takes his place at the head of the table. Behind him are several gold images of the Buddha arranged in a tier-like fashion, along with pristine color photographs of Their Majesties the King and Queen of Thailand.

Fifteen distinguished-looking policemen and significant members of the community are already seated around the table. Other attending leaders—twenty-eight, to be exact—are seated in two rows of folding chairs that arc around the central table. I am aware that attendees are not seated randomly. Those at the main table are deemed to have more face than those seated on the outside. The chief asks me to sit in an empty chair at the far end of the main table.

As we are being served water, cookies, and coffee, there is a subdued bustle at the doorway. The member of parliament (MP) is arriving with his entourage. He sports a dyed coiffure and a light blue silk *prarachathan* jacket.[2] Everyone greets him with great deference.

He is invited to sit at the head of the table next to the chief of police. The members of his entourage are seated to his right. Each is careful to lean slightly in his direction as if ready to spring to his assistance. The new arrivals are served coffee and cookies—first the representative, then his posse.

The chief of police calls the meeting to order. A ranking policeman reads the reasons for the town meeting—to serve the community more effectively. As his hands grip the text, I note he is wearing a diamond-studded gold watch and an ostentatious gold ring. A businessman next to him, dressed rather casually, is wearing a large gold ring that flashes diamonds and a gold Rolex watch. A thick 22-karat gold bracelet adorns his other wrist.

The chief introduces all guests, beginning with the MP. Gathered here are managers of banks, owners of large businesses, headmasters of schools, subdistrict officers, and hospital administrators—in short, most of the influential people of the district.

The chief moves the meeting along according to the agenda. After a few status reports, the MP is invited to speak. He is careful to mention how he is brokering many benefits for the community.

The chief then opens the floor for anyone who wishes to express an opinion. Those sitting around the main table remain seated while speaking. Those in the outer rings often stand hesitantly before respectfully offering a viewpoint.

Just before adjourning, the chief introduces me and asks me to say a few words. I stand to greet the assembly, stating that it is an honor to be here. "I was born in Thailand," I say. "Presently I am doing doctoral research." As I speak, it strikes me that I am being given honor and face. I also sense that my presence may be lending a fractional amount of face to this historic gathering.

The meeting adjourns. The MP approaches me, talks briefly, and gives me his business card.

The whole group heads downstairs and outside. Policemen hover attentively around the MP as he points to a spot near the gate of the compound. He tells the chief that he's going to pay to have a small rain shelter built there.

We take a group photo in front of the police station. The chief is careful to place me between him and the MP. We then line up respectfully to *wai* the MP as he climbs into his pearl white, chauffer-driven SUV and leaves.

I am due to eat lunch with the chief and some businessmen, so I quickly go back to the meeting room to gather my backpack. Upon returning outside, I am surprised to see that the MP has returned, and he will be joining us for lunch.

At the restaurant I am seated next to the police chief. To my other side is the MP, who grandly announces that the entire meal is on him. A wealthy businessman quickly protests, insisting vehemently that he would be very honored to play host. During the meal, this same man shamelessly flatters the MP, saying how fortunate the community is to have such a great patron. He also states that since the police assist the community, members of the community must assist the police. "That way we walk together," he says.

Toward the end of the meal the chief leans toward me and casually says, "You should go with the MP to the community event he's attending this afternoon."

"That's an attractive idea," I say. "But didn't we have a focus group scheduled this afternoon with some of your subordinates?"

When the chief acts as if I just spoke a sentence in Swahili, not Thai, I instantly get it. The good money is on a plan to join the MP's afternoon entourage. I should just stop talking and cooperate.

Before I know it, I am in the back seat of the MP's Land Cruiser. He first takes me to his very large house and proudly shows me around. A few minutes later we are back in his vehicle, driving to a nearby subdistrict. He points out a large sign that spans the highway. Glistening with gold trim, it features oil-painted images of His Majesty the King. The MP is careful to inform me that he ordered the structure to be built with his personal donations. Sure enough, as we pass under the arch I look left to catch a quick glimpse of a plaque announcing him as the benefactor.

We arrive at the subdistrict police station for the yearly competition of large temple drums. Our vehicle stops in front of a line of policemen standing at attention. They scramble to open the doors so we can descend. Then it hits me. This afternoon I am in the glow of this leader's personal radiance.

The event is being staged on a soccer pitch adjacent to the police station. An impressive array of a dozen or so temple drums stands like a row of cannons along the opposite sideline. Each has a monstrous megaphone attached for the purpose of amplification. Villagers crowd the near side of the pitch, squatting on the ground with great anticipation.

We are ushered into a tent reserved for dignitaries, where the MP and district officer are invited to sit on a cushioned vinyl couch. I am seated with others on plastic chairs set off to the side. They offer us drinking water—the MP first, the district officer second, the local chief of police third, me, and then others. The workers serve us on their knees.

I glance to my left toward a huddle of villagers squatting on the grass. I see only their backs, but one figure catches my eye. He's wearing a white T-shirt with red letters printed on the back. The words jump. There—plain as day—is the MP's name along with words written in the local dialect: "Our village's representative in parliament."

When it's time for the MP to give his ceremonial opening remarks to the gathered crowd, he steps out to a microphone just in front of the tent. The district officer, the police chief, and two other men stand behind him in a show of support. Their bodies form an arc, a kind of reflective shield, you might say. The local chief then turns to me and insists that I join them. I quickly comply.

The MP welcomes everyone to the event, recognizing certain prominent individuals and thanking local temples for their participation. He calls on all things sacred to bless the event. When he declares the festivities to be officially open, there is a loud echo of applause.

Very shortly afterward, the MP begins to stir as if he is preparing to leave. Clearly, the centerpiece of his face presentation is now complete. He informs me that I will be staying at the festivities because my friend, the other police chief, will swing by to pick me up at the end of the day.

The MP's exit toward his vehicle is grand. With dignified steps he glides slowly down the entire length of the field, treading close to the squatting masses. His entourage, including me, follows at a measured distance behind him. As he passes each cluster of villagers, they show him respect by smiling and lifting their hands high in traditional *wai*s held fast against their faces. He, in response, walks with a constant *wai* held to the middle of his chest. Making his way, he gazes upon his subjects with an untiring cherubic smile. This poignant scene captures it all. They need his great charity. He needs their respect and their votes.

As he reaches his vehicle, a fawning policeman opens his door for him. The higher-ranking policemen and I stand at rigid attention until his car turns away and heads out of the compound. We are then free to return to the competition that is underway.

Two hours later, my friend—the host of the town meeting earlier that morning—arrives to pick me up. Sitting together in his police car, we discuss my impressions of the afternoon.

"Do you know what that was all about?" he asks me. "Do you know why you were invited along?"

"Why?" I ask.

"It's because your presence as a *farang* gave the MP greater face," the chief continues. "With you in his entourage, the villagers probably thought, 'Wow, what kind of leader *is* this, that he even attracts foreigners—people of international stature—to our event!' Those villagers assumed that you and the MP were conversing in English, of course. That boosted his image as well. In fact, that MP returned to have lunch with us for *one reason*—to snag you as a member of his entourage for the afternoon. *That* is how things work. That's what it's all about. Gaining face!"

Indeed, face is right before our eyes. If we pay attention, we can hardly miss it. Like an invisible currency, it is everywhere. Hiding like a mysterious code in the daily behaviors of leaders, it promises great insights into how Thais gain the cooperation of their fellow citizens.

2
ALL THAT GLITTERS

"THE FACE OF THAI PEOPLE is of grave importance," writes one intellectual (Snit 1975, 505). Anyone familiar with this country and its culture would readily agree. But Thai face can seem as ethereal as thick fog shrouding an unfamiliar mountain path. It's right there before our eyes, but to explore its properties is disorienting. What exactly is this precious abstract treasure? What are its dimensions within the Thai worldview?

The starting point for understanding face is not altogether clear. Thais do not use the simple word "face" (*na*) to refer to this psychosocial phenomenon. That term all by itself merely connotes the visage of a human face. To enter dialogues about face, you have to ask about those who "have face, have eyes," or those who have "face-eyes" (*nata*, หน้าตา).[1]

No English phrase perfectly captures the meaning of this idiomatic expression, "to have face-eyes." The best translation is "having the appearance of prestige," or what we might simply call prestige. This is the first critical piece—the entryway—for building an understanding of Thai face.

Take careful note that having face in Thai society is broader and deeper than the idea of having "face-eyes." Every competent Thai social actor behaves as if he or she has face. Every person can lose face or gain face.

A poor man's father dies in a village and he has no money for the funeral. What does he do? Often he feels compelled by societal values to borrow a large sum of money to pay for customary village-wide feasts that others deem appropriate for such occasions. He does this because he can't stand others gossiping that he has no face. Upholding the honor of his family and relatives, he must be able to say, "I gave it my best shot." Then in the ensuing months he attempts to repay his debts. Thais use a fascinating idiomatic phrase to describe this common phenomenon: "the dead are selling the living."[2]

It's not just the host that cares about face at public ceremonies and celebrations. Common people who attend festivals at village temples often feel an irrepressible need to wear gold necklaces, bracelets, and rings in order to make an impression on others. They will go to great lengths to obtain this jewelry, even going into debt. These are not wealthy people, but they still want to enhance their standing in the community. "They do this so that others will socialize with them," says an office worker.

The nation is awash in face talk. Listen carefully, and you will hear Thais of every status in all circles of society refer to their possession of face. For example, when you feel embarrassed because of a harmless gaffe in front of peers, you can say, "My face is broken!"[3] Everyone will have a good laugh. That's hardly the case, however, when someone from your ingroup—a parent, a boss, or a good friend—says to you, "You sold my face."[4] Now you should feel immediate distress and the threat of shame. You should rush to apologize and seek to remedy the situation.

My point is that face talk—whether it is playful or deadly serious—is common to all speakers of the Thai language. The most nondescript person in society staunchly defends and maintains his or her possession of face. In fact, Thirayuth Boonmi, a well-respected Thai intellectual, claims that Thais "believe the maintenance of their faces to be the most important thing in life" (1999, 275).

Yet only certain people have "face-eyes," or the appearance of having prestige. Among this elite group, face presentations are pronounced and highly visible.

Just whom are we talking about? The most prevalent connotation in modern Thai society is that a person with this kind of social capital *has money.*

"Face-eyes is money," says a judge. "The economy, public acclaim, gold and silver . . . it's all about face-eyes." If you can flash gold or make a statement with the right clothes, the right hairdo, or the right car, people will take notice. And they will likely defer to you as one who has a certain amount of legitimate social power.

Think back to my story in chapter 1. At the town meeting, participants are careful to wear gold, precious gems, and expensive watches. The MP arrives and departs in one of the nicest vehicles money can buy. Before he and I attend the public event that afternoon, he stops to show me his expensive house and his team of maids and gardeners. These examples help us visualize how Thais claim worth on the basis of possessing "face-eyes."

Athajak Satyanurak (2006, 7–8) traces contemporary society's emphasis on the "external" back to the behavior of Thai nobles from the nineteenth century onward. In response to materialistic values introduced by increased contact with Westerners, nobles began to measure honor by their ability to live a "civilized life." The atmosphere among nobles became highly competitive. They strived to obtain new possessions—automobiles, jewelry, and "toys," such as cameras from Europe. Nobles who lacked money to buy and flaunt these desirable goods felt inferior. They were identified with a pejorative term: "lords without shrines." As nobles continued to parade their possessions in front of one another, their symbols of wealth began to epitomize heightened honor and societal status. This is how feelings about honor became entwined with the practice of consumption.

Try a little exercise. Ask your Thai friends, "Would you like to 'have face, have eyes'?"[5] Many—if not most—will answer, "Yes."

Cultivating this form of capital is a wonderful thing. "My goodness, it is the *most* important thing, this 'face-eyes'!" says a wealthy businessman. "Every Thai person wants to gain face whether he admits it or not. Thais are more covetous about 'face-eyes' than anything else. They want possessions, money, and gold, and all along they are thinking, 'How much face does this give me?'"

Society grants highly desirable privileges to people with this dimension of face. It's like having good credit. They have clout. Life becomes more convenient, more comfortable. They are immediately more acceptable, more respectable, and better liked. Other members of society approve of them with ease, giving them preferential treatment. They receive frequent gifts and favors. They gain valuable connections. People cooperate with them more readily. In short, these people have social capital to spend in public situations.

When Thais are asked to identify people in society who have this form of social capital, their thoughts often gravitate to individuals with prominent public profiles: the prime minister, privy councilors to the king, ministers of the cabinet, senators, members of parliament, the supreme patriarch, governors, district officers, mayors, movie stars, sports stars, well-known singers, and the very wealthy—or the "hi-so,"[6] as they are sometimes called.

We shouldn't make the mistake of defining "face-eyes" as fame, however. There is another Thai word for that dimension of face, and we'll get to it soon.

Most people with "face-eyes" are *not* famous. Every local association, brotherhood, business, club, community, fellowship, fraternity, guild, league, order, sodality, school, temple, university, union, or village is likely to have at least a few individuals with "face-eyes," or prestige. We're talking about the village headman, leaders in local communities, men and women successful in business, abbots of renowned temples, popular priests, and individuals who truly benefit society—doctors, teachers, soldiers, and policemen.

Prestige is valuable, but it is by no means rare or unattainable. Although this term usually connotes a person with money, sometimes it simply describes a person who is in some way excellent, gifted, or virtuous.

Thais use this word as a gloss for any of the other forms of social capital granted by society. In other words, if you have honor, public acclaim, or accumulated goodness (terms I will introduce shortly), other members of society will most likely consider you to be someone with "face-eyes" as well. Social values assume that anyone with one or more of the many dimensions of face must possess a certain amount of prestige as well.

To say that someone has "face-eyes," then, is the most common way to say that a person "fits" into Thai society. If you can create the appearance of having prestige, you can project a claim to worth that others must take into account. If you do this frequently and convincingly, your efforts to present yourself will garner the approval of others. To have "face-eyes" is to possess an unquantifiable amount of social power.

This is the "umbrella phrase" in all Thai speech about human worth. It is the most inclusive of the five key concepts that form the anatomy of Thai face.

"Face-eyes" is also the veneer of Thai face, the most superficial level. Society often awards this description based solely upon outward appearance. Members of the public study external cues—surface impressions of a person's self-presentation—and on the basis of those cues they judge him or her to be worthy of acceptance, respect, and special favors. This type of social capital is granted most often on the basis of things like wealth, skill, beauty, intellect, performance, success, and influence—things that have little to do with a person's inner being or character. As the shallowest dimension of Thai face, it is utterly pervasive.

Someone with alleged prestige, or "face-eyes," casts a compelling appearance of worth into social space. At times there is real substance behind the presentation. At other times it is mere window dressing. But we should not underestimate the certified value of this form of capital.

Façades—surface impressions—are both highly convincing and dreadfully important in Thai society. With few exceptions, people who deliver convincing self-presentations in public are deemed worthy of honorable treatment. It doesn't really matter whether or not that sits well with you. This form of face is simply too potent, too effective, and too valuable to dismiss as meaningless or worthless.

We will come to see, however, that the Thai view of worth is anything but one-dimensional. Consider, for example, a rich man who exploits the poor. He is shown honor in public because of his social power, but few people regard him as truly honorable. His prestige glows with a superficial candescence, but others see it as a charade.

That's because surface impressions are often hollow and misleading. They gleam and sparkle, bedazzling the eye. For brief moments they can charm us sweetly. But they can disappoint us just as quickly, leaving us with a gnawing hunger to experience some true standard of worth. In other words, all that glitters is not necessarily genuine gold.

3

A CASCADE OF WATER

LET'S EXPLORE A SECOND DIMENSION of Thai face known as *kiat* (เกียรติ). English speakers commonly refer to this form of capital as "honor."[1]

Reflect on my anecdotes in chapter 1. Recall how the municipal leader proudly shows me his children's university diplomas. Envision the police chief's uniform, hanging neatly pressed and laden with decorations and symbols of rank. With your mind's eye, see that large sign spanning the highway, glistening with gold trim and featuring oil-painted images of His Majesty the King. Consider how the most comfortable seats at the temple drum competition are reserved for the most prominent leaders. Imagine the MP as he takes that dignified stroll down the sidelines of the soccer pitch in front of squatting spectators who show respect by holding *wais* fast against their faces. All of these vignettes feature honor as a centerpiece.

True honor commands genuine respect and approval. It carries more weight than simple prestige. Honor conveys an aura of *legitimacy*. A person with honor has the approval of others because he has claim to a smidgeon or more of unquestioned value.

Honor is a powerful lifter. It says to others, "This person truly deserves to be shown respect. Listen to him." It elevates certain people above others in such a way that they begin to be seen and known from a greater distance away. Still, this attribute is not a matter of breadth or girth. When you hear this term, think ascendance, think height.

"This society is starved for honor," claims a wealthy businessman, laughing heartily. Awards, citations, certificates, prizes, promotions, and trophies elevate certain citizens above others, conferring significant social power upon them. Titles and ranks do the same. Positions of authority confer honor, usually signified by adding official prefixes to names. Members of the military and the police often feel this sense of worth.

The Thai understanding is that honor comes from above. Honor descends. It trickles down hierarchies like water down a cascade. "The king is the fountain of all honors," says a powerful retired banker.

To really capture this, it is helpful to envision the entire population as a giant triangle with His Majesty the King at the top. Most Thais inherently desire to raise their level of *kiat* to be as close to the king as possible. Thai citizens still view government employees as honorable because they are considered representatives of the king, serving His Majesty in helping the citizens of his kingdom. People frequently cite the *ongkhamontri*, members of the king's privy council, as having tremendous uncontested honor because they're people whom the king has examined and declared to have "made the grade." No other seal of approval can top that.

There is also a strong correlation between honor and virtue.[2] "Enduring honor is not dependent on things like silver and gold," insists one religious leader. "It's not dependent on duties or titles. It's dependent upon goodness, upon inner qualifications—an inner life that we nurture, things like being honest, being sincere with others, backing up words with actions, being responsible, and being honorable in our comportment around members of the opposite sex."

Some Thais go so far as to say that without virtue a person does not possess honor, because the two are not detachable. Need proof? Watch when a person with honor commits a major violation of moral standards. When the broader public catches news of the incident, that person's reservoirs of social capital can evaporate faster than a fleeting rain shower on the sizzling sidewalks of Bangkok. Honor rests on the moral bedrock of virtue.

Possessing *kiat* is something more than possessing power. It is more than wielding influence because of one's position or wealth. It's more than being excellent, skilled, or gifted in some special way. It's more than being well known or famous. To qualify as one who possesses honor, you must be virtuous. Or, to put it more delicately, you have to *look* as if you have virtue.

Honor, therefore, is both *something that society bestows* and *something within*. This insight points us to two intriguing thoughts. Sometimes society bestows honor on people who lack honor in their inner being. Their character and their honorable status are disjoined. At other times, people are honorable inwardly yet lack the corresponding echo of affirmation from society. Honor often goes unheralded.

It is advisable, then, to distinguish two types of honor: the quality of being truly honorable, regardless of awards or titles, and the honor that has to do with rank and position. The first is tethered to a person's true inner goodness. The second is an echo of response that society gives to certain individuals—some deserving, some not so deserving.

Another way of explaining this is to say that honor has its counterfeits. Those with true honor win genuine, spontaneous respect from others. They perform their duties faithfully and assist others with fairness and few ulterior motives. But there is false *kiat*. Many Thais argue that if a person holding a position of honor is dishonorable in the ways he treats others—for example, if he uses his position for selfish and dishonest gain—then he does not possess "true *kiat*."

A person with superficial prestige and a person with honor will both be treated honorably by other members of society. But it is possible to have honor without prestige (to be highly respected, but to live a simple and unassuming life), or conversely, to have prestige without true honor (to have wealth and influence but to lack the genuine approval of others). We should not miss these immensely important distinctions.

"Having prestige is something lightweight and frivolous," says a community leader. "It's tied to your outward form. But 'honor eats deeply to the center of your being.'"[3]

Yet prestige and honor are so interlaced that many Thais—perhaps even most—easily confuse the two. It's remarkable, really. Here we have two forms of social capital monumentally different in quality and essence, yet they appear together so often that they seem indistinguishable.

This may seem like a case of harmless misjudgment, something hardly worth our interest. Not so. This cloudy thinking has grave consequences. It is precisely what sets the stage for the subversion of honor in society, a topic I will address with greater frequency as my central argument unfolds.

Although honor is great in height, it often has a rather narrow base. Associations, institutions, and other entities frequently confer titles, awards, certificates, decorations, and trophies that carry deep meaning for a small subset of the population. These accolades grant real social power, but that power is usually limited in scope. Someone right next door may feel entirely unmoved by a given declaration of honor if he or she is not a member of that circle or ingroup. Because of this quirky aspect of what Thais call *kiat*, a person with "face-eyes" often cuts a broader swath of societal recognition than someone with honor.

For the most part, Thais do not view this form of social capital as something endogenous, or self-generated. Ordinary individuals can behave in honorable ways that win respect, but living a noble life is rarely the pathway to attaining legitimate honor. Laws and codes sanction this notion of *kiat*. In fact, it is almost impossible to acquire this dimension of face unless you are in a position of authority and do things to benefit others.

Yet this dimension of Thai face remains solidly entrenched in virtue. "We have to discern the roots of a person's honor," argues a community leader. "Is it honor born of virtue, or honor spawned by mere influence?" She pauses for a moment before resting her case with a shocking coup de grâce: "In that sense, it is possible for a beggar to have more honor than the prime minister."

Countless Thais would scoff at such a claim. So often, honor is cut loose from virtue and defined solely by status and position. Men and women who lack good character find ways to win awards, titles, ranks, and positions of power, and when they do they demand approbation from others.

Honor is that quality in human beings that commends them to others as being genuinely worthy of acceptance and respect. It confers value based on the merit of two things: excellence and virtue. Even in the cynical, cutthroat world of politics and power, that combination is compelling. It yields true legitimacy in the eyes of others. Like a refreshing cascade of water, honor descends from above to lend a sense of security and contentment to all who attain it.

4
A DRIFTING FRAGRANCE

A THIRD DIMENSION of Thai face is *chuesiang* (ชื่อเสียง). In contrast to honor, which is all about height, this word is all about breadth or girth. Think horizontally. Are you gifted or outstanding? Well, who knows about it? Are you an emerging politician? How big is your stage?

The most common connotation of this word is "to be known or broadly recognized by others." The etymology of the word is revealing. *Chue* is "a word designated [for use] in addressing a person," or to put it simply, a name. *Siang* is "something received by the ears," or a sound (Dictionary of the Royal Institute 2003). If someone has *chuesiang*, his or her name has reached the ears of others. This kind of face is like a fragrance that drifts a long distance. I refer to it as "public acclaim."

Again, reflect back on chapter 1. The town meeting is a stage for the police chief to expand his public acclaim. His face is enhanced by the attendance of many powerbrokers from his district who will return to their daily responsibilities and (hopefully) speak well of him. In addition, the presence of the MP at that meeting is a boon to the public image of the police chief because it associates the chief with the broad reputation of a prominent public leader.

Also, recall how the MP makes an appearance at the competition of temple drums. This calculated use of his time is highly advantageous to *his* public acclaim because he is on display before hundreds and hundreds of villagers who will return to their friends and family to talk about him. In days past, the MP has broadened his visibility by distributing free T-shirts with his name printed on the back. Today he has a foreigner in his entourage, suggesting that his renown extends across international borders.

In both of these vignettes, we see eminent leaders working intentionally to expand the reach of their public recognition. Both men see the great value of this particular dimension of face.

Let's now imagine that we are asking some Thais about the characteristics of this form of social capital. They look puzzled and ask, "What *type* of public recognition?" They are alerting us to something very consequential. There is both good public recognition (*chuesiang di*) and bad public recognition (*chuesiang mai di*). Our cultural informants are wondering, "Which kind do you want me to talk about?"

It is difficult for Thais to elaborate on this word without first giving it a moral rooting. If you ask enough Thai friends about the notion of public recognition, you will discover that they inevitably shape their comments to the backdrop of some standard of virtue.

Honorable behavior plus public awareness equals positive public recognition, or public acclaim. To maintain this kind of reputation you must show evidence of possessing strong moral values. You must benefit society by practicing generosity and doing good things for the sake of others.

It is important to separate the meanings of "face-eyes" and public acclaim. These two words are coupled so often in daily speech that many Thais are prone to believe they are nearly synonymous. That is not the case.

Prestige is flatly amoral. It can be earned by honest means or bought by dishonest means, yet either way it grants substantial social power to individuals. It is a form of social capital that society will rarely scrutinize for signs of legitimacy.

Public acclaim, by contrast, is a two-edged sword. It is wonderful to be known widely for good things. But when a prominent person falters or fails, a different kind of reputation spreads. Just as a fragrance can drift a long distance, so can a stench.

Obviously, only positive notoriety gives you valuable social capital in society. Public acclaim engenders vast amounts of general *acceptance*. When a man with this kind of face meets people in public venues, they graciously receive him and spontaneously accept him. They have confidence in him. They want to interact with him and cooperate with him. He is known broadly and accepted implicitly.

This concept of public acclaim is tricky, however. A "good reputation" can have two subtle but distinct meanings: (1) being truly selfless, generous, righteous, and beneficial to society—that is, renowned for being virtuous, and (2) being the object of the interest and adoration of others.

Picture an actress at the height of her profession. People in broad cross sections of society recognize her, like her, long to see her, crave to observe her talents, and spontaneously express adoration for her. This celebrated individual is considered "good" not because of a truly virtuous life, but because she is in some way unique: wealthy, gifted, prominent, skilled, nice to look at, excellent, or all of the above.

Modern Thailand is abounding with emphasis on this latter type of "good reputation." Sectors of the media prey on the cravings of throngs of people who love to idolize entertainers, athletes, politicians, the top brass in the police and military, as well as the high-society crowd. The impact of mass media has never been more potent, especially with the advent of personal computers, the Internet, smartphones, and an explosive appetite for social media.

Members of the general public have little personal contact with these famous people. Fans cannot and do not know what kind of people they *really* are in private. Magazines, newspapers, and social networking platforms continually portray contrived and retouched images, accentuating over and over again the winsome qualities of these high-profile individuals. Why? It sells print, news programs, movies, and merchandise. It's like hypnosis, like candy to a baby.

This creates a puzzling sociological phenomenon. A mesmerized public often grants to those who are famous an aura that they are also *morally good* people. Their perceptions are not based on careful judgments that measure the level of true virtue. They are merely expressions of euphoric idolatry in response to mythic, bigger-than-life images that make a huge splash—images that can be as vacant as a hologram when measured in terms of true virtue.

Among a populace that understands true virtue because of the goodness of their king, a person with this other kind of "good" reputation—captured by the English words *fame* and *popularity*—is much like an imposter.

A second case of duplicity occurs when someone seeks to buy the image of moral goodness by orchestrating a show of generosity. A Thai expression for this is "to place gold leaf on the *front* of an image of the Buddha." This wordplay is a twist on a familiar idiomatic phrase: "to place gold leaf on the back of an image of the Buddha."[1] It alludes to the practice of making merit by affixing small, thin sheets of gold leaf to a Buddhist statue. A person who performs a noble act with no ulterior motives is like someone who quietly affixes the gold leaf, purposely standing where others cannot see him because he doesn't want to be noticed or credited for his act of reverence. In vivid contrast we have those who do good works for the purpose of generating valuable social capital. They want to make a show of their charity.

But self-aggrandizing behavior does not always generate a genuinely good reputation. In the slums and *sois* (lanes) of Bangkok as well as in villages across the country, Thais maintain a healthy skepticism when evaluating face-gaining behaviors. If a person is suspected of having done good works with ulterior motives, his or her "good reputation" can actually diminish. To want to gain face or "grab" face is unsightly behavior.

So a genuinely good reputation is more difficult to acquire than simple public acclaim. Behavior is judged according to the exacting benchmark of virtuous teachings. You have to prove your truly good qualities over an extended period of time. Often your impact has a smaller radius than simple *chuesiang*, but it commands a deeper level of respect. Local people know you well, and in knowing you they cannot deny that you are worthy of honor. This kind of public acclaim renders feelings of worth that are of greater substance than the positive vibes provided by mere fame.

Yet all public acclaim—regardless of its foundation—is extremely valuable. To possess a good reputation is to be held in esteem as being exemplary and respectable. People praise you. They extol your worth. It can help you get *what* you want *when* you want it, and you can do that much faster than someone hidden in the faceless masses.

Take special note that this dimension of Thai face is *volatile.* It ebbs and flows. Public adulation is based on diverse opinions and preferences, and it can be extremely fickle and unstable. Especially if popular recognition is due to grandeur rather than goodness, it can evaporate in a heartbeat if you are hit with a rash of bad press, or if the driving forces of the media decide to shift their collective attention to fresher rising stars.

In ancient Siam, the public acclaim of prominent individuals had a small geographical radius. When reputations were disassembled by wildfires of gossip, it took time for news to travel geographically. How different things are these days! Modern mass media add a ghastly speed to processes that expand or diminish a person's public acclaim. Networks like Facebook, Instagram, and Twitter have given voice to the masses like never before, and little wildfires of gossip can easily rage into destructive infernos. This uncontrollable synergy—the media fueling gossip and gossip feeding the media—strikes fear into the hearts of prominent public figures.

It also works the other way around. This kind of notoriety is much easier to buy back or "redeem," as the Thai express it. To reclaim this kind of face once you have lost it, you simply make another stab at success and then work the mass media to recall the mercurial affections of the public.

"Thais easily forget bad reputations," says the managing director of a music recording company. "Wait six months. Try a new approach. Simply build a fresh image for them." In other words, those who pursue this superficial form of *chuesiang* should keep in mind an old saying: "Easy come, easy go."

Different rules constrain the public acclaim of a person whose reputation rests on the goodness of honorable living. This kind of capital is much more difficult to acquire. It is also far less capricious. It is more credible than popularity based on grandeur, and it is also more resistant to the attempts of others to tarnish it. But if it is ever lost due to immoral behavior, it is extremely difficult, if not impossible, to redeem.

A virtuous reputation is something that you achieve. Very rarely is it ascribed. People often deem the son of a morally upright man to be good because he shares the family name. But if that son does not behave in virtuous ways, society will withdraw its genuine approval no matter what his surname may be.

People with ranks or titled positions (*kiatiyot*) usually enjoy public acclaim, but some of them sorely lack a good reputation. Cultural codes dictate that others must show them respect. But if they are dishonest or selfish or greedy, often they cease to command true respect. They continue to receive oblations of respect, but in the eyes of many they are not worthy of respect.

It is fair to postulate that the dimension of honor, or *kiat*, signifies quality, while the dimension of public acclaim signifies quantity or extensiveness. Both lend significant social capital to those who possess them. To have either is to have a valuable form of "face-eyes." If you're ever able to put the two together, you have an extraordinarily potent combination.

But the real genius of public acclaim lies in the fact that it is one of the least scrutinized forms of capital. You don't have to be honorable to profit from *chuesiang*. You just have to be excellent in some way, then noticed, and then pushed into the limelight. At that point, the ignorant enthusiasm of the masses is usually enough to sustain you.

Chuesiang is electrifying social capital, and it can be highly intoxicating. Like a giant amplifier, it exaggerates the greatness or goodness of a person through the agency of expanded recognition in society. Like an echo, it is society's response to a person's cache of social power. This societal feedback magnifies both greatness and dishonor. It is like a fragrance or a stench that drifts a long distance.

5
A LARGE TREE GIVING SHADE

IN THE UPPER REACHES of what is truly honorable lies something that Thais refer to as *barami* (บารมี). It is absolutely pivotal that we understand this form of social power because it is supremely valuable and uniquely indigenous to the Thai worldview. It is the pinnacle of honor in society.

This particular dimension of face is founded upon the practice of underived generosity. Looking back on the narrative in chapter 1, when the MP speaks to the town meeting he documents all the benefits he is brokering for the citizens of that district. After the meeting, he is careful to showcase his role as patron of the police by pointing to a spot in the compound where he has decided to build a small shelter from the rain. During lunch the local businessman strongly insists on paying for the entire meal as a show of monetary force through the medium of generosity. And at the base of the memorial to the king spanning the highway is a plaque etched in bronze that serves as a beacon to spread the name of the generous politician who paid for its construction. All of these are examples of leaders pursuing a reputation of having *barami*.

No single English word covers the nuanced meanings of this dimension of face.[1] We can think of *barami* as "accumulated goodness," something based upon a leader's perceived "moral strength." I will use both phrases to refer to this facet of Thai face.

The etymology of *barami* builds a case for the glosses I propose. Traced back through early Theravada Buddhist texts, this word meant highest position or complete achievement. Subsequently it took on the meanings of excellence or complete mastery of teachings. For example, the Buddhist faithful were exhorted to practice ten *barami*, or ten perfections.[2]

Like honor, modern Thais envision this form of social capital as something that flows downward into society from the king by means of his example of virtuous leadership. For commoners, the ultimate stamp of *barami* is to be appointed by His Majesty as one of sixteen privy councilors that serve as advisors to the throne. For the most part, public opinion resoundingly confirms the accumulated goodness of any member of this highly distinguished council.

But this form of capital can also be found outside of that elite circle. Members of society commonly attribute this dimension of face to thousands of leaders in Thai society. Everyday conversations often link *barami* to a concept of sacral power that may or may not be related to moral strength. The word is attributed to a wide range of people: "kings, magicians, the meritorious, or prominent gangsters in the countryside . . . those with great power who have a great number of attendants or people serving them" (Thirayuth 1999, 270).

One scholar documents at least four connotations of *barami*: (1) an ideal moral sense of being truly virtuous; (2) a prestige sense of being someone significant on the social scene; (3) a negative sense of having dark influence that is to be feared; and (4) a charismatic sense of possessing a winsome ability to impose one's will on others (Johnson 2006, 168).

These several shades of meaning hint at something we dare not miss. Connotations cluster into two general categories. One is based on virtue. The other is based on hegemony or raw dominance. Common parlance has separated the concepts of virtue and power to such an extent that great power alone can be enough to qualify a leader for this ascription of accumulated goodness.

If this is true, what is at stake? Imagine a leader who practices generosity "with strings attached." He provides assistance and resources only to people who bring him personal gain. He treats all other people with indifference at best and contempt at worst, even to the point of exploiting and harming some. Members of his entourage regularly attribute *barami* to him. Many who have benefited from his largesse whisper the same.

Does this man have accumulated goodness? It depends, of course, on what connotation of the word you embrace. I have found that many Thais contend that the central meaning of this ancient word is still anchored in a standard of virtue displayed by a righteous monarch.

So whenever this word is ascribed to certain non-virtuous patrons who are selectively "good" to their entourage and other clients, don't be surprised if onlookers judge it to be a case of false attribution. Too often in contemporary society, attributions of *barami* are the fruit of bogus propaganda generated by a leader who wants to gain a valuable form of face by subverting the honor system. That kind of leader is altogether different from a leader with virtue as his or her moral compass.

Thais find it easy to describe a person with this form of capital. They will tell you that to qualify he or she must have a truly noble heart that responds to others from the perspective of what is righteous and fair.

The findings of one social researcher confirm this. David William Connor conducted ethnographic research among Thai leaders and found that *barami* "originates in the moral goodness" of an individual and drafts power from the perceptions of others who have observed and benefited from the leader's consistent expression of "meritorious selfless behavior" over a period of many years (1996, 240–42, 275). A person who qualifies for this accolade is not self-serving. He or she uses social capital to mobilize others to work together for the good of the collective.

An indispensable characteristic of someone with accumulated goodness is that he or she possesses substantial resources and uses them for the good of others. In other words, moral goodness is judged to a great degree by the way that it frequently and consistently expresses itself in selfless assistance of others. A leader who practices this as a lifestyle catches the attention of people and builds a wide audience, expanding and solidifying a good reputation.

This form of capital is not accrued by just any act of kindness, however. People with moral strength must be kind toward others with no strings attached. They must not act for the purpose of receiving reciprocal kindness. They must not use wealth to manipulate others, moving them around like pawns on a chessboard. This cardinal stipulation disqualifies a legion of shrewd leaders that wish to purchase the affections of the masses by practicing contrived generosity.

Although *barami* can generate considerable social power, individuals with this attribute do not set out with power in mind. They neither seek power nor abuse power. Nevertheless, they win a potent influence over others when people respond to their kindness by rallying around them in loyal support.

Of the five kinds of Thai face, accumulated goodness is the scarcest. It is increasingly rare today. Why?

To simply do good works or make merit is not enough. To qualify, you must demonstrate that you have a noble heart. But the spoils of power and money dilute the virtue of many contemporary leaders by wooing them to pursue these things as goals in and of themselves.

Another reason for the paucity of *barami* is that leaders must be extraordinarily consistent and durable over the long haul. Years may pass—sometimes even decades—before others will wholeheartedly ascribe this to them. Leaders must serve honorably and successfully, often within the bounds of positions of authority. They must nurture good relationships with others over a long period of time, negotiating with fairness through relational and political fractures that often occur due to frequent disagreements and contention. These tempests shipwreck the best intentions of many leaders. They learn to compromise ethically and morally just so they can survive.

To say that someone has accumulated goodness is to say that he or she has great honor, but not all who possess honor have accumulated goodness. In fact, very few do. Society attributes this accolade to people who—over a very long period of time—display a truly upright heart and work to solve the problems of others with no thought of what they will receive in return. These people use goodness, not position or power, to gain the cooperation of others. In response, others accept them willingly. They want to follow someone who is ethical, someone who keeps their best interests in mind.

In the chapters that follow we will learn that people with true accumulated goodness tend to have little interest in gaining face. They do everything with sincerity, with a pure heart, without thinking of what they might gain when the other party reciprocates. They are motivated by love and mercy. They do not cling defensively to their repository of prestige.

Are we talking about a completely unattainable ideal here? Do we need to get our heads out of the clouds and take a look at the actual political landscape? Is there really anyone who fits these lofty descriptions? And if not, why are we wasting time on this topic?

Against the backdrop of today's political brinkmanship characterized by zero-sum battles, incessant allegations of corruption, power plays, rancor, lawsuits and countersuits, polarization, and reciprocal demonization, it appears that we have lost forever that virtuous knight in shining armor who will point the way to reconciliation and justice for all. But the ideal of *barami* will not fade easily. It is buried deep in the hearts of the Thai people, calling out to them like a lonely siren, enticing them to wish for more in their leaders.

We must understand that the toxicity of politics on the national stage does not define all of Thai leadership. Below the surface are thousands upon thousands of leaders in lower-level government, in business, in non-governmental organizations, and in religious communities. Among this vast pool of leaders, there are some who actually practice the principles of *barami*. They are not perfect, but they are fair and kind and intent upon doing what is most beneficial for the collective they serve.

This facet of Thai face is based on the foundation of respecting others. People with this quality consistently show deference to the face of others[3] and readily honor those who are worthy of respect. Through this consistent behavior they accumulate a reputation of having moral strength. They slowly garner a rare form of social capital, not by actively pursuing that capital, but by sticking to their principles. Their *barami* is simply a byproduct of their virtuous leadership.

People like this—people with bona fide *barami*—are awarded monumental amounts of the other forms of social capital as well. Their positive impact upon others leaves a lasting glow. It radiates long after they leave their positions of power or influence.

"If someone has accumulated goodness, you can see it," says a judge. "There is no need for him to build it up. It is a personal characteristic that simply emerges."

This is the most valuable of the five abstract treasures that are comprised in Thai face. To possess accumulated goodness is to have the most secure form of face in Thai society. It is the height of honor.

To remember this facet of Thai face, imagine an enormous rain tree casting a spacious swath of shade at the edge of rice fields. Weary workers approach it with anticipation of escaping the brutal heat of the sun by resting in its shadow. It is always there, always welcoming. It provides something indispensible without asking for anything in return. It is forever a favorite place in their memories.

That is how common people feel about someone with accumulated goodness. They delight to rest in his or her shade.

6
A PLACE TO STAND

IF YOU WILL SUMMON your powers of concentration, we will now dissect the concept of *saksi* (ศักดิ์ศรี), the most arcane of the five dimensions of Thai face. Ask any Thai to isolate the central meaning of this word and he will struggle. He may even wince. He's likely to contradict what the other chap said. The word seems vague and loose, with a legion of connotations. It is *beyond* abstract, but it is integral to any discussion about face in Thailand. "Thai people believe that *saksi* is more significant than any other thing," says a high-ranking police officer.

Once again, let us recall the police chief in the first chapter of this book. He proudly shows me five precious amulets that he wears every day under his uniform. Why does he wear them? He says that they give him confidence and inner energy. In other words, they bolster his personal sense of having value. They reinforce his belief that he carries honor with him wherever he goes. These self-assured descriptions hint at *saksi*, the cornerstone of Thai face.

In terms of etymology, the word *sak* comes from the Pali and Sanskrit languages. It has three related meanings: power or ability, strength, and status (Dictionary of the Royal Institute 2003). The word *si*, also from those ancient languages, carries the meanings of shining brightness, auspiciousness, beauty, and progress (ibid.). If we combine the meanings of these two syllables we have intriguing translations: "strength that shines brightly" or "radiant power."

One scholar describes *sak* as "abstract sacred power" that has emanated from the monarchy for several hundred years. The king grants this sacral power to others to confer rank and authority (Keyes 1987, 31). Another calls it "cosmological" power and contrasts it with the word *amnat*, which has a stronger earthbound connotation (Zehner 1991, 161). Yet another calls it "power in the sense of resources" (Akin 1975, 102). This word has so many connotations that I hesitate to give it an English gloss. Its shades of meaning must emerge inductively through description.

In the minds of many Thais, *saksi* is a giant tangled ball of conflated terms. But despite its whimsical adhesion to many notions, this word stands quite distinct from the other four facets of face. It is difficult to unmask the phantom-like qualities of this word unless you study Thai face.

At its heart, *saksi* is an independent, individualistic force at work within every competent social actor in Thai society. It stands against society's strong collectivist sanctions and pressures to conform. It is a substratum in the psyche that lends freedom for an individual to think and choose for himself. It is the wellspring of personal convictions and principles that enable him to stand up for what he thinks is right. It frames the bottom-line, non-negotiable issues that he is willing to defend.

In a society of people traditionally known for their easy-going mien and lack of rigidity, *saksi* appears to be an anomaly. It is the essence of being your own person. Some might call it autonomy or willpower. Some Thais describe it as "having a place to stand."[1]

We are talking about endogenous worth—the amount of worth a person grants to himself or herself. The other dimensions of Thai face are judgments of worth awarded by society. This word is different. It connotes a personal sense of honor that hovers in the bottomless chasms of the Thai psyche.

This aspect of face is rooted in the self. "The Thai are first and foremost ego oriented, characterized by the highest ego value of being Independent [*sic*]—being oneself," writes Suntaree Komin (1990, 133). "Thai people have a very big ego, a deep sense of independence, pride and dignity. They cannot tolerate any violation of the 'ego' self.

Despite the cool and calm front, they can be easily provoked to strong emotional reactions, if the 'self' or anybody close to the 'self' like one's father or mother, is insulted."

A German sociologist, writing over a century ago, captured the Thai notion of the ego self well: "An ideal sphere surrounds every human being . . . into which one may not venture to penetrate without disturbing the personal value of the individual," he writes. "The radius of that sphere . . . marks the distance which a stranger may not cross without infringing upon another's honor" (Simmel 1906, 453).

This is curious. Buddhist teachings avow that the self does not exist. "There is no such thing as real 'self,'" pens one writer. "Ultimately, the entity which we commonly refer to as the 'self' has no permanent existence and is merely a combination of ever-changing physical and mental forces" (Chai 1998, 33–34). The behavior of many Thais, however, suggests that most have a clear sense of self and they stand ready to defend it.

Saksi is the epicenter of face attachment. It drives all attempts to gain honor and broad recognition. To have this treasure is to acknowledge that the societal rules of face are important. It means that you as a social actor are willing to behave in ways that demonstrate your worth, and you will defend that worth in social space. You are saying, "I have value." This claim-right to honor initiates all face behavior.

This keystone of face—endogenous worth—is the reason many Thais strive to avoid a loss of face at almost any cost. In the throes of interpersonal conflict, Thais often use a vulgar personal pronoun to refer to themselves: *ku*. This pronoun communicates that they are making a stand, holding ground, resisting a threat of intrusion, or willing to put up a fight for what they see as valuable. *Saksi* invokes the use of this pronoun in face-threatening situations. It functions as a counterforce to the constraining pressures of highly collectivist Thai society. An oft-quoted saying epitomizes this defensive behavior: "You can kill a real man, but he won't let you despise his worth."[2]

Decades ago, anthropologists documented and debated the "loosely structured" or "loosely woven" aspects of Thai society, observing that individual behavior is often shaped by free will in spite of existing social pressures (Ayal 1962; Embree 1969; Evers 1969; Kirsch 1969; Phillips 1965, 1969). But when we grasp the radical role of *saksi* in molding social behavior, we gain valuable insight into paradoxical displays of individualism.

This claim-right to personal worth is powerful. Often it lies dormant, but it is always there, forever ready to spring into action at a moment's notice.

In situations of abuse due to asymmetry in power, *saksi* lends courage to the lesser party. If a certain patron does not show proper regard for the worth of a client, *saksi* can empower that client to turn on a dime and pursue a more favorable patron. In fact, S. N. Eisenstadt and L. Roniger (1984, 136–37) document that Thai clients tend to show a shallow loyalty toward patrons who do not treat them well, a characteristic that distinguishes them from clients in other Southeast Asian countries.

Get a Thai talking about *saksi* and the word "myself" will surface repeatedly. "*Saksi* always adheres itself to a person," says a policeman. "It is something within us that we establish ourselves." This flatly is not the case with the other four words we have explored. Although *saksi* is many things to many people, in present-day Thai society it is typically conceived as an inward quality.

"We commonly believe that everyone has his own *saksi*," writes Thirayuth Boonmi. "*Saksi* has abstract characteristics that are concealed within every person" (1999, 265).

The Thai constitution refers to *saksi* as something every person possesses at birth, regardless of ethnicity, skin color, gender, language, religion, political views, or other things. This connotation of the word is similar to the Western concept of basic human dignity. *Saksi* is innate, not manufactured or fabricated. It is a possession from birth. It is the "resident locus" of a person.[3]

"It can't be bought with money," says a judge. "It isn't something that we can acquire by going out and getting it. It is already within human beings."

Can this sense of personal worth wax and wane over the course of time? Can it be accumulated in greater quantities like prestige, honor, reputation, or accumulated goodness? Can it erode or implode?

Yes, for many Thais *saksi* seems alterable. This is especially true when the word assumes the connotation of self-confidence, something dynamic and expandable. It can be boosted by success in the social arena and damaged by failures that go public. It seems to ebb and flow. Yet few Thais claim it can become so damaged that it disappears altogether.

Be forewarned. Modern Thais will seem to contradict themselves when talking about *saksi*. In one breath they'll tell you that it's self-determined—an inherent sense of worth—and in the very next breath they'll admit that it's vulnerable to all that transpires in social space.

This should not surprise us if we keep in mind that, despite frequent displays of individualistic behavior among Thais, most sectors of society are still highly collectivist. Collectivists assume that "the self is interdependent with the surrounding social context and it is the self-in-relation-to-other that is focal in individual experience" (Markus and Kitayama 1994, 97). In other words, the membrane between "self" and "other" is porous.

This helps us to understand why conversations about *saksi* commonly drift into contexts that are the domain of one of the other four aspects of face. This happens so often that endogenous worth can begin to feel like an external possession. For example, when people lose face badly they often will claim they have lost *saksi*. What they are really saying is, "This is an affront to my personal power."

Saksi is maintained, Thais will claim, by "behaving appropriately according to your status." If a person with great prestige eats at a noodle stand alongside the road, he can lose *saksi*. If he entertains guests at home or in a restaurant, he must ensure that the event is first class, or he can lose *saksi*. These two vignettes really have to do with maintaining prestige, or *nata*. Yet many Thais see a connection with *saksi*.

Successful members of society often link their private sense of worth to status, rank, or titled position attained through sacral power and good fortune. "In Thai society *saksi* is important in establishing the 'place' or position of people in society, and it has to do with other terms, such as honor and rank" (Thirayuth 1999, 269).

This notion of *saksi* as an external possession—a public decoration or citation denoting worth or radiant power—almost certainly predates the modern emphasis on *saksi* as an internal matter defined by the self. During feudal times, society judged the worth of a person by the amount of *sak* he possessed (Akin 1975; Keyes 1987; Zehner 1991). The contemporary tendency to tie a private sense of worth to status is quite likely a vestige, a lingering memorial to times past. It is prominent among those with royal lineage, descendants of the nobility, soldiers, policemen, and the very wealthy—people who are continually treated as though they have more worth than common citizens.

Thirayuth (1999, 265–66) notes a connection between endogenous worth and external objects, claiming that since ancient times Thais have attached *saksi* to material possessions, women, and certain vocations. "For example, nobility in past eras cared deeply about *lom phok* [a *chada*, or a headdress, worn to display one's rank]. It had to be stored in an appropriate place. If someone else touched it or acted disrespectfully [toward it], that action would bring contempt into the relationship . . . certain material things had absolutely no dispensable value except as symbols of *saksi*."

In modern times, conceptions of *saksi* remain conjoined with the external world. People create symbolic attachments between themselves and physical objects or public personas around them, turning them into "honor spheres." If anyone disrespects these external spheres of personal honor, it feels like an assault on their *saksi*.

Saksi is also linked with virtue. "The human animal is good," says a religious teacher, "but how much virtue does a given human actually have in his heart? That's human *saksi*. If we share resources, if we assist others, our *saksi*—like a lotus—will be very alluring."

A person's actions can either certify or cast doubt upon the *saksi* he or she claims to have. This is why Thais frequently judge the *saksi* of their fellow citizens. Consider a woman who sees her neighbor lying in his yard inebriated and shouting profanities at eleven in the morning. "He's behaving as though he has no value," she says in a huff of pity and disgust. She accuses him of lacking *saksi* because alcohol emboldens him with courage to disregard the conforming pressures of face rules and sanctions. His behavior says to others, "I don't believe in your rules. They are inconsequential to me." Others condemn him because he appears to have given up his fight for social respectability.

The rationale behind these judgments of worth can seem complex and arbitrary. Let's ask a middle manager in city government if beggars have endogenous worth. "No," he responds, "because they don't take responsibility for themselves. They obviously don't have a sense of their worth as human beings." He goes on to tell us that road-sweepers have worth because they are law-abiding and do their work. Disabled members of society have worth, but not if they go begging. However, a blind beggar who makes a living on sidewalks by singing over a portable sound system has worth because he or she gives something in return for the generosity of others.

This dimension of face is intrinsically bound to the theme of shame. To "have *saksi*" is to feel a delightful sense of worth. To "not have *saksi*" is to feel shame. It is to feel morally reprehensible and worthless, as though you are completely outside the acceptance and embrace of others. When other members of society accuse you of being in this state, they demean your basic worth. When you allow those accusations to define you, you can feel utterly worthless.

If someone violates a moral code or a widely shared social convention, other members of society are prone to utter the same damning phrase. "He has no *saksi*!" they say with disgust. If that contemptuous judgment becomes broad public consensus, it can decimate any "face-eyes," honor, public acclaim, or accumulated goodness that society may have previously granted to that person.

Still, it is crucial to understand that public sentiment alone cannot determine an individual's *saksi*. Ultimately, individuals must decide for themselves if they agree with society's opinion of their worth.

Saksi is organically related to the other dimensions of Thai face. Visualize the forms of Thai face as parts of a living organism so interconnected that if someone threatens or damages any one of them it is felt in all the others. If we assume this perspective, we can understand why a significant loss of one or more of the other four abstract treasures often raises immediate concerns about personal honor. If you "touch" any part of a person's storehouse of face, often he will feel it instantly in the depths of his sense of endogenous worth.

Thai face is founded upon *saksi*. This vital treasure is the proprietary space within every citizen, the space from which every social actor speaks. It is the critical core of Thai face, the starting point for the accumulation of prestige, honor, public acclaim, and accumulated goodness. One must demonstrate honor within before society will agree to confer a public grant of honor.

Saksi is a view of Thai face from the inside looking out. We cannot capture its many complex shades of meaning with just one English word. It carries connotations of autonomy, self-determination, dignity, self-esteem, self-confidence, conscience, pride, and sometimes even rank or status.

Despite its many meanings, we can best conceive of it as endogenous worth. It stands unique in the constellation of five words because it is an inward sense of having value. It offers a place to stand.

7

THE ANATOMY OF THAI FACE

YOU ARE NOW FAMILIAR with five vital kinds of social capital that make up Thai face: prestige, honor, public acclaim, accumulated goodness, and endogenous worth. We have examined each one until its unique facets have flashed like the cuts of a diamond. Evidence is strong that each is integrally related to all the others. It is time to explore those relationships and plot them together in a way that shows the big picture.

This is a challenging task. We are probing into unplumbed depths of tacit cultural knowledge, investigating things that very few people have scrutinized, dissected, or analyzed. For most Thais, these psychosocial notions are muddled together to such a degree that they seem indistinguishable, but my ethnographic research has clarified the elemental meanings of each form of social honor. My claims do not contradict the popular perception that these concepts are intricately fused. They merely pose an exciting new question: "If these forms of capital are clearly distinct from each other, then how do they combine to form a whole?"

Let's create a visual model of the anatomy of Thai face that portrays the meanings of these very abstract concepts. This macro view will explain both how these forms of capital differ and how they adhere to one another. We will build this model piece by piece by looking at each concept in turn and seeing how it links together with the others. Let's begin with the notion that anchors everything.

Endogenous worth, or *saksi*, is the bedrock of Thai face. Think of it as the underground foundation that supports the weight of all other forms of social capital. Although *saksi* is a highly abstract indigenous concept, it is of pivotal importance. It is the only treasure not granted by society. It lies below an imaginary plane that divides a person's internal and external worlds. *Saksi* is the sacred, inviolable treasure of every human being. This sense of endogenous worth is a springboard for the pursuit of the four other coveted forms of social capital. *Saksi* offers Thais a place to stand.

Honor, or *kiat*, is the guarantor of Thai face. It is what lends (and denies) genuine quality to every avowal of worth awarded in social space, whether it be "face-eyes," public acclaim, or accumulated goodness. We might conceive of honor as a cone, a kind of monument to worth that is earned in public space. You have a cone. I have a cone. Everyone has one. Some are impressively tall. Others are quite short. But every competent social actor builds some kind of public monument to worth.

Because facework is rife with tactics subversive to these standards of true honor, we must concede that *many of the cones of honor we see on a daily basis are actually riddled with chasms of dishonor*. On the surface they look good. They may even be highly convincing. But often they deceive us.

Genuine honor is legitimate worth displayed in social space. It trickles downward through hierarchies. To be a steward of this valuable treasure is to be given many avenues for gaining greater face and power in Thai society. Honor—when it is morally founded—denotes true worth.

Public acclaim, or *chuesiang*, measures the sweeping reach or range at the base of a person's cone of social capital. If someone is powerful or talented or worthy of respect, this dimension of Thai face answers the question, "Who knows about it?" It measures the breadth of a person's public recognition. For most people it is constrained to rather narrow local circles. But for a few choice citizens, the radius of their renown extends countrywide.

The bare word *chuesiang* usually connotes something positive, something good—like a drifting fragrance. But it can be either positive or negative. We can think of it as a double-edged sword.

Good public recognition is an obvious asset, but negative public recognition is an unwanted liability. It erodes social capital.

This form of face is highly volatile. All dimensions of Thai face can be damaged, but public acclaim—much like prestige—is less stable, less secure, and far less enduring than honor, accumulated goodness, or endogenous worth.

Accumulated goodness—also known as moral strength or *barami*—is the most highly coveted dimension of Thai face. We might envision it as the tip of a person's cone of honor. But remember, this form of face is relatively rare. For most Thais, the tips of their cones of social capital are not graced with the crown of *barami*.

This is the most secure and enduring form of social power in Thailand today. It is also the most effective approach for winning the hearts of followers and gaining the cooperation of other members of society.

Prestige—called "face-eyes" or *nata*—is best thought of as a sparkling veneer that covers the aggregate of social capital controlled by an individual. It is the umbrella phrase that Thais use to describe anyone with social power in society.

Similar to public acclaim, this kind of face is often bestowed on the basis of things like wealth, skill, beauty, intellect, performance, success, and influence—things achieved through some show of prominence or dominance. The qualities that generate this kind of capital do not necessarily pivot on a person's character. In other words, just because someone with *nata* sends signals to others that he *deserves* to be treated honorably, that does not mean he is *truly* honorable.

This form of capital is the shell of Thai face, the most superficial layer. Though it is often just skin deep, it is by no means inconsequential. In fact, it is astoundingly significant. In Thai society, outward impressions matter greatly.

Prestige is a flashpoint for the other four kinds of social capital. It is innately tethered to a person's reservoirs of honor, accumulated goodness, public acclaim, and endogenous worth.

This kind of face is closer in meaning to public acclaim than it is to honor or accumulated goodness. When compared with forms of genuine honor, it is easier to acquire and much easier to lose. Also, it can easily deceive us. So often it creates a façade that frustrates our best attempts to judge the presence or absence of true honor. The beguiling sparkle of all that glitters can often blind us from things that truly matter. Because this dimension of face is so highly disinterested in the question of inner virtue, the "face-eyes" of any given person is often a poor measure of his worth.

Now for the model that represents the anatomy of Thai face (see fig. 1). This model shows how the five very distinct dimensions of face are organically related to each other. Take a few moments to study this visualization of what is, in essence, a Thai view of human worth.

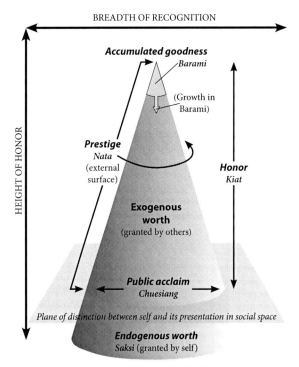

Fig. 1. The anatomy of Thai face

To make sense of this model, let's suppose that we ask an imaginary Thai to step forward for the purpose of conducting a full body scan to measure his reservoirs of social capital. He graciously agrees. After the scan, his results appear on the screen of our laptop, looking something like figure 1. How shall we interpret what we see?

Begin by taking note of two vital dimensions that map the edges of facework in Thai society: the dimension of height, representing the amount of honor, and the dimension of breadth, representing the extent of that honor.

Next, notice the thin horizontal plane of distinction near the base of the cone. That imaginary plane separates this person's sense of self from what is going on in social space. Everything below that plane represents *endogenous worth*—the amount of worth granted to himself by himself. This is *saksi*.

We can safely say that honor subsumes both the height and the depth of genuine value. Why? Everything below the invisible plane represents honor within. Everything above that plane represents honor granted by society. In other words, the theme of honor runs from the bedrock of *saksi* to the pinnacle of *barami*. Honor is the gold standard of worth.

Everything above the invisible plane represents a form of *exogenous* worth—something entrusted to that person by society. Consider the proposition that society reserves the right to rescind any grant of face that is conferred in public space, whether it be prestige, honor, public acclaim, or accumulated goodness.

Beginning from the bottom of this figure and moving upward, let's comment briefly on each aspect of the anatomy of Thai face.

Note that *saksi* is the foundation of Thai face. It is organically related to the other constructs. This reminds us that whatever happens to a social actor in the outer dimensions of personhood will often be felt at the very core of his self-esteem.

Directly above endogenous worth is *kiat*, or honor. Honorable individuals often receive the echo of society's acceptance, approval, and respect (also known as public acclaim). But that is not always true. Sometimes a bona fide person of honor is not very widely known. His honor is evident to all who know him well, but his exemplary life does not receive the amplification of public acclaim. We can adapt our model of Thai face to demonstrate this phenomenon, something we might call a case of "unheralded honor" (fig. 2).

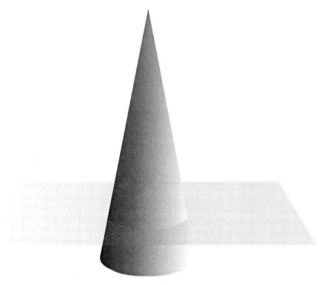

Fig. 2. Unheralded honor

This person's "cone of honor" is tall, but its base has a rather narrow radius. Is there honor? Absolutely. Does he enjoy much public acclaim? Very little.

Now, for the sake of comparison, glance back once again at figure 1 and notice the width of the cone at its base, just above the imaginary line of distinction. That diameter measures the reach of a person's (allegedly) honorable reputation—his or her *chuesiang*.

It is not hard to identify cases of public acclaim that have everything to do with true honor. Consider the wide recognition given to a soldier or a policeman who displays indisputable bravery in the line of duty. Consider the politician who establishes a foundation to protect the rights of abused women and children. Consider the owner of a small business, a woman of her word who always treats the customer right. All three of these examples argue that honorable living can generate a form of public acclaim that spreads far and wide.

But very often in modern society public acclaim lends potent social capital to people who have done little or nothing honorable. Take the case of a widely celebrated, handsome actor who—when off screen—is snarky and self-absorbed. His kind of *chuesiang* connotes fame, popularity, and stardom. It's all about making a splash, putting on a contrived presentation.

I call it simple public acclaim, shown by figure 3. This kind of public acclaim is broad at the base but very short in height, meaning that even though this person is broadly known, he or she lacks true honor. This cone of honor contrasts sharply with the cone in figure 2.

Fig. 3. Simple public acclaim

Now direct your attention to *barami* at the tip of the cone in figure 1. Not only does our imaginary volunteer have honor, but he is also one of those rare Thais whose graciousness and generosity have given birth to deep respect in the hearts of many.

Notice that a small arrow points downward from the tip. That subtle detail acknowledges that the noble reputation of this person with moral strength is growing. As he accrues new material resources and social capital, he willfully chooses to use those assets to assist others. He regularly shows kindness. He puts the good of society over his own vested interests. As he pursues this lifestyle with sincerity and consistency, his goodness accumulates and spreads downward to define the quality of his honor.

Again in figure 1, notice the thin, tilting arrows pointing upward and downward from the word *prestige*. One arrow points to the tip of the cone, the other to its base. These arrows tell us that "face-eyes" should be conceived as the external surface of a person's entire cone of social capital—much like gold paint or gold leaf sometimes overlays one of those conical, spired stupas that dot the landscape in Thailand. Prestige is the glint, the dazzle of the cone. Its purpose is to catch the attention of passersby.

This completes our brief sketch of the anatomy of Thai face. Distinct layers and dimensions form a constellation of highly complex values built around five abstract notions. Each is a form of social power.

What are some takeaways from this theoretical view of Thai face? To begin with, there is no doubt that contemporary Thais vary in their understandings of these notions. They often conflate them in their thoughts and speech. But to contemplate the anatomy of Thai face is to begin to understand with exceptional clarity that *these varied kinds of capital are not one and the same.* Once we have grasped this fundamental concept, it is not difficult to discern that having the appearance of honor can be altogether different from being genuinely worthy of respect.

Yet certain individuals—especially leaders—are delighted when prestige, honor, public acclaim, accumulated goodness, and endogenous worth are lumped together in one tangled mess. Why? *When society conflates the meanings of these five words, the public perception of what is truly commendable becomes profoundly murky.* Individuals who acquire one of these precious treasures—especially the wealth of "face-eyes"—will often find society quite ready to grant many of the other treasures as well.

I am arguing that as long as these terms adhere together as an undefined mass, power-hungry people will find it easier to take dishonorable shortcuts. Competitions for social capital are rife with fabrication, deceit, hidden agendas, bald lies, manipulative ploys, power plays, unethical choices, illegal activity, and exploitation of the weak. Daily quests for social capital are so riddled with dishonorable tactics that we feel, at times, like raising our arms in helpless surrender. Worse yet, we regularly reinforce this behavior by rewarding those who use these tactics. We show them respect. We award them with trophies, citations, promotions, special titles, and some of the highest positions of power. Sadly, it pays handsomely to be dishonest.

This lack of discretion is fallacious and unfortunate. To grant honor is to judge the worth of a human being. It ascribes value.

Whenever we catch ourselves doing that, it would be good to ask a penetrating question: "What standard are we referencing?"

Beneath the flurry of face interaction in Thai society there is a primordial tug-of-war over the standard for measuring honor: is it power or goodness?" It seems advisable to answer, "power." People with power and money control society. It is prudent to show them honor, because to do otherwise can attract credible threats to our well-being. Survival instincts beg us to feign respect whether or not we really feel respect in our hearts.

But do our acts of pretense declare that a person is truly honorable? We know otherwise. Something within implores us to quietly question what is going on. "You are powerful, you have money," we think to ourselves, "but do you have true honor?" To suppress that thought is to suppress the very *notion* of honor.

People with prestige are in some way dominant. They have greater wealth, smarts, charm, beauty, skill, authority, or influence. But we should separate these things from honor altogether. There is nothing inherently honorable about having a bigger piece of the pie than someone else. As long as Thai social actors continue to treat all attributions of "face-eyes" as though they are equally valid, then wealth, excellence, and raw power will threaten to replace honor and virtue as the foundation of Thai face. If every extraordinary trait is honorable, it is not long before we can get that uneasy feeling that all true standards of honor have evaporated into thin air.

"If a leader maintains his form—regardless of his level of virtue—Thais will easily believe in his credentials to lead," laments a respected religious teacher. Her words address the duplicity that leaders often employ to coerce others to grant to them more esteem than they truly deserve. In every society "some people are being rewarded for their skill in affecting others' responses and decisions, rather than for their merit" (Goode 1978, 235).

Leaders should never forget the subtle but profound difference between receiving a show of respect and being truly accepted and respected.[1] When followers say that they "respect the face, respect the eyes"[2] of someone, they are probably paying tribute to perceived moral goodness in that person. They are saying they *sincerely* accept and respect him or her. There is no equivocation. This phrase signals a divide between those who are truly esteemed and those who merely appear to enjoy the esteem of others.

As we now turn our attention to the dynamics of Thai leadership in part 2, a simple argument is already forming. A leader—to be worthy of the spoils granted to him—must be more than great. He must be morally good as well. That's why we shouldn't treat every flash of brilliance as something of great value. Not everything that glitters is gold.

For centuries, Thais have liberally provided their leaders with commodious opportunities for subverting honor. Contemporary leaders—especially those who subvert prestige processes—may not appreciate the greater clarity we now possess. But if an increasing number of people begin to comprehend the true shape and form of Thai face, that simple measure of lucidity may catalyze a healthy public dialogue about what is truly honorable.

The five dimensions of Thai face are distinct, one from the other, yet they form a whole. Many Thais tend to treat them as a whole in all judgments of honor, but the truly discerning will keep them distinct in their thinking and living. Any society that desires justice must be careful to make these distinctions.

PART 2

THAI LEADERS AND FACE

8
NOTHING GOLD CAN STAY

A NEW MERCEDES BENZ is pulled over for violating a traffic law. The driver, a wealthy businessman, casually mentions that he knows a few important people.

But the policeman isn't intimidated. "Excuse me, sir," he says. "May I please have your driver's license? I must write a ticket. You can reclaim your license at the police station."

This prestigious man considers it a big loss of face to be forced to pay a traffic fine, so he hurries over to the local station to meet with the police chief. After a brief conversation, the chief dismisses his ticket. To take the chief out for a 5,000 baht dinner feels better than paying a 200 baht fine and sensing a loss of endogenous worth.

This anecdote is puzzling. It is truly remarkable how far this community leader goes to avoid looking at fault. A popular saying reveals potent values that compel this man. "Lose silver, lose gold," the saying goes, "but never allow yourself to lose face."[1]

If we want to understand Thai leaders, we must explore their facework and their underlying beliefs about face. That is precisely the subject we will pursue in part 2 of this book.

Try something. Ask your Thai friends a plain question: "Is having 'face-eyes' important to leaders?" The average response will be a resounding yes. "The two can't be separated," says a seasoned government employee.

Having "face-eyes" is indispensable fuel for leadership in all contexts that are Thai. Leaders spend this invisible currency to gain things of great value: influence, productivity at work, a large network of relationships, opportunities to move up hierarchies, better income, recognition, respect, acceptance, honorable treatment, convenience, comforts, self-confidence, contentment, and family pride. Who wouldn't want all that?

Leaders deeply cherish these caches of prestige. Shining like gold, face is one of their most precious treasures, something to be protected at any cost.

It is also precarious. "Prestige comes and goes," laments a high-ranking policeman. "It's hard to acquire, but easy to lose."

Face is fleeting. Too often, it is at risk. And leaders have a particularly strong aversion to loss. Any significant loss of face puts them on high alert. Their faces may look unfazed, but you can be sure that inside they are disquieted, defensive, and feeling most uncharitable. At times they can retaliate in ways that escape the bounds of rationality. If you intentionally cause a leader to lose face, you will probably make an enemy for life. If that person is very powerful, you will pay for it. If that person lacks the immediate means to hurt you, he will wait to inflict revenge because he deeply resents you. Even if you accidently offend someone's face, you may risk a permanent break in that relationship unless you rush to apologize and ask what you can do to set things right. So if you want to foster friendships and forge alliances—if you want to *thrive*—you should never dare to touch what is sacred. For all Thais—but *especially* for leaders—face is inviolable.

Let's examine the phenomenon of face loss in circles of leadership. First we will explore what a loss of face feels like. Then we will consider what leaders try to avoid as sources of loss and options they entertain when dealing with loss.

This concept of "losing face"—what Thais call *sia na sia ta*[2]—has worked its way into many languages around the world. Non-Thais who are not familiar with this concept will need to brush aside cultural baggage long enough to appreciate and validate *what Thais feel* in the throes of a loss of face. To have proper empathy, it is best to slip into their shoes.

Every Thai knows what a loss of face feels like. It is simply part of the terrain of facework. As social actors navigate relationships and strive for a sense of acceptance and respect, face loss is bound to happen. It is inevitable.

Mild losses—blunders, missteps, mispronunciations, lapses, flubs, and goofs—are relatively harmless, even for leaders. Miscues conjure a sense of embarrassment that can be light or intense, depending on the context and the way others interpret the incident. But if you can own them and laugh with others about your obvious loss of form, that is often enough to remedy the situation. A little self-deprecating humor goes a long way. This kind of mild face loss—being slightly out of form—is a common experience in many cultures. We need not strain to understand how a Thai might feel when it occurs.

However, a *serious* loss of face in Thai society is something altogether different. It happens when a social actor is publicly exposed as having said or done something that violates sacred cultural values. Perhaps he has committed an immoral or unethical act. Perhaps he is the object of harsh public ridicule, gossip, or slander. Perhaps a former ally has gone over to the other side to expose some embarrassing secrets. The scenarios are endless.

A serious loss of face feels very different from mild embarrassment. It feels awful, like you are suffering a vicious assault on your psyche, even on your very life. It feels as if your inherent worth has been devalued. It is not a simple feeling of regret for slipping up. It has moral connotations. A person who loses face doesn't just hear, "You did poorly." He hears, "You are not good. You are *morally defective.*"

Do not miss this point. A serious loss of face in Thai culture, psychologically speaking, conjures a powerful sense of *shame*. It's a feeling that you have lost an undetermined amount of regard that others once had for you. You are less than acceptable. You have been pushed outside of an embrace that once surrounded you. This evokes excruciating emotions, and it can leave you questioning, "If I am now unacceptable to others, what remaining value do I have?"

Shame is linked to feelings of exposure and vulnerability. It is a feeling that some unsightly aspect of your personhood has been exposed and your *true worth* as a human being has been challenged, damaged, and diminished. It is an emotion that makes you want to hide (Wurmser 1994).

Serious losses of face are especially painful for leaders. They are people who have achieved a level of respect and ascendancy. Daily their egos have been fed by the acceptance of others. When this very precious "nectar" appears to vaporize into thin air, they feel shamed and rejected. That withdrawal of affection represents a break in relationships with people who used to regard them in a positive light—people they care about and people they need. This long fall from lofty heights is intensely painful.

For most Thais, but especially for leaders, *loss of face under any circumstance is flatly unacceptable.* It damages the state of well-being known as "having face, having eyes." It violates a sense that life is safe.

Conceive of face possession as a glass of water filled to the brim. A Thai with prestige has a sense of homeostasis when his glass feels completely full. A loss of face is like spilling some of that water—even a smidgeon. At that point, his attention becomes riveted on what has been lost, not on the bounty of his remaining caches of face.

If this sounds like oversensitivity, it's likely you've been raised as an individualist. A person soaked in strong individualist values has an *independent* construal of the self. He evaluates his behavior in light of his "own internal repertoire of thoughts, feelings and actions, rather than . . . the thoughts, feelings, and actions of others" (Markus and Kitayama 1991, 226).

Someone shaped by collectivist values, however, is very different. Members of most ethnic groups in Thailand share an *interdependent* construal of self that is deeply embedded in social relationships. Their emotions are influenced profoundly by the thoughts, feelings, and actions of *others* (ibid., 227). In fact, their definitions of self can reach beyond the bounds of their skin to include significant others.

"The unit of analysis is not the individual, but the *individual-in-relations,*" writes a prominent Asian face scholar (Ho 1994, 269). This is why public humiliation is so devastating for collectivists. They deeply cherish the affirmation of members of their ingroups.

For Thais, the pain that accompanies face loss is heightened because their sense of well-being is rooted in the approval of other members of their primary circles of relationship. The threat of losing that approval functions as a significant social sanction.

"'Face' is a powerful sanction for the Thai in encouraging or discouraging certain behaviors," writes one scholar (M. Ukosakul 1999, 17). That's because it functions as a system of merits and demerits. To receive face from other members of society is wonderful. To lose what you once had is highly distressing. The possibility of withdrawal of respect and approval is a threat, a mechanism that curbs undue displays of immoral, overly individualistic, or self-aggrandizing behavior.

A loss of face is a change in perspective from two viewpoints: the way others view a leader and the way she views herself. Something in her behavior or circumstances has forced these changes in perspective. They are *real* changes. Things are not as they were. This loss of homeostasis is distressing to the leader's psyche and potentially damaging to her relationships and stores of social capital.

Some offending incident, caused either by the leader herself or someone close to her, is perceived to have depleted her store of face. This creates a feeling that honor has been lost, followed by emotional reactions that the leader may or may not express to others. Three stages—an offending event, a sense of a loss of honor, and emotional reactions to that change—all constitute a "loss of face" (M. Ukosakul 1999, 115–24). The experience is both psychological and social.

Always keep in mind that face loss is a very subjective experience. Consider a leader with a degree from a Thai university who socializes with leaders educated in England or the United States. He feels inferior because those leaders send their children overseas during summer breaks, and he can only afford to send his children to another province. He feels a loss of face when they mention things like the orchestra, the ballet, a Van Gogh, or a Picasso, because he has no knowledge of those things. But in each case, the sense of loss is a private experience.

Suppose a host overlooks a prominent leader at an official gathering. Even when others are not aware of the blunder, the neglected leader can feel a private sense of loss.

This scenario can be reversed. It is possible for others to feel a leader's loss of face before he becomes aware of it himself. Sometimes—even *after* he is made aware—he may refuse to feel shame. Reflect on the army general who feels perfectly comfortable driving a Toyota. Others whisper to one another, "Can you believe he drives that thing instead of a BMW?" But he doesn't care. Is he losing face? It is hard to say. What seems apparent is that when leaders choose not to live up to certain public expectations it can help them sidestep, to some extent, some common sources of face loss.

No leader chooses to lose face. That much is certain. Very often, threat of loss or actual damage is the handiwork of his adversaries who wish to do him harm. But if it were that simple, a leader's store of face wouldn't be as vulnerable as it truly is.

The problem is that a loss of face can be triggered at any time by a leader's *own efforts* to present himself in public space. These unintended and unwanted self-presentations represent something I call "face leakage"—the inadvertent projection of a negative image into the public arena. Thais describe this as "selling your face."[3]

It is easy to assume that impression management is a highly deliberate and proactive exercise, a simple matter of controlling and tweaking an image in the public arena. But much of facework is unwieldy and unpredictable.

When creating impressions, leaders cannot control everything or be aware of everything. There are times when, try as they might, they forget important details crucial to the positive outcome of their self-presentations.

Leaders can be profoundly unaware of unintentional impressions they make. Suppose we have a man who perceives himself as being very generous. People who know him well have concluded otherwise. They perceive him as being insufferably stingy. He is blind to his negative personal baggage, but others are not. So, when he attempts to present a generous image to others, they fail to believe that image.

Much of facework is passive. It is inadvertent, undevised, unintended, and extemporaneous. Thai leaders commonly attempt to manipulate and control a desirable public image, but the fallout from passive facework can sabotage their best efforts to succeed and gain power. Face leakage can thwart their finest attempts to lead.

So for leaders, the terrain of life is pockmarked with landmines that can cause face depletion. To be a leader is to deal continually with the fear that you may lose what you have. The stakes are high because face is precious social capital, and many leaders have plenty to lose.

How exactly do leaders lose face? What things must they avoid? Let's explore what constitutes a loss of face for most leaders.

First, leaders lose face by *failing to produce*. Failure in leadership tasks quickly erodes their prestige. Repeated failures insure that they will fade off the scene as people who no longer have face. "You must not fail," says a highly successful banker. "You must not fail in the big things."

Any poor decision can lead to face loss. "If a decision doesn't work out right or bears little fruit," says the owner of a language school, "it's a very, very big loss of face. It shows a lack of giftedness in planning, as if he doesn't see the big picture, or lacks wisdom, or isn't smart enough."

A leader can lose face if he proposes a plan in a meeting but it is not adopted. Suppose the chairman of a committee announces a plan to make merit at a temple in a nearby province. He intends to give 10,000 baht. He asks the vice chairman to give 5,000 baht and the other members to give 3,000 baht each. But one of them responds, "No, that's too much," and the others agree. When he fails to sell his idea, he feels a loss of face, and he may complain, saying, "My allies wouldn't lend me a hand."

When leaders perceive that they've spoiled something or failed in a big way, sometimes they feel a loss of inherent worth, or *saksi*. However, much depends upon the individual. Certain leaders feel that deep sense of loss, while others are saddened by a poor outcome but don't take it as hard. They might quote the familiar saying, "Four-legged creatures stumble; even sages make mistakes."[4]

Similarly, leaders lose face by *not delivering on promises*. A prime minister in recent history declared that by the end of that year there would be no more poverty in Thailand. "But instead, the poor actually became poorer," recalls one religious leader.

Political candidates are famous for promising help to their constituents and equally famous for failing to deliver when given the chance. Budgets can be woefully insufficient for all those promises, and political opponents often attempt to inflict damage by voting down proposals. In the end, broken promises bring a loss of face.

Leaders lose face when they are *exposed for wrongdoing*—things like getting involved with the "dark elements" of society, making money through corruption, getting caught for driving under the influence of alcohol, or sleeping with an underage woman. If it is disclosed that they have built up prestige through former (or continued) involvement with illegal practices, such as selling drugs, they experience a great loss of face. And because leaders share face with their families, even wild or unlawful actions of a family member can cause them to lose face. They must try to keep their home lives stable.

The gravity of any misstep is a critical factor, of course. If a leader can convince others that an infraction was unintentional, the loss may not be so serious. Leaders who know their followers well and understand the pulse of society can usually redeem mild losses of face with a little effort. But if people judge a leader's wrongdoing to be deliberate, the crisis is much more sobering. Serious violations of social norms, religious teachings, or the law constitute a grave situation, and they can draw a public reaction so strong that there is no way for a leader to regain his or her former status. At the end of the day, a leader's positive image can be sullied by the public exposure of any major miscue, failure, loss of form, inconsistency, legal infraction, or moral violation.

Leaders lose face through *public criticism*. They can be very sensitive when others disparage their work as flawed. Some leaders cannot and will not tolerate being censured or challenged.

If leaders are criticized openly in any public forum, there is a high possibility of damage to their face. It can be particularly harmful if someone criticizes their motives or disputes the way they have appropriated finances. They can lose face when people contest their policies and decisions.

Here we have a prominent community leader who has fostered a friendship with the president of a university. Over the years this leader has accepted numerous invitations to address various student convocations. The president has also helped him to register several underprivileged students at the university. But when the president issues a new policy that every student must have a laptop computer, the community leader calls him to protest. He requests the university to provide computers for financially disadvantaged students. The president does not flex. In fact, he announces that students will not be able to take their final exams without a laptop. At that point our leader decides to make a stand. He goes to the defense of the poor by personally arguing his case with the trustees of the university. In the end, the policy is changed.

"I understood that my actions might cause the president to lose face," says the leader, reflecting on this experience. "But there are times you must put right principles above relationships."

If a boss criticizes a lower-level leader in front of others, that subordinate loses face. Conversely, if a subordinate publicly disagrees with his or her boss—an exceedingly rare scenario—it is viewed as a serious attack on the face of the boss.

Let's ask a wealthy banker if a leader loses face when publicly criticized. "Oh, nobody dares!" he exclaims. "This kind of thing doesn't happen in our society." He thinks for a moment, then quickly qualifies: "Political enemies do this, and newspapers make it their vocation."

Leaders can lose face because of *gossip* and *slander*. They worry about what people say behind their backs, and they often feel shame when people are gossiping.

A relatively small incident can be fodder for scuttlebutt. When donating to a cause, one must give an amount appropriate for someone with "face-eyes." Prestigious leaders must be generous when placing money into wedding cards. At funerals, if they give just 100 or 500 baht like a common person, it can spark gossip: "Hey, why did she give so little when she has that level of prestige? Why is she being so stingy? Does she lack the resources? Ah-ha! Maybe she's struggling financially!"

In many societies, gossip is the language of the disempowered, and Thailand is no exception. Those who lack the power to challenge the hegemony of a leader often will resort to this potent and effective weapon. It is a tool that tempers the abilities of leaders to establish undue asymmetries in power.

Slander is particularly harmful because it can diminish the devotion people feel toward a leader. "In the district where I live, there was a very promising candidate who was winning admiration," recounts a policeman. "Just days before the election, a rumor appeared in newspapers alleging that he abused his wife. That's all it took. His public acclaim came tumbling down. What did he do to solve the problem? He hastily held a news conference to insist that it wasn't true. He had to get the news out to attempt to fix his image."

Leaders lose face when they're *overlooked at public ceremonies*. At such gatherings, the focus of attention is on the host and his special guests of honor. The host commonly invites distinguished guests up to the microphone to say a few words—usually to praise the host and the event or speak words of blessing. But the host might unintentionally overlook a person of higher status in favor of someone with less status. When bypassed, slighted leaders often feel a loss of face. Others who notice can feel his loss as well. If the "mistake" is intentional, disrespected leaders will interpret it as a competitive effort to "break their face."[5]

Leaders lose face by *misspeaking in public*. If they declare something to be true but facts surface to expose their words as untrue, they can lose face. If they misspeak due to a lack of adequate information, they appear incompetent or unprepared. Others consider this to be very bad form.

Leaders lose face by *having to admit that they are wrong*. Listen to an author and speaker as he recalls a childhood experience:

I once had a dog I loved very much. If someone pretended they were going to hit me, this dog would protect me. Man, I loved that dog! One day I came home and asked, "Where's my dog?" My mother said, "I sold him to a family of foreigners for three hundred baht." I burst into tears. She said, "We'll buy you another one." But she never apologized to me. This is deeply embedded in Thai society. Deep down, did my mother know she was wrong? She knew. I knew she felt bad. But she couldn't say the words. Fathers and mothers never say "I'm sorry" to their children because they feel it's a loss of face. They are leaders. Leaders never make mistakes. This is the way Thai people think. If a person makes a mistake, he is not a leader.

It is not easy for most leaders to acknowledge fault, let alone apologize. "It's most rare—almost impossible—to find anyone willing to confess wrongdoing publicly," says a religious leader. "It's equivalent to destroying your prestige. Sometimes, a leader would rather die than reveal sins or weaknesses."

Let's now shift our focus to ways that leaders respond to face loss. At the slightest hint of loss, most leaders display a survival instinct that catapults them into hyper vigilance. They are highly motivated to recover lost honor, and they will do all they can to avoid loss, or at the very least, to alleviate undesirable consequences. They exhibit enormous energy and determination to repair what has gone wrong. Thais call this "redeeming face," "restoring face," or "retrieving face."[6]

The split second leaders become aware they have lost face they begin to experience some powerful thoughts and emotions. "I think to myself, I must protect my 'face-eyes,'" says one leader. "I must try to contain the damaging information so my shame doesn't spread more widely."

Some leaders immediately get angry because they think that they alone are right. "Those with great 'face-eyes' like to be a one-man show," explains a female leader. These leaders do not tolerate any loss of face. They are vindictive. They will view the person who caused them to lose face as an enemy.

"There is so much quarreling among leaders in Thai society," observes a religious leader. "They're constantly causing each other to lose face—sometimes intentionally, sometimes unintentionally. In the national parliament, dissension is rife because they forever cause each other to lose face."

If someone "pounds" or "rips"[7] a leader's face, the leader will often nurse feelings of hurt and anger with a desire for revenge—an emotion Thais describe as *khaen*.[8] You may be surprised, then, to learn that outward passivity is a common initial reaction to face loss. Emotional detachment is a routine coping mechanism among Thais (Chaiyun 1994). When leaders sustain face loss, their phlegmatic responses are calculated ploys to contain damage. To admit shame is to make the crisis even worse, so they choose to look impassive. "See, after you've lost face—if you don't show that you are hurt—you can deflect the gaze of others so that they stop thinking about it sooner than later," explains a university professor.

Still, loss of face is a highly anxious experience. Leaders worry, "Who knows about this and what am I going to do?"

A key factor in determining emotions is whether or not leaders accept that they are truly at fault. False charges almost always stir up a "fight" response. But even if the damaging information is true, many leaders will tenaciously fight the charges. They get angry and insist, "I'm not wrong. I won't lose face. The other party is at fault." They reject any blemish on their reputation, a stance captured by a curious idiom: "to stubbornly insist that the rabbit has but one leg."[9] Only when the evidence becomes overwhelming will some leaders implode with shame, sadness, hurt, or fear.

"Those who are weak will feel shame. Those who are strong will feel bitter," claims a wealthy businessman. "If you can't afford to be bitter, then you feel shame. If he has a 'big face,' a lot of power, or if he's more defiant, he doesn't have to feel shame. He can always inflict harm in retaliation. You can have a kind of game theory about it. If a stronger man slaps you in the face, naturally you don't slap him back, but if he's weaker than you, then you beat the living crap out of him! It's very natural."

Not all Thais would agree with that perspective. Some would argue that a person with strong moral values should feel remorse about wrongdoing.

Shame plays a dominant role when leaders lose face. Strong feelings of rejection and loss can give way to sadness and remorse. Self-esteem and self-confidence feel depleted. Leaders describe this as a loss of inner power.[10] "Some leaders become priests or find a quiet life somewhere, or they just disappear. They don't want prestige anymore," says one leader. "Their hearts are weary, burdened, and despondent."

When leaders experience a confirmed loss of face, they have options: they can blame it on someone else, insist that they have done nothing wrong, show sadness and apologize, or hide for a period of time until things blow over and the issue loses its force.

But for the most part, lost face must be redeemed. The most common way to redeem face is to offer excuses or counter with information or evidence indicating your innocence.[11] If the loss of face is not severe, many leaders simply lie. "Immediately lie. Save yourself!" says a leader, with a touch of sarcasm. "Then if you're caught in your lie you can always say, 'I just couldn't bring myself to tell the truth. I was embarrassed.'"

An embattled leader often works his webs of influence by telling others about the injustice done to him. He claims he has been singled out. He blames it on someone else. "Whether or not the 'evidence' is true or false isn't the point," says a chief of police. "Just refute the information." Prominent national leaders do this through the mass media. "You just 'fix' the news," says a high-ranking border patrol policeman. "You say, 'It's not like that. It's like this.' Just find a platform and fight back." These tactics are called "embracing everything good, but pushing evil onto others."[12]

There are other creative ways to respond. Leaders can change the topic, use humor to diffuse the situation, or get others to look beyond their blunders to their shining successes.

If leaders experience a major loss of face due to adversarial attacks, they commonly want revenge. At the very least they will nurse grudges. They will bad-mouth their enemies and actively avoid them. These days it is increasingly common for leaders to pursue full-blown retaliation. Legal arenas are filled with defamation lawsuits and countersuits. Some leaders with great power and influence will even break the law to exact revenge.

"The reaction of many Thais is vindictive," says a successful businessman. "Very few people will try to amend things. *Very* few, I think. People are vindictive. They will try to inflict some kind of harm or injury on the other party. Their response is, 'Don't you know who I am?'"

Leaders must exhibit restraint, however. If assailed leaders redeem face with harsh public words, that course of action can actually be counterproductive, causing them to lose even more face. Because of this, most leaders keep a careful watch on their words. They avoid speaking sharply, showing anger, or using words as an excessive show of force.

Timing is a huge factor in fighting face loss. Leaders must move as quickly as possible to restore their face. The longer they let the situation go unattended, the greater the potential for widespread damage. If they do not rush to redeem face—if they just brush the whole incident aside—they risk losing even more face.

Loss is calculated in stages. Before they do anything else, leaders seek to confirm if significant others are waning in their acceptance and respect. If this appears to be true, they begin to feel an uncomfortable threat of loss, a damage to their "face-eyes." In other words, they acknowledge (at least inwardly) that an undesirable turn of events has *temporarily* disturbed the equilibrium that sustains the goodwill of others.

The story, however, is not yet over. Leaders enter a liminal period when they cannot determine the severity of their losses. In fact, it may be too early to conclude whether true loss will occur at all.

However, if their loss of face is staggering in scope, leaders know that all their social capital is potentially at risk: their prestige, public acclaim, honor, accumulated goodness, and perhaps even endogenous worth. In this liminal period, these treasures become like temporarily frozen assets. They remain in question until leaders effectively redeem loss through one of the many techniques available. *During this tenuous stage, society is beginning to question the right of the leader to lead.* Those who wish to be fair will withhold their final judgments. But enemies or competitors will seek maximal damage by pouncing upon the incident.

In the end, leaders may be unable to redeem face if their infractions are serious—such as a violation of law or common standard of morality. In these most severe cases, leaders can lose their entire caches of social capital in a kind of "domino effect."

The last of the treasures to be threatened, of course, is *saksi*, or endogenous worth. It is at risk only when a violation is judged to be particularly egregious. Many Thais argue that it can never be lost entirely. Yet when it feels damaged by severe face loss, the pain is excruciating. To question the endogenous worth of any person—let alone a leader—is to question his or her intrinsic value.

If broad public consensus regards a leader as having lost honor at her deepest core, it is exceedingly difficult for her to redeem face. If, however, she can successfully redeem her "face-eyes," the other forms of social capital are usually returned to her as well—although not necessarily unscathed.

It should be blatantly obvious that leaders consider the experience of losing face to be highly undesirable. There seems to be only one satisfying trajectory: *upward*. It is entirely unacceptable to lose ground, backtrack, or wane in popularity, influence, and respectability. When loss does occur, it can be taken very poorly by the psyche.

Face to a leader is like money to a miser. He can never have enough of it, and to lose the smallest farthing (or *satang*) of an accumulated treasure feels tragic.

The face needs of leaders in Thai society have a significant influence upon their motivations and decisions. Like an invisible force, they powerfully shape the contours of leadership behavior. That is why an awareness of this topic of face loss is fundamental to the study of power and governance in Thailand.

Face is highly variable. Like a valuable cache of gold, it is always at risk. For leaders in Thai society to lose any amount of this form of social capital is enormously stressful. It can shake feelings of well-being to the very core. Loss of face impairs their efforts to lead effectively. That is why leaders strive diligently to protect themselves from any and all losses. But sometimes it feels as if "nothing gold can stay."[13]

9
GUARDING YOUR TROVE

THINK BACK TO the retired municipal officer I once visited in Bangkok (chapter 1). Do you remember the immense care he took to groom himself before stepping out of his front gate for a stroll in the lane? He wore new clothes. He peered into the mirror. With precision, he coaxed each hair into place. He cautiously checked every detail of his physical appearance. Only then was he ready to go.

Was that self-infatuation? No, it was behavior designed to maintain his stores of face by avoiding potential causes of face loss.

Leaders are stewards of priceless stashes of social capital. Some treasures are magnificent; others are modest. But all are extremely dear. Because of this, leaders are tireless in sidestepping potential losses of face. These attempts to protect and preserve face are known as *raksa na*.[1]

This kind of behavior is common in all social circles, not just among leaders. You will recall that every person, regardless of status, behaves as though he or she has face and takes measures to preserve face. Consider the practice of social smoothing known as *wai na khon uen*,[2] or protecting the face of others. Everyone does this to some degree. The goal of this behavior is self-preservation. By showing deference to the face of others, you are asking for the same kind of treatment in return. You do this by smiling a lot, greeting others appropriately, avoiding unnecessary confrontation, suppressing feelings of disagreement, and speaking in ways that give honor to others.

Even people of humble means will sometimes staunchly defend their inherent worth. "I once tried giving money to a poor man collecting recyclables out of garbage bins," says a leader. "He bristled and refused, insisting, 'I am not a beggar!' He was protecting his sense of endogenous worth as a human being."

But common people do not practice face maintenance to the same extent as those who have prestige. Leaders must maintain face to a far greater degree than their followers because they face greater consequences should they fail to do so. They control greater amounts of social capital. They simply have more to lose. "The higher you are, the more you have to exercise caution," says a university professor.

Having prestige can be burdensome. That's a strange sentence to write, but it's true. "Those without prestige experience a freedom," says a community leader. "They can wear rubber slippers or torn shirts. But those with prestige—no way! They have to maintain their image because society has expectations about how people with 'face-eyes' should speak, dress, act, and be."

"Those with 'face-eyes' are to be pitied," muses a religious leader. "They can't lose face. If they do, it's equivalent to not having value. I think these people are often anxious and fearful about losing face."

Leaders must grow skillful in evading face loss. They maintain a high public profile. They are easily recognized in their spheres of responsibility and influence, so they must be ever conscious of their self-presentations. They must be aware at all times. They must remember that others are carefully monitoring their words and actions—especially enemies and competitors who would love to discredit them. So leaders educate themselves about situations that can lead to a loss of face. They choose conduct that keeps them in zones of safety. Just how do they do this?

Leaders *speak sparingly.* They always watch their words. As we've already noted, misspeaking can damage their public acclaim. Even words spoken in jest can create problems if someone takes them seriously. Often leaders avoid making decisions on the spot because they fear making a mistake and losing face in front of others. "Because you are on top," says a chief of police, "even the smallest incident can have an impact on your 'face-eyes.' You must exercise great caution in your speech so that loss won't occur."

Leaders must be skillful at *guarding others from a loss of face*. When they treat those around them with respect, face maintenance becomes more manageable. Failure to do this can cause unwanted ruptures in relationships. "Thai people avoid offending others because it signifies a break in personal relationship. It is irredeemable," says a powerful businessman.

Leaders constantly *monitor their public appearance and demeanor*, something Thais call *wang tua*.[3] They want to look good at all times. They pay close attention to the way they dress.

It is good to keep in mind, however, that rules of comportment differ according to situation and locale. Leaders in villages can usually afford to be more relaxed than leaders in towns and cities.

"I went to Chonburi," recounts an influential community leader. "A local leader took a bunch of us leaders out to eat. He wore slippers, shorts, and an undershirt into the restaurant. The rest of us were wearing neckties. But when the owner of the restaurant greeted him, he raised his hands high against his face and bowed in deep respect! This kind of leader doesn't care. He knows he has money and he's a leader in the community, yet he doesn't care about his comportment." Thais describe this kind of leader as "gold wrapped in rags."[4]

But for most leaders in Thai society, shows of wealth are an important veneer. Leaders project an appearance of prosperity because it helps to gain the respect and cooperation of others. It is one of the most generic and tangible ways to say, "I have prestige, and you should treat me with honor."

"Wealth is fuel for the journey," says a district chief of police. "This way of gaining credibility has ancient roots."

For many leaders, the quest to find money is relentless. They are constantly compelled to find fresh means to maintain and increase their levels of prestige. "It is because of 'face-eyes,'" says a villager. "They want to possess, they want to acquire."

Leaders commonly borrow money to maintain their prestige. At large public gatherings, prominent leaders must wear expensive clothing, designer shoes, rings, diamonds, and gems, so as to avoid feeling embarrassed before others. "We don't have the means, but we have to purchase consumer goods, even if we accumulate debt," says a subdistrict officer. We call this behavior "going beyond our abilities."[5]

One cannot merely put on a show, however. People doggedly monitor the generosity of their leaders. A decrease in a leader's benevolence can lead to a decrease in his power over his entourage. Leaders at all levels of society must play the role of patron because *being generous is one of the most common techniques for expanding power in Thai society.* It is the primary reason why leaders must be so unflagging in their quests for financial resources.

Even local village leaders must dispense significant amounts of money so people will remain dependent on them. They are approached by a constant stream of visitors with requests for assistance, especially financial help. An age-old idiom describes this ancient practice: "The base of the steps is never dry."[6]

This never-ending quest to ferret out fresh financial resources is a headache. If leaders lack influence to secure resources needed by the collectives they serve, they can lose face. If they make money by breaking the law, they worry that someday they may get caught. If they borrow money with no plan for repaying, they can become deeply indebted to people of influence.

But the leader as patron is a widely entrenched prototype with deep influence at almost every level of modern society. Leaders must often acquiesce to an implacable financial burden. They simply cannot afford to ignore the economic quotient of face maintenance.

Lack of privacy is another burden of face maintenance. Prominent leaders find it difficult to appear in public without being noticed. Wherever they go, people know them. They must nurture an ever-increasing number of strategic relationships that can sap their time and energy. "You become tired and have fewer chances to rest," laments a chief of police.

The status of leaders thrusts them into the spotlight and makes them vulnerable to criticism. "If a woman with no prestige gets pregnant out of wedlock, who's really interested?" asks one leader. "But if a famous television host gets pregnant out of wedlock, who *isn't* interested?"

"If we're going to accept or admire anyone in Thai society, he must be good in every way," explains a judge.

Many leaders in Thai society seem to *embrace a standard of utter perfection*. They feel that they must never—under *any* circumstance—appear weak, incompetent, misinformed, or at fault in any way. They deal with constant anxiety that their prestige will depreciate due to bungled self-presentations.

"None of us is always perfect," says the owner of a small business. "At times we get tired or sick, or we feel down, or we make mistakes, but we're pressured into feeling as if these things aren't allowed to happen. It's stressful."

In short, leaders are held to an impossible standard: always get it right. Never slip up. Why do leaders agree to this unforgiving standard? Apparently they have little recourse. Society is quick to expect it of them.

To maintain this guise of perfection, leaders must embrace a level of hypocrisy. Especially when they harbor shameful secrets, they must put up a false front. "Part of maintaining face is lying," states an office worker. "Lying to others and deceiving yourself. The most immoral thing is lying to yourself all the time."

This penchant to appear perfect varies, however, from leader to leader because of differences in perspective, temperament, and character. "We cannot make mistakes," says a well-known Christian pastor, weary of bearing unrealistic expectations. "I say to my followers, 'If I were to conduct a survey asking what you expect from your pastor, I guarantee that not even angels would want to apply for the job.' So I say to them, 'You must love me as I am. I cannot be all that you expect me to be in every way. I'm trying to be a good person, but I'm not good in every way.'"

Another palpable pressure for leaders is that they cannot "tread water." They must be *relentless in acquiring new knowledge, skills, and resources*. If they fail to do this, one day they might lose face by appearing incompetent and misinformed.

Even in retirement, leaders give thought to face maintenance. When leaders with titles and status retire, watch carefully. They will attempt to find other positions of honor to replace the one they had.

They welcome opportunities to serve as directors for corporations and organizations. "It doesn't matter if that position is not much of anything," says a leader. "It's still better than going from everything to nothing."

Techniques of face maintenance are *preventive* in nature. They serve as a prophylaxis for face loss. For example, we've noted that leaders play the role of patron. This creates a buffer that protects them from face loss because their indebted clients usually come to their defense. A leader might speak to the police on behalf of a follower, or bail a follower out of jail, or lend a follower money in exchange for a personal check. In every case, those who benefit from a leader's kindness will be prone to protect his face in future days.

It often takes a team to maintain the image of a leader. That is why many leaders find and nurture a group of close subordinates to serve as "their people."[7] Entourages help to alert leaders to early signs of danger that might be on the horizon.

We've noted how success helps to protect leaders from face loss. Leaders must be truly productive. They must research what is expected of them in each new leadership context and give special attention to the requests and needs of key players who can determine the success of each project. At times they can minimize failure by choosing projects that have the best chance of success. They do this because they know that when respect is high, criticism is likely to be low.

Leaders cultivate harmony in their relationships. They nurture relationships with important patrons—people with influence in the community, or leaders in high positions of authority. If they are successful in building these alliances, others who know of these tertiary relationships will think twice before attacking them.

There is also strength in numbers. If at all possible, leaders listen to the majority opinion of their followers. To choose an unpopular course of action and then fail is to invite a substantial loss of face. But if most followers support their leadership choices, leaders often can avoid a great deal of damaging criticism.

Another secret to maintaining face is to live a morally good life. Leaders can shield themselves from unnecessary face loss when their actions are consistent with their words. Leaders with accumulated goodness, in particular, practice few defensive techniques other than being honest, fair, and generous in the exercise of their duties. "Do what is right," says a village leader in the Northeast, "and you will always have the truth to explain your actions."

Some leaders seek protection from face loss by denying others the right to criticize. Consider the wealthy prime minister who, when criticized by a prominent newspaper, threatened to buy a majority stock in the company. Such tactics often backfire, however, because members of the public tend to dislike leaders who care too much about face.

Face is difficult to obtain and even more difficult to maintain. Leaders must bear the burden of preserving their prestige by learning the defensive postures and skills of face maintenance. This is serious and toilsome work. If they do not maintain what they have, their stores of capital can dissolve with frightening speed.

But another maxim is about to emerge. If leaders do not continually *gain* face, they can lose their capacity to lead.

10
LET THE GAMES BEGIN

SEVERAL YEARS AGO the governor of Bangkok proposed to extend the elevated railway across the Chao Phraya River. If he could have completed that major project, it would have brought him a fine gain in face. But the prime minister preempted the governor's plan, saying, "Let's wait on this. It is the responsibility of the Department of Transportation."

These two competitors were from opposing political parties. Each party had drawn up its own plans for mass transit in Bangkok. Both leaders intended to extend the elevated railway, but neither wanted the other to succeed. This is a compelling illustration of how the desire for face can be a powerful motivator for politicians.

In all fairness, you might be thinking, "Wait a minute. Were these men competing for face, or was it power that they really wanted? Were these political games with face consequences, or face games with political consequences?"

The answer is, "both." There is no doubt that they were locked in a tug-of-war over power and control. But they were also competing for greater public acclaim among the residents of Bangkok. Both men knew that a big gain in face could tip the scales in an upcoming election.

Most Thai leaders actively pursue face as treasured social capital. If that sentence seems colorless, you might want to reread it, noting first that the bald pursuit of face for the sake of face is deplorable behavior in the eyes of most citizens of the kingdom.

Yes. Three phrases describe the intentional pursuit of face: "promoting face," "grabbing face," and "wanting to gain face."[1] All three elicit negative feelings in most Thais. Ask them how they feel when they see someone behaving this way, and the words *mansai* will almost surely fly from their lips. It means they feel a mixture of disgust and envy. They may even call the person a *sueak*, or a "damned brownnoser"[2] (Flanders 2005, 207–8).

I am not sure why this response is so widespread, though I suspect that part of the answer rests in Buddhist teachings. A central tenet of the faith is that cravings are the root of all suffering, and they should be repressed or—even better—completely extinguished. Translated into everyday living, we might say that it's poor form to desire anything badly, and it's especially poor form to *look* like you desire it badly.

So conventional wisdom discourages aggressive face acquisition. If leaders are too obvious in their efforts to gain face, it can easily backfire. They risk the chance that others will talk negatively about them, generating unfavorable gossip that can frustrate their efforts to rise. This common response to "grabbing face" serves as a social sanction against those who would unashamedly seize power and advantage.

All attempts to grab face, therefore, involve a calculated risk. Leaders must handle them with a delicate touch. They can pursue face actively as long as they appear as passive as possible. It is best to act as though they care most about the collective and very little about personal gain.

But this sanction does not, by any means, eliminate competition for face. On the contrary, *competition for face thrives*. Most leaders deeply covet greater "face-eyes." Like any other scarce and valuable resource, desire for this abstract treasure triggers a flurry of competition in leadership venues across the nation—top to bottom. There are many contestants on a similar quest.

"The real truth is that competition for face is the nature of high-level leaders," says a wealthy banker. "If you don't want face, then don't become a leader, that's all. If you are going to be a leader, you must want to acquire face."

Members of the public weigh a leader's face by comparing him or her to other leaders. This act of comparison inevitably sets the stage for competition. If you are a leader, it often feels as if you are the protagonist and any proximate leaders are antagonists. In order to thrive, you cannot merely protect yourself from loss. A strong defense with no offense is a poor formula for success. You must be proactive in gaining face.

Especially among politicians, there is intense competition for prestige. In certain contexts—pitched electoral battles between political rivals, for example—society at large shows greater tolerance for shameless acts of pursuing face. Everyone accepts that a competition is underway and it will not be over until there are clear losers and one clear winner. In these situations leaders will pursue face with abandon. They will interpret the face gains of perceived competitors as a threat to their own stability. They will work to frustrate and erode those advances, even to the point, if necessary, of damaging the face of their competitors.

Such competitions can be costly to the public. Let's say that the opposition parties in parliament present a decent plan for addressing a certain public concern. Their proposal has great potential for benefiting needy sectors of the populace—perhaps even more so than the competing proposal of the ruling government. But the majority party will not acknowledge those ideas. To do so would feel like a loss of face.

"Sometimes politicians maintain face rather than doing what is right and fair," says a judge. "They give their own face maintenance more consideration than they do matters that will benefit the citizens."

Efforts to gain face often occur in the context of competition for what appears to be a limited amount of social capital. This "zero-sum" game is most prominent whenever the coveted goal of face gain is a rare commodity, such as when many leaders are pursuing the same official titled position.

"Peaks are sharp. There are few high positions," says a long-time government employee. "Everyone is fighting for titled positions," adds a religious leader.

"When the Chinese bless one another, they say, 'May you develop and prosper,'" observes a community leader. "But Thais will say, 'May you be successful in becoming the lord and master of others.'[3] It's in our veins. We believe that entering a high position of authority is something important. This has been fixed in us for hundreds of years. In the early days, people pursued an education with a view toward working for the government. It was so we could become 'big'[4] — someone able to command others—so that others would bow down to us and show us respect."

Titles confer legitimacy to their holder. To possess a position of authority in Thai society is one of the clearest ways to make an uncontested claim to honor, although the amount of honor varies significantly according to the position. In other words, while having prestige is valuable, for many leaders that is not enough. They desire to possess honor that is unequivocal. Competition for titled positions, therefore, becomes unusually intense.

A key variable determining a leader's choice of face behaviors is whether or not he assumes this zero-sum perspective. If he is convinced that the coveted prize is in short supply (i.e., a political office, a promotion to higher military rank, a title bestowed by royalty, or a reputation for having the "biggest face" in a community), he will consider every competitor's gain in face to be a loss in face for himself.

A leader who assumes this perspective will be serious, intense, proactive, tenacious, and sometimes even brutal in competition. Thais refer to this level of rivalry as "life and death"[5] behavior.

When most leaders—not just politicians—feel strongly challenged, they are interested in the *disempowerment* of their adversaries. Once things have developed to that point, their pursuit of face is highly competitive and sometimes vicious in nature.

But do all leaders in Thai society compete for prestige? "Oh, all the time," replies a prominent leader. "They vie for prominence."[6]

Throughout society there is competition for this precious commodity. To lead a business, a university, a community association, a temple, or a work team—you must accumulate face. The intensity of competition may differ significantly according to the context of leadership, but competition for face is prevalent among leaders at most levels.

"They don't know what 'enough' is, so they have to keep climbing," says a government employee. "It is hard to become champ," she continues, "and even harder to defend the championship."

With very few exceptions, all Thai leaders want and need to gain face. If they choose to tread water, they will find themselves drifting downstream from their positions of dominance. In other words, a leader's daily behavior must continuously manifest his or her "face-eyes" in convincing new ways.

Why? If someone is already abundantly rich in face, why must he continue to gain face?

One answer lies in the engaging idea that face, like other forms of capital, must be expended with use. "Status," writes Peter Blau, "can be considered as capital, which an individual can draw on to obtain benefits, which is expended in use, and which can be expanded by profitably investing it at interest" (2005, 132). This insight is enormously helpful for explaining why leaders must continue to gain face.

The state of possessing face is not static or inert. It is dynamic and ephemeral. Social exchange theory teaches us that every time a follower complies with a leader's wishes, it is equivalent to paying back (to an undefined extent, to be sure) a debt of cooperation he owes that leader. If the leader wants to continue to expect compliance, he must continue to procure new capital. He must make fresh acquisitions of face to reconfirm his superiority and justify his ongoing claims to preferential treatment.

Taking this theory even further, we can think of efforts to gain face as risky attempts to reinvest capital so as to make a profit. "It is by taking this risk of losing some or all of his power that the superior earns surplus profits, in the form of increased power and other rewards, if the chances he takes pay off" (ibid., 136).

So leaders are foremost among members of society who proactively pursue face. Leaders are on the move. They are devotedly intentional about using rules of face interaction to climb established hierarchies.

How, then, do they do it? How do leaders cultivate greater prestige? What are their time-proven strategies for gaining face?

Let's begin by paying proper respect to untold thousands of capable leaders in diverse sectors of society who, on a daily basis, perform their duties well and serve their collectives admirably. Their examples point us to one of the most obvious sources of face gain. Leaders gain face by *being competent and productive.*

It takes more than a superficial show for leaders to advance. To gain lasting face, leaders must produce. They must solve the problems of followers. They must win the respect of others by demonstrating genuine talent and ability. They must be true to their word and true to their responsibilities. Success eventually brings the accolades of others, and it can lead to rock-solid gains in face.

But leaders employ many other tactics as well. Foremost among all strategies is this: leaders gain face by *playing the role of patron.* Generosity toward others is one of the most powerful means of gaining face in Thai society. A leader must become a "father who takes care of others."[7] "Society today shows acceptance toward those who give," says a leader in an agricultural cooperative.

Leaders must present an image that they care. They want to appear kind and generous. They leverage their social capital to survey the needs of constituents, offer assistance, donate money, impart knowledge, find resources, improve conditions, and solve problems. At school events, rites of passage, public celebrations, and official openings of public projects, leaders look for opportunities to gain face. They offer the use of their cars, distribute bottles of drinking water, pass out free T-shirts with their names on the back, or give table fans to each family. They focus on the felt needs of those under their care in order to win their hearts. "Whatever you have," explains a prominent police officer, "you must give it first in order to receive the acceptance of society."

Politicians look for ways to "buy face." They direct budgeted funds toward high-profile projects that make a splash rather than tackling much more critical issues. Why? They desire to gain face.

A leader's role as patron is demonstrated by his perceived generosity in making donations. "Let's say that they're selling tickets at work to raise money for a charity, and each ticket is 1,000 baht," says a municipal manager. "Leaders who really want to gain face will commit to buying ten—maybe twenty—tickets. Do they have that kind of money? No, but they'll go to their subordinates and say, 'Hey, look after this.' Each subordinate will take two or three tickets. If he can't sell them to friends, he'll buy them himself. Then they'll gather the money and take it to their boss, who'll give it to the charity and say, 'See, this represents my ability.'"

There is a solid gain in face for leaders who donate money, provided that the amounts of their donations are made known to the public. People with "face-eyes" gained great amounts of face by donating money after the 2004 tsunami. Across the country, television screens flashed the names of donors and the amounts of their great charity. Cynical observers could hardly resist the sense that these donors were simply grabbing face. "People that do this aren't really helping others out of a true desire to help," says a high-ranking border patrol policeman. "There's a hidden agenda—to maintain their 'face-eyes.' They're merely using a tool, that's all. They're insincere."

Leaders also donate to temples. The key is to make sure that news reporters document their generosity. Not everyone is impressed, however. "When I give money for *kathin* [a Buddhist merit-making ceremony], I remain anonymous," says a disgusted businessman. "But others want it broadcasted. 'This person donated however many tens of thousands of baht.' They gain face. Making merit has everything to do with gaining face."

Leaders also gain face by *hosting public gatherings*. Whenever people gather in large numbers—whether for banquets, ceremonies, festivals, rallies, concerts, marriages, or funerals—certain individuals have an opportunity for significant face gain.

"It is remarkable," writes a Thai intellectual, "that we often use the phrases 'lose face' or 'gain face, gain eyes' on occasions when we have large gatherings, when there is a crowd or a certain group of people present. If in such assemblies we receive value or a symbolic role— such as receiving an award, praise, or being chosen as a representative to give an oration—we feel that we gain much face" (Thirayuth 1999).

On the village level, when someone with status—perhaps someone with a lot of rice in his granary—sponsors an official gathering for the purpose of making merit, he will invite the whole village to a feast.

He will kill a cow, offer liquor, obtain the services of a *mo lam* (a singer who tells stories through a genre of country music), and provide other entertainment. Villagers who are invited will treat the host with great respect. Often these events last many nights in a row. The host wants to gain wide recognition and "face-eyes" from his investment.

"People spend beyond their means in order to . . . keep up their faces," writes a Thai scholar (Ubolwan 1997, 66). That's because you can't skimp in hosting these events. The keeper of royal wealth in a former era once wrote: "You cannot have a shortage when providing a feast for monks or for people. To provide a feast is to provide so they can eat as much as they want, with no restraints or barriers. The host of the feast must prepare enough to provide adequately. No matter what costs might be, pay them. Because if you are killing a water buffalo, why lament over the peppers?" (cited by Thirayuth 1999, 274).

This expectation of abundance is tethered to the threat of shame. If a host lacks enough money for the event, somehow he must find it. This puts immense pressure upon leaders, but they're not the only ones who suffer. "A family might be extremely poor, with hardly enough food to eat," says a bookkeeper, "but when it comes time for a son to be ordained, they have to do everything in their power to make the gathering grand. Instead of sponsoring a modest meal—no way! They fear losing face—they must have a huge feast with plenty of food left over, and they want a large crowd to attend. They feel pride, but they lose out because they go into debt. It's like 'making curry paste and dissolving it in the river.'"[8]

A popular writer shares the following personal anecdote. "When I got married I thought of having something small with my parents and a few friends, with some food afterward. My father said, 'No! Two hundred tables!' I was thinking as they do in the West. But my father needed to have 'face-eyes.' This has been buried deep in Thai people. They must grab face."

Leaders understand the calculus of face at such events. The host of a gathering stands to gain the most face, but this is true only if the gathering goes splendidly, with no kinks. The amount of gain depends upon many variables, such as who attends the gathering, the number of guests, the amount of food, and the quality of the food. "If he doesn't do it right, if it's not to public expectations based upon his economic status," says a judge, "people believe it's a great loss of face."

If common people attend in great numbers, the large crowds reflect upon the host's perceived generosity. Does the host receive wider public acclaim? That depends upon whether the media and gossip mills spread details of the event to a wider audience. The clever host will ensure that this indeed does take place.

To legitimize a gathering, a host must be able to find a special guest with recognized honor who is willing to attend. At the village level, the host invites the village headman. At the district level, he invites the district officer. In province-wide gatherings, the governor must commence ceremonies. This is mandatory for ensuring major face gain. This extends a splendid opportunity for special guests to gain face. Leaders with rank and title exercise discretion in accepting invitations. They will decline invitations to smaller events that yield little in the way of wider recognition, believing that they now are worthy of much larger gatherings. They "choose their stage," to put it bluntly.

The presence of a special guest demonstrates to the masses that the host has connections. He knows a "big person." The guest attends "to bring honor to the ceremony."[9] He publicly speaks words of blessing and praises the host.

This ritualized behavior effectively enhances the host's "face-eyes." His or her face gain is commensurate with the level of honor of the special guest. "If someone meritorious like the king attends an official gathering, everyone believes that the gathering has received the highest honor," explains a district police chief. "The king receives 'face-eyes,' public acclaim, acceptance, honor, and recognition for his accumulated goodness. The host receives 'face-eyes' from the king and reciprocates with loyalty from his heart—highest respect towards the king. As if he were a god."

Sometimes attendees at these events have opportunities to gain face as well. When government workers attend birthday ceremonies for the king or queen, they can gain face when panning cameras show them seated in the background with their white garb and royal decorations. At smaller, more localized gatherings, prominent community leaders attend local events simply to be seen and thereby gain a little face.

At public gatherings, face in the form of honor trickles *downward* like water over a cascade, a phenomenon we noted in chapter 3. Here is an indigenous model of empowerment that illustrates how someone with prestige can decide to give face to someone else, thereby increasing that person's social capital. "This is the way they give honor, give 'face-eyes,'" says a chief of police.

Leaders gain face by *projecting an image that they are morally good.* Thai society likes and compliments good people. Leaders who appear to speak the truth, follow through on their words, and govern with fairness and empathy are held in high esteem. When leaders do good works with little fanfare, it can significantly increase their prestige.

Some leaders—perhaps many—"do good" explicitly for the sake of gaining face. They want their attentiveness toward needy people to be seen. They "create an image"[10] that they are virtuous, refined, generous, and kind-hearted. They "advertise themselves"[11] by arranging photo ops at orphanages or scenes of disaster. These gracious self-presentations are disseminated by the news media, giving leaders increased public acclaim. It reifies and solidifies their stores of face. Especially in politics, it is a key strategy for climbing the hierarchy from village to district, district to province, and province to the national stage. Leaders should avoid outright bragging, but they must speak of their own goodness. A televised press conference is a golden opportunity. A positive front-page magazine article is invaluable.

One common tactic for self-promotion is to claim credit for a completed project. Consider the opening of Bangkok's Suvarnabhumi airport. "Actually this project was on the drawing board for over forty years," says a high-level leader. "But it was completed under a certain prime minister's tenure, so he rushed to sit in the first airplane to land at the airport. He went there to claim credit. He gained face."

Self-promotion can be subtle. If a younger leader always makes sure he is in the background of a prominent leader at news conferences and public events, viewers may begin to wonder, "Is this a rising star?"

Time has a way of exposing leaders who like to gain face by putting on pretentious shows. But not always. Superficial appearances matter greatly in Thai social settings. If this tactic always backfired, it would all but disappear. On the contrary, public leaders make generous use of it.

Leaders also gain face by *winning the hearts of their superiors.* "It is mandatory to find others to lift us higher and higher," says a leader. "You cannot climb all on your own."

Leaders search for ways to win the hearts of their bosses. "Grow close to him because he has the ability to pull you upward. The boss will choose the subordinate he loves the most. He will give him the most chances," says a professor.

"My father's friend had the big boss visiting from Bangkok," the professor continues. "He learned that the man loved to play cards and gamble. What did he do? He arranged to have several of his friends play cards with him and the boss, and—knowing that the boss didn't like to lose—he gave his own money to his friends and told them to purposely lose. He did this on the boss's subsequent visits as well. I don't know where he got the money, but he found it somehow. It paid off. When the time came for the next key promotion, he got it."

In countless hierarchies of business, government, and even the non-profit world, leaders who want to "climb the stairs" look after those who are "bigger," as Thais phrase it. By winning the favor of their superiors they have a better shot at gaining acceptance, praise, titles, and greater wealth.

"I often thought, 'Why are some of my friends spending so much time looking after the boss, brownnosing him?' says a former government employee. "Especially the men would follow the boss around: carrying his brief case, showing through body language that he's the boss and they're inferior, working late, spending time with him outside of work hours, and going with him wherever he went. After a short period of time, these colleagues would be promoted—very fast. They had a drive to gain face. Other subordinates who didn't like those tactics felt that they couldn't compete. They were never chosen, they had little money, or they didn't have time to make the effort."

A related tactic is to keep your work in front of the boss. Employees must attempt to catch the boss's eye—becoming a special assistant, doing projects of interest to the boss, and even performing tasks that the boss himself should be doing.

The game is played upward, not downward. While it is important to treat your subordinates well, it is far more important to win the hearts of those above you.

"It works like a magnet," explains one leader. "When someone is promoted, others below will treat him as he treated his superior in order to be drawn upward."

Leaders gain face by *promising benefits to others*. The very act of promising shows self-confidence, and it can yield a gain in "face-eyes." When leaders claim to have ability and a certain amount of power, it gets people talking.

We have already noted that politicians do this to get elected. "No matter how hard or how easy it might be to deliver, just give your word in advance," advises one leader, mimicking smooth-tongued politicians.

It's easy to over-promise and under-deliver. Some promises are gratuitous and unsound—if not delusional. Others have substance and potential, but once leaders are elected their good intentions may be thwarted by political quarrels and other realities.

Leaders gain face by *displaying wealth*. You are well aware that a show of wealth in Thai society is a powerful claim to prestige. Leaders build up social capital by amassing financial capital. It matters very little to casual observers how riches were acquired—whether through corruption, exploitation, or by assuming heavy debt. What matters is that leaders have wealth to put on show.

Leaders gain face by *earning educational degrees*. This is as much about status as it is about proving they have the knowledge necessary to give direction to others. Degrees from prestigious academic institutions, especially in America or the United Kingdom, can raise the level of a leader's "face-eyes."

Leaders gain face by *accumulating titles*, by becoming chairpersons of community associations, hospitals, businesses, or organizations.

Consider what a former city official did many years ago when a district of Bangkok was flooded and the city lacked funds to address the problem. He took ten wealthy local businessmen out for seafood and paid the entire bill. During the meal he was frank about the need and asked his guests to serve as members of a problem-solving committee. They donated the needed funds and their names were then posted publicly, giving each man a boost in face.

A few years later, this same municipal manager was helping a committee for the preservation of Thai culture to prepare for the Songkran festival. He was asked to find money to purchase chairs for the event. What did he do? He approached a man in the community who, in his words, "liked a big face."[12] He flattered him, saying that there was no one in the community bigger than he. He asked the man if he would kindly serve as the honorary chairperson of the festivities, and then casually mentioned the need for one hundred chairs. The man agreed to serve, and a few days later a check arrived to cover the expenses. The community leader wanted to gain face, and he understood the wordless message that he was expected to provide the needed chairs.

Leaders gain face by *attaching themselves to other prominent leaders*. They build networks of "friends" in the right places and then use those relationships to their advantage. They are also careful to show their faces[13] at high-profile gatherings of important people.

This is face gain by association. Leaders do this because society judges the level of their prestige on the basis of those whom they socialize with as equals (Blau 2005, 133). Also, there is little profit in socializing with common people. Leaders work their webs of relationship upward in an effort to gain face and power, a topic we will tackle in future chapters.

Leaders gain face by *cultivating personal entourages*. Here we are not talking about face gain generated by a leader's generosity with his entourage. We are identifying the entourage itself as an effective tool for gaining face during forays into public space. The very sight of an entourage in public increases the level of interest and respect of onlookers, thus increasing their estimations of a leader's prestige.

Whenever a leader ventures into public surrounded by a group of attendants, it signals to all that he is a person with "face-eyes." This boost in recognition is a precious payoff from his efforts to build and take care of his entourage.

"On the level of the district or the province, wherever you go, take an entourage with you," says a high-ranking policeman. "If you go alone, you feel like you have no power, like you still have insufficient 'face-eyes.' But if you have an entourage or a group of people to cheer you and support you, it helps."

Leaders gain face through *the honorific speech of others*. The impact of honorific speech is subtle but powerful. When others use terms of honor to address a leader in public, it can lead to face gain because it reinforces and sometimes intensifies respect. Special pronouns like *than*, *khun*, and *phrakhunchao* (used with priests) give honor to their recipients. Those present and listening, including bystanders and virtual strangers, tend to think more highly of the leader.

Last, but certainly not least, leaders gain face by *causing competitors to lose face*. This approach is driven by the thought, "Your loss is my gain."

To put it lightly, facework between leaders is often agonistic. It is no secret that political enemies are out to discredit one another, but this behavior is not by any means limited to politics. It is rampant in all levels of leadership across the kingdom.

When leaders feel threatened by the gains of adversaries, they must find ways to embarrass them and damage their public image. They criticize their efforts to solve problems, lodge accusations, fabricate stories, leak hurtful information, and sabotage their proposals and projects. These and other face-damaging tactics are referred to as "cutting the chair"[14] out from under a leader. They actualize a strategy to gain face by bringing a competitor down.

We will now shift gears to consider competition for face in a unique context—among members of an entourage. In other words, we will study the leader as a *client* competing with fellow clients for the favor of the same patron.

Patron-client dynamics exert a robust and pervasive influence on most contemporary Thai relationships. The scholar Lucien Hanks observed this many decades ago, and it still rings true: "With the probable exception of the bond between husband and wife, every liaison between people in this society takes on some forms of this patron-client relationship" (1975, 200). He calls this pattern of social exchange "not just the mortar but the rods and rivets that hold Thai society together."

Hanks duly reminds us that most leaders are but a single point in a vast matrix of hierarchical relationships. We dare not miss this. In other words, almost every leader is both a patron *and* a client—a patron of some, a client of others. We can benefit greatly by looking at competition for face amongst *peers* in entourages and organizations.

Due to indigenous patron-client patterns, fellow members of an entourage often must compete against each other for the heart of their patron. They flatter the boss, speak well of him to others, display gratuitous honor toward him in public, and find ways to assist his efforts to gain face. Thais describe this fawning behavior as "sucking up to" or "licking the shins and the legs" of the boss.[15] When members of an entourage adopt this kind of opportunistic behavior, all understand that a competition is underway.

Like all competitions, inevitably there are winners and losers. If a subordinate is promoted above his peers—whether due to merit or favoritism—it is sure to trigger reactions from other members of the entourage.

After a promotion, peers often conduct a period of informal investigation. They want to know, "Is this a good thing? Why was he chosen? Was it because of true ability, relational connections, or celestial luck?"

Envy is extremely common. "Among groups of people of relatively equal rank and 'face-eyes,' if one of them rises, the others will feel dissatisfied, as though each of them has lost face," explains a judge. "The rise of a new leader can actually cause his peers to lose face."

It does not help matters that promotions are often based on favoritism. When certain colleagues are unjustly favored over other more worthy candidates, feelings of envy can be intense. Disenfranchised peers can feel disgust toward colleagues who get ahead by brownnosing.

Envy is not the only response, however. Some peers may be genuinely happy for their colleague, and they will say so. Others may use similar words of affirmation, but it is flattery for the purpose of "sucking up" to the rising colleague and aligning themselves with his power.

If you talk with Thais about competition amongst peers, they will frequently cite the same proverb: "Do good, but don't become prominent or you will be in danger. No one wants to perceive you as more prominent than he is."[16]

Because of intense competition for face, many Thai leaders have a strong aversion to seeing others look good. Out of envy they will often frustrate a rising colleague's ability to function and flourish. "There is this tendency to pull ambitious people down," claims a community leader. "Others around you become easily annoyed if you elevate yourself too much."

This is a key insight. Members of an entourage who begin to gain face will often be subject to a distinct egalitarian pull downwards. This common reaction is not necessarily good because leaders should be allowed to rise if they are competent. But in many circles of Thai society today, when groups of clients of equal rank share the same patron within the same entourage, there is an intrinsic pull downwards that retards the empowerment of any one of them. This downward tug is clearly a competitive tug, not a tug to preserve harmony. It surfaces because groups of equals assume zero-sum thinking about their shared pursuit of a coveted goal.

Leaders in Thai society compete intensely for face. They contrive and implement strategies to manipulate patrons, undermine competitors, and dominate subordinates. Their facework is rife with stealth, chicanery, rancor, and envy because all contestants are in hot pursuit of social capital that is essential for true success and contentment.

11
WHAT GOES AROUND COMES AROUND

ONE DAY A HIGH-RANKING border patrol policeman in Aranyaprathet allows an employee and his friend to hitch a ride into Bangkok. When they stop along the way for a bite to eat, the officer pays for their bowls of rice porridge. Years later this same employee, spotting the officer at the national headquarters of the Border Patrol Police, politely asks if he remembers him. The officer smiles and says, "Yes."

"Sir, I still have not forgotten you," replies the employee. "You were the assistant chief in Aran, and one day I rode into Bangkok with you. I will never forget that bowl of porridge."

"I hadn't thought anything about it," says the officer, recalling the incident. "I was willing to help out. I had room in my car. I didn't think it was anything special, just something I normally do for my subordinates. But he interpreted it as something grand."

A world of cultural meaning hides in this anecdote. It illustrates the quiet power of uncalculated acts of kindness in Thai society. Authentic generosity often creates fond memories that linger not only for years, but for decades—or in some cases, for generations to come. Generosity usually initiates a *cycle of reciprocity* between giver and receiver. It is a major player on the landscape of social exchange.

We have already highlighted that leaders are patrons. They are givers. This is an essential characteristic of the Thai way to lead. Leaders must continually reify their social capital by being charitable with their followers. They generously take care of family, relatives, friends, subordinates, and allies. A leader's largesse can reward him or her with economic power, large numbers of clients, and valuable relational connections.

That's because reciprocity is what makes the Thai world go 'round. To grasp that is to step into a wide portal of understanding regarding Thai leadership. Patterns of social exchange reveal much about how leaders gain the cooperation of their followers.

To explore this topic, we begin with a simple word that has powerful meaning: *bunkhun*. The word has two root meanings: "merit" and "virtue" (Haas 1964, 292, 93), but when you put them together, no one English word does justice to the sublime layers of meaning, so I will avoid using a gloss.

Bunkhun is a deeply indigenous social phenomenon that shapes the fiber of relationships in Thai society. It has everything to do with leadership processes that surround us on a daily basis. We should think of it as relational reciprocity triggered by generosity. Suntaree Komin calls *bunkhun* "indebted goodness," and describes it as "a psychological bond between someone who, out of sheer kindness and sincerity, renders another person the needed helps and favors, and the latter's remembering of the goodness done and his ever-readiness to reciprocate the kindness" (1990, 139).

The essence of a *bunkhun* relationship emerges when a person does something to benefit someone else and the grateful recipient reciprocates in some way. *Bunkhun*, therefore, falls solidly under the rubric of social exchange.

Because most pockets of society are so thoroughly hierarchical, social exchange usually occurs between people with disparate amounts of social power. Holmes and Suchada state that the concept of *bunkhun* is "perhaps the most fundamental value that has emerged out of the vertical nature of Thai society" (1997, 30). Egalitarian forms of *bunkhun* do exist in contemporary Thai society (we will touch on that in a moment), but most social exchange occurs in the context of asymmetry in hierarchies. It takes place between patrons and clients.

Patron-client patterns exert a powerful influence in circles of leadership and followership in contemporary Thailand. As we study these patterns of reciprocal obligation in the next two chapters, we will gain fertile insights into contests for power that occur daily between leaders (patrons) and followers (clients). But let's first return to the seminal word that lies at the heart of Thai social exchange.

Bunkhun is relational indebtedness that gives way to gratitude. A word that epitomizes gratitude is *katanyu katawethi*.[1] One scholar translates this couplet as "to remember and eventually reciprocate," but that doesn't fully capture the richness of this phrase (Akin 1975, 110). I think that "loving indebtedness expressed through grateful behavior" is closer to the mark.

Thais have valued gratitude for centuries. *Bunkhun* was prominent in patron-client patterns during the early Bangkok period (1782–1873), when it held much the same meaning as it still carries today (ibid., 110–11).

In past generations, groups of villagers carried coconuts to the king, or they sent him an oxcart full of rice, or they gave their children into his service. In contemporary Thailand, when villagers visit someone important like the district officer, they often take him a gift—perhaps food, perhaps money—even though he already receives a salary for his duties. The villagers do this to show affection, to "display water from the heart."[2]

"I think that—of all nations of the world—Thailand has some of the clearest examples of patron-client behavior," says a judge. These patterns can be traced back to the feudal system that dominated Thais in past centuries. The masses were held under the governing control and influence of a few individuals who had great economic power and authority to rule. When people received protection and care, they always found ways to reciprocate toward their benefactor or patron.[3] They were at his service, and their loyalty was often so consuming that they were willing to die for him.

Take careful note that *bunkhun* was forged in the context of enormous social disparity in ancient Thai societies. Simply put, this form of social exchange emerged from a history of relationships in which one of the exchange partners had considerable power over the other. Cycles of reciprocity arose between people of unequal power and status.

"Thai society is still based upon the feudal system," says one leader. "We believe that there are both 'big people' and 'little people.'"[4]

"In our past history we've had monarchs to look after the sufferings and the joys of the people," says a graduate professor. "We have come to expect that he who is high must look after him who is low. Just like water that flows from high places."

These words allude to the example set by King Ramkhamhaeng of the Sukhothai dynasty, who referred to himself as "father king."[5] "He ruled the rest of the kingdom through vassal lords over whom he presided like a strict but affectionate father" (Griswold and Prasert na Nagara 1975, 44).

"Thais have a patron-based system[6] that dates back to the *sakdina* days," says a government worker. During that period of Thai history, kings looked after princes, princes looked after nobles, nobles looked after commoners, and all of them were superior to slaves[7] (Wales 1934). Each of these matchups had the tenor of "master and servant." The master cared for the servant in every aspect of his life. The servant served his master.

Faithful servants often became like family. "Back when many people in the Northeast had no surname," says the owner of a bakery, "when it came time to pick a name, people approached a successful, established patron to ask if they could use his surname and become a part of his larger community."

Patrons demanded explicit compliance and faultless loyalty. At the same time, they provided clients with a valuable hedge of safety.

But a dash of common sense tells us that patrons were not always benevolent and clients were not always sincere. This is a weighty point. Acts of "kindness" were often like double-edged swords because the benefactor, if he was kind, was also powerful. Punishment was allotted to clients who did not show proper gratitude. To this day a saying is reserved for people who fail to show gratitude: "The sky and the earth will punish you. The earth will swallow you up."[8]

In short, patrons in ancient eras showed a mixture of kindness and judgment. Clients felt both love and fear. It was a world of antipodal extremes. This insight should tempt us to wonder if *bunkhun* in modern days might also assume two very different forms, but let's hold that thought until the next chapter.

When Chinese immigrants arrived in Thailand, they brought cultural values that cherished affectionate reciprocity in relationships. It is possible that these values reinforced Thai beliefs about the merit of gratitude.

To this very day, many Thai-Chinese approve of someone who recognizes kindness and responds appropriately. This theme of gratitude can be seen in their custom of cleaning the gravesites of their ancestors and leaving food there. They know that their deceased loved ones no longer have bodies that need to eat, but it is an expression of deep gratitude.

Many modern Thais readily feel their indebtedness to the kindness of others. When they enter a warm reciprocal relationship, they describe either the other person or the relationship as "having *bunkhun*."

These relationships are guided by a well-known proverb: "Love gratitude, recognize kindness."[9] When kindness is shown to them, most Thais feel as if they want to give something back. "That is the heart of the Thai people," claims the managing director of a large music corporation.

Kind acts of generosity often generate "feelings of loving indebtedness."[10] When pure *bunkhun* emerges in relationships, clients feel indebted but do not begrudge that indebtedness. Instead, warm feelings of connection surface to complete the *bunkhun* cycle. The recipient says, "Hey, this person was good to me. I want to reciprocate."

Over time, both parties—the patron and the client—can grow to feel fond of their bond of attachment. When they do, they experience a sense of affection and desire to be generous with one another.[11]

"If warmth is lacking, it is not real *bunkhun*," asserts a villager in the Northeast. Not all Thais would agree, but the comment points to the centrality of affection. Without that warm sense of attachment, clients will often balk at the thought of reciprocating.

It is not polite to ask directly for payment of relational debt. "You can't say, 'I gave you this. You should really feel obligated to me,'" says a retired banker. "To do that is to 'tear a person's face.' You don't do that, no matter which party you are."

Bunkhun is a feeling that can last for a lifetime. For example, clients of a consistently generous patron will continue visiting him long after he has retired from leadership in society. You may have seen photos of this in the newspapers—a posse of admirers, bouquets of roses in their arms, visiting a retired public servant on his birthday. They will continue giving him honor and face for the rest of his life.

That is the shape and form of asymmetrical *bunkhun*. But Thais, especially those who live in villages, also practice an egalitarian form of mutual indebtedness. Thais call this "family *bunkhun*" or "kindred *bunkhun*." Exchange partners assist one another on the basis of friendship or family obligations.

Suppose someone from the Northeast visits Bangkok. He will stay and eat with a friend at no charge, but when he first arrives he won't forget to have a gift in his hands—perhaps produce from his village. This kind of exchange is also present when peers help one another with homework, or when a neighbor becomes ill in the middle of the night and someone drives her to the hospital.

"When someone helps you, you want to help them in return," says a farmer's wife. "Sometimes we don't have money to send our children to study, so we borrow it from relatives. But we will always teach our children that when they finish their studies and begin working they must reciprocate in some way—either by using their knowledge to help those relatives, or by returning money to them. And if those relatives come upon difficult times, we use our money to help them, or sometimes we will just take them some good food that we have made."

Consider an elderly woman of Chinese descent who is the oldest sibling. She has prestige in the family because she is financially stable and she has a generous heart. Years ago, during a financial crisis, a relative borrowed a large sum of money from her. "Do you believe it," says her daughter, "even though this relative repaid the money, every single New Year's Day she visits my mother, bringing fruit. My mother helped her just once when she was in need, yet that act has carried meaning for the rest of her life."

These are examples of kindness shown between approximate equals. But talk about *bunkhun* long enough and your conversations will often return to the familiar theme of a greater party helping a lesser party.

In every village you can find people who control resources, people who never ask for financial help from anyone. These individuals have prestige. They gain social capital by being generous. Let's suppose a villager with prestige frequently sponsors merit-making ceremonies at the temple. Each time he does this, he asks for the assistance of other villagers. With time, he grows fond of some who frequently help him out. If one of those villagers happens to fall into need, this patron lets him borrow money to pay for medical care or cover the tuition costs of his children. In response, the client gives this patron unconcealed respect.

"If a patron becomes ill, we will go to his house and help out," says a farmer, "because we revere him as someone who has shown affection toward us."

Manifestations of *bunkhun* differ in their intensity. The first factor determining the level of intensity is *the amount of genuine altruism.* If a person of means does something generous for someone with no strings attached, the intensity of *bunkhun* can be quite significant. Especially if that patron had no imaginable obligation to help the client in the first place, the client's desire to reciprocate will be intense. If, however, kindness is shown with strings attached, then the intensity of *bunkhun* is lessened.

Intensity also depends upon *the size of the act of kindness.* A great act of graciousness is likely to create a stronger sense of *bunkhun* than a smaller act of kindness.

The *timing* of an act of kindness is also critical. *Bunkhun* is intensified when the act of assistance is timely and crucial to the survival of the client's family. In this case, the client usually will attempt to reciprocate in many creative and humble ways. A Thai saying expresses this so well: "Even unto death, I am willing to die for you."[12] A reciprocal bond is further intensified when acts of kindness are *repeated over and over again.* Patrons can "build *bunkhun*" by consistently showing generosity to a person's children and grandchildren. When this happens, that patron commands great respect, gratitude, and loyalty.

Intensity also depends upon *the character of the client*—the amount of devotion a client genuinely feels and expresses toward his patron. This can vary from individual to individual. An extremely grateful client, by his response, helps to thicken the bond. Clients who willingly reciprocate are identified as those who "know *bunkhun*."[13] But not all clients are equally grateful. Those who do not reciprocate are considered ungrateful and without loving indebtedness.[14] These latter labels are pejorative and harsh.

Last of all, the *bunkhun* bond seems to grow very deep when *patrons do not emphasize their power* over clients. Gardeners and housemaids often work faithfully for employers for many years, not just because of the pay, but because they feel at ease in the relationship. These employees know that—no matter what—they will be cared for. "In my father's era he kept paying employees long after they were old and no longer productive for the company," says a wealthy businesswoman. "They didn't do much, but we knew that they had loyalty toward their boss. I think we loved each other. It was as though we were from the same family."

If patrons don't have what potential clients want or need, they exert little influence over them. For example, suppose a subordinate is transferred into a new corporate job. She is an outsider. She has no history with the head of the department and little interest in any of his resources. She fulfills her responsibilities, but she doesn't "look after" him or cooperate with his intentions as his loyal followers do. In this scenario, the leader has significantly less power over this particular follower.

But a bit of generosity, when accepted, can garner handsome returns. This is especially true when clients lack the resources to pay back patrons *in kind*—in other words, when they cannot return *exactly* what they have been given. In this case it becomes unclear just when or how debts might be fully repaid. In fact, clients begin to wonder *if* debts will ever be repaid.

The dynamics of *bunkhun* serve to perpetuate social ties. Relationships founded upon indebtedness often last a very long time, and to a great extent this is because clients are left wondering just how much it will take to fully repay a patron's act of kindness.

Clients tend to reciprocate with abstract gifts of the heart: compliance (or in some cases, abject obedience), loyalty, faithfulness, respect, affection, gratitude, and words of praise. These gifts render formidable amounts of social capital to the patron (or leader).

Patrons, on the other hand, tend to provide concrete and tangible things—most often, money, but also promotions, opportunities to shine, and many other favors. Over time, some patrons offer their clients intangible gifts that are even more precious: a warm sense of being attached, a sense of belonging in mutual bonds of affection.

This hints at a secret to true success in Thai leadership. Rather than simply lording power over followers, leaders can choose to nurture warm relationships with them. It is an approach that preserves and perpetuates the bond between leader and follower. It lends longevity to relationships, and it also arouses a valuable sense of harmony in local collectives.

An almost fail-safe way to gain the cooperation and assistance of others in Thai society is to provide generously for them. Patrons wield power over clients because they give them access to resources they sorely need. Thai leaders know this dynamic well and they put it into practice with great finesse.

As you navigate relationships in Thai society, always remember: to accept a considerable act of generosity is to *relinquish power to a patron*. From that point on, you must give face to that benefactor on a regular basis and you must never disappoint him. It is as though you have received a substantial loan and you've chosen to live in a state of indebtedness.

Thais will tell you that relational indebtedness can feel light or heavy, depending on the patron. But one of the most striking things about gratitude created by an act of *bunkhun* is how long it can endure in the heart of a client. What goes around truly does come around, and it continues to do so for a long, long time.

12
WARM FUZZIES AND FEARFUL HEARTS

"TAKE A GOOD LOOK at someone with prestige or public acclaim, someone who rules over others," says a judge. "He'll try to recruit people. He'll build influence over them for the sake of his own personal profit. We call this 'building up your arms and legs'[1] so you gain power. He *must* build this group up. If he doesn't have them—he's dead, he's finished. You can't become capable or prominent all by yourself. To become a good leader, you must have close subordinates and clients under your control."

This man's words signal to us that the world of *bunkhun* is more complex than it may first appear. Two categorically different approaches to generosity exist side by side. One patron gives out of affection with little calculation and no intent to manipulate. The other gives with strings attached. Simply put, he is making an investment. He expects to reap a return.

Both approaches begin with an act of generosity. Both create relational debt. But they are two dramatically different patterns of social exchange. "On the one hand, both parties are sincere in giving to each other," explains a university professor. "On the other hand, the patron wants to 'help,' but the client feels burdened. If he doesn't reciprocate, he feels very uneasy."

Clients, or followers, experience indebtedness in two very different ways. Some feel affection and devotion. Others struggle with feelings of being used. What factors determine such disparate feelings? How is it that *bunkhun* can be experienced so differently?

If we listen to Thais talk we will understand. We hear them allude to "false *bunkhun*" when describing benefactors who hope to gain something valuable in return for their generosity. We can recognize this approach as instrumental social exchange—a contest of power between exchange partners—and nothing more. Recipients feel an uncomfortable burden of debt.

In contrast, Thais also speak of "genuine" or "righteous" *bunkhun*.[2] This approach stirs up good faith and true sincerity between exchange partners. Patrons are generous with clients because they truly desire to help. Recipients feel a sense of loving indebtedness. "When it is real *bunkhun*, says a religious teacher, "the benefactor gives freely, devoid of any secret desire for a particular response or payback."

Considering the cutthroat atmosphere of most competitions for face, we can safely assume that "false *bunkhun*" is far more common. Still, Thai voices bid us to shed our cynicism long enough to believe in a notion called "real" or "morally right" *bunkhun*. They warn us that *bunkhun* must be kept from contamination or it can become a different thing altogether. They argue that most contemporary patterns of exchange have drifted so far from the original essence of *bunkhun* they do not deserve the label.

Yet to insist on a utopian, pure form of *bunkhun*—to disqualify "contaminated" expressions of it—can quickly become polemical and counterproductive. Since Thais use this word to describe both patterns of generosity and indebtedness, I recommend that we think of *bunkhun* as a continuum of relational behaviors of similar ilk, but with differing dynamics.

Figure 4 makes a clear distinction between uncalculated acts of kindness and acts that expect a client to reciprocate in a manner profitable for the patron. Each approach is a fully indigenous form of patron-client behavior.

Affectionate *bunkhun*   **Instrumental *bunkhun***

Fig. 4. *Bunkhun* viewed as a continuum

At the far ends of this continuum we have two divergent types of social exchange that look deceptively similar. On the one hand we have pristine affectionate *bunkhun*. On the other hand we have instrumental *bunkhun*, typified by *rabop uppatham,* the ancient patron-client archetype that retains poignant influence over many, if not most, asymmetrical relationships in contemporary Thai society.

Acts of generosity that lie in the middle of the continuum contain elements of both blueprints. This is extremely common. In fact, most social exchange between patrons and clients is probably some blend of these two polar opposites.

For the sake of clarity, let's review the contours of affectionate *bunkhun*. A patron generously helps a client in her time of need. This display of charity is willful and spontaneous, free from the coercion of others. The patron is sincere and other-centered. He simply desires to show kindness with no thought of reaping benefits in return.

The client feels indebted. She realizes that she cannot pay the patron back in kind, and she may never be able to pay him back in full, but it is not a heavy feeling. Because she is the object of generosity rooted in genuine kindness, she feels a deep, enduring affection for the patron. She responds with a lifelong pattern of spontaneous and sincere acts of kindness—both tangible (small gifts, favors) and intangible (obedience, loyalty, respect, love, praise, and gratitude). Her motivation is *intrinsic*, not extrinsic. She responds not because she must, but because she *wants* to. She feels genuine affection and deference toward the patron.

Curiously, this sense of indebtedness catalyzes a cycle of relational warmth that many Thais crave. "True" *bunkhun* influences behavior as long as both parties remain alive, and sometimes even longer. "We must engrave the memory of a patron's kindness in our hearts for a lifetime. We must tell it to our children and grandchildren," says one religious leader. A Thai proverb expresses the same sentiment: "Indebtedness to *bunkhun* can never be eaten away."[3]

The other strain of generosity is very different. Here are the contours of instrumental *bunkhun*. A patron generously helps a client in his time of need. This display of charity is premeditated. It is designed to create indebtedness in the client. The patron's motive is self-centered, with a view to reaping some benefit in return. He is making an investment and he expects to collect on it. He is "purchasing" the loyalty and assistance of the client.

The client feels burdened by debt. He realizes that he cannot pay the patron back in kind, and he wonders if he will ever be free of his obligations. He feels manipulated. He would like to repay his debt once and for all so as to be free of the *bunkhun*, but often the calculus of repayment is kept so vague that he can never be sure of just how much is enough. He reluctantly responds with required acts of assistance. His motivation is *extrinsic* and he reciprocates because he *must*. He fears the patron and dreads the consequences he might face if he fails to respond.

This outside-in pressure on the client is a textbook characteristic of instrumental *bunkhun*. An awkward sense of indebtedness settles upon victims of calculated kindness. "If a patron performs an act of *bunkhun* just once on behalf of a client, the client fears that the patron will ask for reciprocation many, many times," says an office worker. "She feels as if she is perpetually indebted, yet at the same time she feels ungrateful if she does not reciprocate."

Few Thais enjoy this feeling. "It is like an endless cycle," says a religious teacher. "Someone does something nice for you, but then one day you're going to have to pay him back. That's why I have some friends who don't want to accept big favors. They're afraid of the payback."

A retired government employee describes this uneasiness:

> When I was a government worker, each year we would be promoted one level and granted a raise. Our boss had the authority to promote a few employees up two levels. He usually did this for those with a heavy workload, or those who assisted him the most. One year I received this special promotion and I knew that I had to go thank my boss, but I felt conflicted. I thought, "Is this promotion an act of kindness, or is it something I deserve? Is this a case of *bunkhun*?" I didn't want to grovel in thankfulness for fear that he would think that he now had some claim over me. At the same time, I didn't want him to view me as a hard-hearted subordinate, someone who didn't

'know *bunkhun*.' In the end, I just went and politely said thank you. But I was so afraid he would view it as [instrumental] *bunkhun*, and I would lose freedom.

Leaders create frames of influence by manipulating the principles of *bunkhun*. They draw people into their webs of control by providing assistance. Once followers become indebted to this type of "kindness," however, the leaders own them.

On the other hand, if more and more people become disinterested in a leader's resources, they begin to slip outside of his control. Consider the example of an agricultural cooperative in a rural district of Chiang Mai province. A group of villagers has pulled away from the influence of certain leaders in the community—not for the purpose of setting themselves up as enemies, but to bring greater justice to the average person. Because their efforts are succeeding, many other villagers are escaping the clutches of these leaders and coming over to their cooperative. The secret, we are told, is to establish independent organizations that do not hope for selfish profit, and then to think of ways to pass profits on to the collective.

"It was very difficult at first because we had to prove that our intentions were noble," says an officer of the co-op. "But after a while, when our alternative began to shine, people exited the old frames and entered the cooperative. The influence of former leaders disappeared. This is what a good society is like."

When clients sense that patrons are taking advantage of them, frequently they will attempt to find other patrons who are good-hearted—leaders who are more restrained in their efforts to take advantage of others. But it doesn't always work. "Sometimes you can't get away. It's like fleeing a tiger to meet up with a crocodile"[4] laments a villager.

In cities across the country, powerful patrons offer "security" to local people. Even honest shopkeepers must comply because they need that security. They will reciprocate with payments of money or other economic opportunities that are potentially beneficial to the patron, such as granting him partial ownership in their company.

Leaders make use of instrumental *bunkhun* to climb hierarchies. A former government employee explains:

The patron-based system is about profiting in some way—both parties profit. The superior profits from those below him who continue to push him upward. His acts of generosity empower him and give him stability. He shares profits with those below him, of course, so that they'll continue doing the things he desires. But it's a sure thing that he doesn't want to stay where he is in the hierarchy. He wants to climb. Even after he reaches the top position of leadership, he wants those below him to "give him a sense of place," you see, to continue to affirm his position and his performance. He nurtures that group of people to buttress his stability.

Often it takes the help of a person with influence to win a good job. "A call from him to the right people, and we have the job. But then we owe him," says a professor.

Consider the true story of a young man who was preparing to take the government exam with hopes of securing a job in the Customs Department. He was told that only one out of every ten thousand applicants would qualify. He took the exam, and because he did so well he was one of ten people selected for a job interview. When he noticed that others were being called in for interviews before him, he asked for help from his father, a government worker who had connections with a certain cabinet minister. His father said, "If you want me to talk to my friend, you'll have the job, no question. But you understand, son, that from now on you will be indebted by this man's *bunkhun*. Once you get the job, if he sends someone to request your 'help' with something, you will have no choice but to comply. I'd like you to be free of that reciprocal cycle. So it's up to you. You can either take the shortcut, or you can wait out your chances." The young man decided to wait it out, and he eventually landed a good job.

Instrumental *bunkhun* grants special privileges to certain individuals so that everything is expedited for them. They simply jump over normal protocol. Several years ago, two sons of a politician were quickly promoted through the ranks as policemen. Many in the public sector doubted that it was because they were more qualified than other candidates. Their father simply had connections.

Patrons often promote members of their entourages to higher levels of authority. Once they have attained those positions, however, they must reciprocate for the favor that has been shown to them. This cronyism is typical of instrumental *bunkhun*.

"In this system it's like, 'My people are good. All others are bad,'" says a retired member of the Royal Thai Air Force. "Gifted candidates who don't practice [instrumental] *bunkhun* will not rise to higher levels of leadership. Those who rise are the ones who reciprocate and do favors for their patrons, yet often they are not the most gifted candidates. This is why our country is developing slowly. For the most part, [instrumental] *bunkhun* dictates the outcome of promotions in leadership."

Typically, patrons have power because they have money. They understand that to gain face they must use their money to benefit their clients. Very wealthy patrons will generously shower members of their entourage with benefits for the sake of gaining a reputation of having accumulated goodness. "When a politician functions this way, it is a matter of maintaining his votes for the next election," says a government employee.

Often clients are not sincere about the relationship. They comply for the sake of money. "Pretend you are very wealthy," says a former government employee. "You give me a large sum of money and I turn around and give it to my entourage of sixteen people—let's say 10,000 baht per person per month. Whenever I return to see you, these sixteen have to come along as well, you see? If just twelve come, you will ask, 'Who are the other four?' And the next time those four get nothing. They are excommunicated. They lose their opportunity. So the other twelve people think, 'Hey, if I don't show up and look after our grand patron, he'll cut the flow of money. No way I'm doing that!'"

In the confines of instrumental *bunkhun*, patrons must maintain the flow of benefits to their entourage or they risk losing clients to other patrons. If they don't stoop down to care for their own, others may judge them as being stingy. The next time there is an election or a power struggle, they lose.

To advance, leaders must do more than indebt their followers, however. They must find "friends" to assist them in accomplishing their goals. These friends must have either legitimate authority to approve a request or significant influence to ensure a favorable outcome. Whether leaders work hierarchies upward or downward, they usually leverage the principles of indebtedness found in instrumental *bunkhun*. That is how they climb, a topic we'll explore in chapter 19.

Patrons who selfishly manipulate clients face a grim reality: clients are respectful and responsive *only for as long as they remain under authority or control.* As soon as they break loose, they often lose interest. Here is a splendid illustration, as told by a border patrol policeman:

> At one time there was a high-ranking officer in the air force. He was a very "big" man, but not at the very top, not the number one guy. He used his power excessively. He didn't show mercy—or what we Thais call *khun*. All he used was power.[5] He didn't show kindness.[6] He never helped anyone. The smallest infraction, he would make a big deal of it. He punished his subordinates harshly. He heaped on the heaviness. Then he retired. One day he went to play golf at a course owned by the military. When he ran into his old subordinates, they acted as if they couldn't care less. Some of them even spit in his direction and spoke sarcastically. That man had no more meaning because he was now retired. No one was interested in playing golf with him. He was nobody. Just an old man. He had no accumulated goodness, none at all. But other officers are different. They give and give, and after they retire former subordinates still visit them and show them respect with sincere hearts.

Another negative aspect of instrumental *bunkhun* is the "tunnel-vision" clients adopt when they indiscriminately reciprocate for the favors of a patron. "Many times personal obligations supersede what is lawful," says a wealthy banker. "Suppose you hit a pedestrian with your car and kill him. If you know someone, when the police report comes out, it's distorted in your favor." This creates a large opening for patrons who wish to subvert the honor system. If they can instill a sense of indebtedness in their clients, strong social sanctions will force those clients to comply with their wishes no matter what they may be. That is how leaders buy prestige.

How does this play out? In elections, for example, people choose candidates to whom they feel the most indebted, not candidates who are most capable or virtuous. Consider the scenario of a long-time MP who decides to have his son run for parliament. Many long-time clients feel obligated to support the son, but not based on his true qualifications. "They'll get him elected," says a judge. "They'll accept him. They'll grant him prestige. But they don't love the son. It's the father they love, respect, and fear. They must support him."

Figures 5 and 6 summarize these two distinct practices of *bunkhun* in Thai society. When we compare the two patterns of social exchange, the differences are truly significant. Let's start with the motives of the two patrons. One patron gives so as to gain personally from his largesse. His kindness has strings attached. The other gives out of genuine empathy. He has no ulterior motives.

Next, compare the clients. They experience two very different feelings of indebtedness. One client is reluctant and fearful. The other is loving and spontaneous.

Also, notice the longevity of each patron's form of influence. The influence of the patron with instrumental *bunkhun* is short-term. It carries force only as long as the patron continues to provide benefits to the client or as long as the patron retains his position of authority over the client. The influence of the patron with affectionate *bunkhun* is constant and stable. His acts of pure kindness win him an almost undying devotion. The client offers a steady stream of cooperation, respect, and praise for up to a lifetime because of the loving indebtedness he feels.

Each cycle of reciprocity pivots on just one thing: the patron's *motives* for assisting his client. That singular variable dictates the entire range of dynamics in each model.

Bunkhun commands a powerful influence over relationships in contemporary Thai society. "You have a giver and a receiver," says a retired banker. "He who gives more is the leader. He who must depend upon the other is the follower."

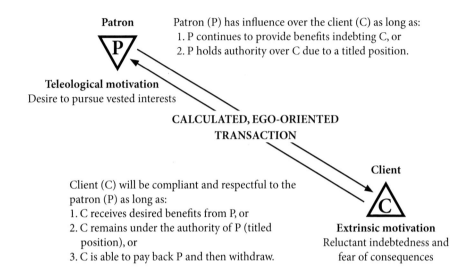

Patron

Patron (P) has influence over the client (C) as long as:
1. P continues to provide benefits indebting C, or
2. P holds authority over C due to a titled position.

Teleological motivation
Desire to pursue vested interests

CALCULATED, EGO-ORIENTED TRANSACTION

Client

Client (C) will be compliant and respectful to the patron (P) as long as:
1. C receives desired benefits from P, or
2. C remains under the authority of P (titled position), or
3. C is able to pay back P and then withdraw.

Extrinsic motivation
Reluctant indebtedness and fear of consequences

Fig. 5. Instrumental *bunkhun*

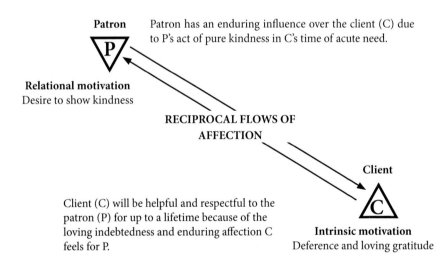

Patron

Patron has an enduring influence over the client (C) due to P's act of pure kindness in C's time of acute need.

Relational motivation
Desire to show kindness

RECIPROCAL FLOWS OF AFFECTION

Client

Client (C) will be helpful and respectful to the patron (P) for up to a lifetime because of the loving indebtedness and enduring affection C feels for P.

Intrinsic motivation
Deference and loving gratitude

Fig. 6. Affectionate *bunkhun*

This pattern of generosity and reciprocity has profound implications for how leaders gain face and use power. Leaders have the opportunity to choose between two very different approaches for extending the shade of their provision.

"A leader is like a large bo tree that gives shade," says a university professor. "Followers are like birds who perch on the branches of that tree."

True. But perching on one tree can feel remarkably different from perching on the next one over. One perch feels warm and secure. The other feels ominous and vulnerable.

13
UNEASY ALLIES

A SUBTLE CONTEST for power brews in the unseen depths of patron-client relationships, and we dare not miss it. Both exchange partners want to benefit. Both use the relationship as protection from face loss and leverage for face gain. Sometimes they collaborate for mutual success. But often they are uneasy allies, each competing for greater personal advantage.

It is surprisingly easy to assume that leader-follower relationships are like well-choreographed dances between satisfied partners. But if we observe with eyes wide open, we will discover a veiled struggle for control of resources.

This is true of most leader-follower relationships for one simple reason: instrumental *bunkhun* is the preeminent choice of most Thai leaders. It is so dominant that it is almost peerless in its popularity. Because of its influence, relationships are not simply about agreeable mutual exchange. They are about attempts to shift existing imbalances in directions more favorable for either the patron or the client.

We will now dig deeper into this agonistic world of instrumental exchange by probing into three topics integral to Thai leadership: 1) how face gain and face loss can affect leader-follower relationships, 2) how leaders attempt to maintain their superiority, and 3) how emerging leaders can find pathways to rise.

To get started, let's review what we have learned in the last two chapters. Leaders who practice pure instrumental *bunkhun* are largely self-serving. They assist clients for the purpose of gaining greater leverage over them. Followers often respond with timidity and subservience, but their allegiance is fragile, if not brittle. Their cooperation is conditional.

Leaders who practice affectionate *bunkhun*, by contrast, assist clients *for the sake of the client*. They genuinely want to help. In fact, they hope for the success of their subordinates. Most of their followers respond with admiration, affection, and whole-hearted collaboration. Their allegiance is fierce and highly durable.

Building on this knowledge, we will learn that followers in instrumental relationships tend to respond with the same manipulative tactics they see modeled by their leaders. That seems intuitive, really. But our next finding may be less obvious: instrumental exchange is highly resistant to the true empowerment of subordinates and followers. By nature it favors the hegemony of the leader.

As we unpack this world of patron-client relationships, I encourage you to think in practical terms. Think of superiors and subordinates, bosses and employees, doctors and patients, teachers and students, parents and children, older siblings and younger siblings, members of the nobility and commoners, the rich and the poor, the powerful and the disempowered. Think especially of leaders and followers.

Thai society is wholly saturated with patron-client exchanges. Simply look around you and notice any two people conversing together. Take a minute to watch how they relate. Chances are very good that you're observing some form of transaction between patron and client. If you then narrow your focus to dealings between leaders and followers, you will be hard pressed to find any interaction that is not on the plane of patron and client.

Because of embedded hierarchies, there is usually an observable difference in social power between exchange partners. But take note that leaders of relatively equal status routinely patronize each other. As a matter of fact, it is extremely common for a leader to ask for help from a friend who shares his level of prestige. If that friend grants a favor, down the road the leader must reciprocate by playing the role of patron himself—that is, by helping his friend accomplish what he cannot do for himself. In the end, both profit economically. Both gain prestige. That is the heart of how leaders use the rules of social exchange to climb established hierarchies—a topic we will pursue in chapter 19.

But very often there is clear disparity in power between patron and client. Leaders, for example, have status and rank. They have more face than people who regularly "depend upon the shade of their kindness."[1] This clear asymmetry dictates the flow of face gain and face loss for each party.

But how? If a leader loses face, does it affect his subordinates? If a subordinate loses face, does it affect his leader? If either party gains face, does it affect the other? It's time to explore the dynamics of empowerment as they play out in patron-client matchups.

Sometimes leaders lose face. When they do, "their people" often share that loss because onlookers view leader and follower as one entity. A superior's wrongdoing can make everyone associated with that organization look bad. Take the abbot of a temple who is exposed as a secret womanizer. He is eventually disrobed, but the good reputation of the temple is tarnished. Resident monks—former clients of the abbot—feel a loss of face in the community.

When a leader falters, members of his entourage usually take the hit because they share face with their leader. Their role is to seek him out and help him solve the problem. They are focused on damage control—making the leader's problem their own for as long as it takes to deflect or dilute the loss of face. They bear the burden of face loss until they successfully redeem their leader's face.

Sometimes close subordinates will experience a contingent loss of face because their leader scolds them, pinning responsibility for his loss of face on *them*. This tactic pushes responsibility for failure downward.

A leader must exercise caution in doing that, however. If his hand comes down too heavily, certain subordinates may be tempted to defect to other patrons.

When a leader loses face, at least two variables influence how much face his subordinates will lose. For sure, it depends upon *the level of relational intimacy in the patron-client bond*. If a subordinate is identified as a close confidant—a member of the leader's entourage— it is more likely that he will lose face when his leader loses face. "If the two share a close relationship outside of the formal confines of work—seeing each other often, drinking together, going to meetings together, taking excursions together—then they both lose face," claims a leader in subdistrict government.

But it also depends upon *the arena of loss*. If a subordinate is closely related to the incident that triggers the loss, he probably will lose face as well. If not, he may be able to find ways to distance himself from his leader's loss, although it will not be easy because of his general obligations as a client.

Let's look at it the other way around. When subordinates lose face, can it impact the face of their leaders?

Absolutely. If a subordinate's failure or disgrace damages the progress of projects under the supervision of a leader, it can cause his leader to lose face. Others will ask, "Whom does this person belong to? How could he have let this happen?"

In cases of severe misconduct, leaders can accuse dishonored subordinates of causing them loss, or "selling their face." Consider the employee who uses her boss's name for personal profit by falsely asserting that "the boss ordered it." When she is caught in her lie, her boss accuses her of selling his face.

But leaders have certain advantages that allow them, at times, to dodge the fallout of a subordinate's loss. "The leader alone is the 'big' one," says a retired air force officer. "Sometimes he won't admit that a shamed subordinate is one of his 'wheels.' He just cuts him off."

Suppose the driver of an influential person shoots and kills a notable member of society. The assailant assumes that his patron will intervene for him. But the patron is in danger of severely losing face because the whole thing has become a high-profile story in the media. In the end, does he accept this as a loss of face? No, he simply disowns his client, and the client goes to prison.

The extent to which a leader takes the hit for his subordinate's losses can vary. Several factors influence the outcome.

Once again, *the level of relational intimacy in the patron-client bond* is a strong determining factor. Obviously, if the subordinate is a family member, the patron almost certainly loses face. Family members—even extended family members—share a collective sense of face. They must work together to maintain and protect it. To illustrate this, note the Thai idiom that heaps shame on parents by identifying their misbehaving child as a "child not taught by his father and mother."[2]

But since most Thais are true-blue collectivists, the scope of familial connectedness often extends beyond blood relatives into other close alliances and associations. For this reason, whenever a leader and a subordinate share a close relationship, the two parties tend to gain face and lose face together.

Another variable is *the severity* of the loss. If a subordinate's loss of face is a small matter, his leader may sidestep it. But if it is due to a grave matter—like a close subordinate caught selling drugs—the threat to the face of his leader is much more real. People tend to suspect the patron, wondering, "Was he behind it? Did he 'use' his client to do this?"

It also depends on *the context of the incident.* Has the subordinate lost face at work, or is it a personal matter?

Due to differences in the ratio of power between parties, leaders have an easier time distancing themselves from subordinates' losses than subordinates do distancing themselves from their leaders' losses. Leaders sometimes have the opportunity to "cut off" a close subordinate who stumbles, saying, "It's his loss, not mine." Subordinates rarely have that luxury. On the contrary, when their leader is in the throes of losing face, close subordinates are expected to draw near to "stop the bleeding" and think of ways to help her redeem face.

What about face gain? What happens when either party gains face?

By now you can anticipate the first variable: much depends upon *the level of relational intimacy in the patron-client bond.* The family and relatives of a cresting leader almost always share in her growing prestige. A common proverb states, "The value of a person depends upon whose child she is."[3]

But subordinates in a leader's inner circle also tend to share in their leader's face gain. Generally speaking, when a leader rises, his people rise with him. "When the public is buzzing about a leader's gain in prestige, the leader is in full view," says a community leader. "And who else do they see? The people who are with him."

Clients can boost their potential for face gain by securing a spot in a popular patron's entourage. When a politician wins an important post, for example, members of his entourage often gain prestige as well. Close confidants are dragged upward and appointed to positions of greater authority.

Another key variable is *whether or not a patron credits his subordinates* when he gains face. If a leader states publicly that his success is due in no small measure to the support of his entourage, his words clearly give face to those subordinates. "But when a person with prestige experiences success," observes a judge, "he usually won't talk about his client base in ways that elevate them. In Thailand, leaders are apt to view supporters as a mere foothold for their upward climb towards achieving more 'face-eyes.'"

Let's flip the scenario around and consider what happens when a subordinate gains face.

If a subordinate begins to be recognized broadly for his excellence or competency, he will often credit his leader for his success. Why? Societal values constrain clients to remember the kindness of their patrons. "This is an ancient custom—that we should always 'show respect to the teacher,'"[4] says a wealthy businesswoman.

When subordinates are promoted to a high post or acclaimed for some great achievement, they commonly cite patrons who have played a role in helping them succeed. This public commendation demonstrates their sense of gratitude and indebtedness. It also grants increased prestige to their patrons.

In addition, people often credit leaders when they have a rising star in the ranks below them. Here we have a soldier rising fast in the hierarchy of the military. His good fortune is due to his own extraordinary competence, but others often compliment his superior officer, saying, "You're doing a good job of looking after him."

Gratitude is an essential value in the Thai worldview. To give face to a patron repays some of the relational debt created by the goodness that the patron has shown to the client. That's why leaders who rise in society often visit their former patrons to report progress and say, "If there's any way I can be of help, please let me know."

In short, leaders are credited for the achievements of their subordinates far more often than subordinates are credited for the achievements of their leaders. One incisive reason for this is that the act of expressing gratefulness and praise—a key ingredient in sharing face with others—is much more likely to flow upwards in Thai society than downwards.

This points to an enlightening discovery. Clients elevated by their patron's face gains rarely, if ever, keep pace with him. Promotions almost always preserve the established hierarchy. Because most asymmetrical *bunkhun* relationships are forged in the furnace of instrumental exchange, *they exist primarily to bring face to the patron.*

Consider the phenomenon of an entourage. A central purpose of the entourage in Thai society is to reflect the face of the patron. Subordinates exist to help their patrons gain more face. That's precisely why patrons make generous use of this tool.

Even when subordinates gain face by successfully manipulating patron-client ties, they rarely outshine their patrons. In grand quests for prestige and power, attention is riveted on noteworthy leaders, not on their subordinates. Rewards of face gain are top-heavy in favor of leaders.

In fact, instrumental *bunkhun* (review fig. 5) is particularly resistant to the true empowerment of clients. Often the act of promoting an underling is merely part of a patron's grand design to increase his or her own prestige. Leaders promote subordinates on the basis of what benefits them personally. "The truth is, patrons never intentionally build up clients for the sake of the client," claims a government employee. "Patrons appoint clients to fill positions so they themselves will gain 'face-eyes' from the move."

Thai patron-client exchanges tend to retain or increase the power distance between a leader and his or her subordinates. Rarely is that gap reduced through the intentional empowerment of gifted candidates in the hierarchy below. Clients do their best to gain social power by manipulating the rules of exchange, but opportunities for face gain are not equitable. The net face gains of superiors are usually much greater than the gains of their subordinates. This accelerates the rise of patrons and squelches the rise of clients.

Just how do leaders perpetuate this imbalance? Those who practice instrumental *bunkhun* learn the delicate art of "nurturing in ways that preclude growth."[5] Somewhat like parents who make every decision for a child, many leaders are deft at cultivating subordinates in ways that keep them dependent and weak. Leaders who practice this technique have a clear goal: to restrain gifted subordinates just enough to deny them chances to blossom. Day after day, they maintain control of their underlings by keeping them dependent.

There can be little doubt that this tactic is designed to maintain or increase power ratios. "The leader says, 'I forbid you to grow bigger,'" says the managing director of a large company. "'You are there, and I am here. If I rise, you can rise, but I forbid you to rise to my level or climb above me.'"

"Leaders don't want subordinates to gain wide recognition—to become prominent or to 'match their own radiance,'"[6] says a graduate professor. "They will attempt to hold them down. They will deny them opportunities and do whatever it takes to keep subordinates from competing with their own public acclaim."

"Don't support your subordinate's progress," advises a community leader. "Don't boost him up so he advances beyond you. Let him be lower. Let him be smaller. Let him be inferior."

"Take care of him in such a way that he never rises to the level where he can compete with your *barami*," says a district chief of police. "Maintain the discrepancy in 'face-eyes' between you and him so that others will listen exclusively to your policies. As the saying goes, 'Two tigers can't coexist in the same cave.' There's also another saying: 'A tree doesn't want its fruit to grow into a tree.' You must nurture in ways that keep them from growing. Otherwise, one day you may find yourself having to obey a former subordinate, and you will lose face and personal power."

"I hold him down, or he will grow bigger than I am," says a community leader, pretending to be a patron who feels threatened by a rising subordinate. "I'll keep you subordinate for the indefinite future," quips another leader. "They say, 'No more. This is as high as you get,'" adds a university professor.

"You are forever an indebted underling," explains a former member of the Royal Thai Air Force. You can look after your patron, but if you want to rise higher than he is—no way."

When certain subordinates begin to excel and rise in power, leaders often will attempt to ensure that those face gains do not disturb the chemistry of their entourage. "There is no feeling of, 'Oh, I'm so happy for you,' says a former member of the military. "The leader says, 'You got this because of me! You must keep looking after me. Get it?'"

When a subordinate experiences a surge in social power, his superior can easily interpret the turn of events as a personal loss of face. The subordinate's gains feel like his loss. The thought of being eclipsed by an underling is a most unpleasant scenario. When a leader feels threatened, he may turn to his peers and bemoan the ungrateful arrogance of the underling, calling him "a student scheming to do away with his teacher."[7]

Consider the case of a CEO who repeatedly promotes a capable subordinate because he makes the company more profitable. But then one day the leader realizes how this gifted subordinate is beginning to undermine the security of his own position. "A leader like that starts to feel shaky," says a community leader, "He begins to reclaim certain responsibilities. He summons the subordinate and says, 'Look, you're beginning to do my work. That's not your place.' He thinks, 'Hey, I molded this person!' The boss doesn't like it. It's a matter of vested interests. He will look for ways to release that employee downward."

Let's be clear about something: when leaders fear competition from below, they are not mere victims of paranoia. Their concerns are often based on credible threats. Smoldering beneath most patron-client exchanges is a contest for power. A dominant leader often puts his entrenched power and influence at risk if he grants too many opportunities to gifted subordinates. He must attempt to control assertive subordinates by letting them function only within narrow confines. "The mango tree is supposed to grow tall," says a community leader. "But if we plant it in a pot, it can't grow. It won't die, but neither will it grow to its full potential."

This habit of precluding growth has several consequences. Obviously, *it enables leaders to preserve their advantageous place* in the hierarchy by retaining (or widening) the power distance between themselves and their subordinates. This protects their repositories of face.

Also, by keeping subordinates in their place, prominent leaders *can continue to use underlings as tools for face gain.* A leader will make it clear to members of his entourage that they have a job to do: they must make him look good.

Another sobering consequence of this approach is that it *tends to chase away many talented and competent members* of an organization or business. Most subordinates targeted by this behavior are intellectually bright, very capable, and high in potential. They are also perceptive. They know the game the patron is playing. Almost inevitably, it seems, they eventually flee camp in search of more benevolent patrons, or they step out on their own to establish their own trail of patronage.

We observe this over and over again in Thai politics. How many times do we see a leader breaking away from his political associations to establish a new party? One reason political parties proliferate in Thailand is that many politicians practice instrumental *bunkhun*— nurturing underlings so they cannot really grow. This style of leadership spawns the formation of highly competitive rival camps. This is true not only in politics, but also in bureaucracies, businesses, organizations, and communities throughout the land.

"In the end it's something that doesn't work," notes a wealthy businessman. "Eventually they leave you and go work for somebody else. If you nurture others so they don't grow, you end up with all the losers. All the winners leave you." In other words, leaders should be forewarned. Hunger for face, unchecked, can become self-destructive. People catch on, they leave you, and eventually you find yourself in the shoes of that retired air force general on the golf course: alone and ignored.

Precluding the growth of subordinates also *tends to create weaker leaders for the future.* Leaders who are jealous of their power grow stunningly shortsighted. They coddle subordinates, arresting their development by denying them opportunities to grow in skill and responsibility. When dominant leaders finally fade off the scene, their successors often lack both confidence and competence.

The practice of precluding the growth of clients is native to instrumental *bunkhun*. It is a vestige dating back many centuries to times when lords and vassals roamed the land. Lords lived according to the following mantra: "I will show kindness only if it benefits me."

That mindset has saturated the value systems of many, if not most, contemporary Thai leaders. A major consequence is that the empowerment of any subordinate is highly dependent upon the needs and designs of his superordinates. Leaders support the elevation of underlings only when it does not threaten their own radiance. The implicit rules of instrumental *bunkhun* sanction and legitimize a leader's choices to be self-serving, and many sectors of society totter under that unforgiving weight. In fact, healthy pathways to empowerment are scarce.

So can clients ascend on their own merits? Can they ever surpass their patrons? It is rare. Many Thais share a prevailing conviction that power distances between patrons and clients ought to be preserved over time. For clients to close those gaps—whether due to their own ability or their clever manipulation of *bunkhun* ties—can fly in the face of some deeply rooted values. "It just feels wrong," says the managing director of a large company.

Shifts in the ratio of power between patron and client, therefore, are of great import. When a subordinate gains face and begins to rise in the webs of *bunkhun* that surround him, you can bet that his run of good fortune will catch the attention of his patron (or patrons). A patron's response will usually vary from indifference (if the patron's interests are not threatened) to affirmation and support (if his interests will be served) to disgust, envy, and resistance (if his interests are threatened). Note that every one of these responses is guided by a fundamental assumption: patrons should conserve the imbalance of power that is in their favor.

So how do new leaders emerge? If we trace the trajectory of rising leaders—the clients of an established patron—we are likely to encounter eight weighty factors that influence their empowerment:

their true capability, their demeanor, their ability to win the heart of their patron, the quality of their relationship with the patron, their patron's level of virtue, the arena of their rise, the timing of their rise, and third-party pressure on their patron.

Emerging leaders who wish to rise on the merits of their *abilities* should be capable, competent, creative, industrious, productive, consistent, and fair in their treatment of others. It is not easy to bypass these criteria. At the same time, it is extremely difficult to rise based solely on these attributes.

The *demeanor* of rising leaders is critical to their success. Clients who rise within hierarchies learn to nurture hearts of gratitude toward their patrons. Leaders tend to feel better about the progress of subordinates who "show respect to their teachers" (their superiors). "Thai society is a society that grovels"[8] claims a community leader. "It gives honor to leaders. So when followers gain face, what do they do? They often say, 'I reached this milestone because of this or that important person.'"

A genuine demonstration of gratitude accomplishes two things. First, by giving face to patrons, clients induce them to show greater support for their progress, something very valuable if they wish to continue to rise. Second, when clients publicly thank a patron, they send him a signal saying, "I'm not trying to grow bigger than you. No matter how high I go, I will always feel indebted to you." That act of obeisance can put certain disquieted patrons at ease.

Emerging leaders must also be clever in *winning the hearts of their bosses*, a topic we have already covered in some detail. This is because the assistance of patrons is nothing short of essential for those who wish to rise from lower rungs of hierarchies. Listen carefully and you will hear Thais comment frequently that their bosses favor just a few people. Whoever the boss likes the most seems to have the greatest opportunity to advance. Especially in politics and in government, leaders tend to give face to subordinates from their inner circle. Subordinates must nurture good relationships with their superiors, keeping close to them and staying involved with them.

Another obvious variable affecting empowerment is the *type of bunkhun* between patron and client. Instrumental *bunkhun* is problematic for worthy clients who wish to rise. To state it simply, the modus operandi of a leader who practices favoritism is this: he must gain at least as much or more from granting a promotion than the subordinate gains by being promoted. This is distasteful to a growing number of Thais because it resists the promotion of the most qualified candidates.

But if the relationship between patron and client is affectionate in nature, leaders will often feel pleased when their subordinates flourish. To understand this dynamic, consider the mutual affection between parents and children, or teachers and students. Each tends to grant face to the other. Each tends to rejoice when the other gains face.

Here is a community leader who wants her students and her children to succeed even more than she has. She delights in the concept of an *aphichatbut*,[9] meaning "a child who does better than his father and mother." In a similar way, teachers are often thrilled to see their students rise to greater heights.

These examples argue that affectionate patron-client relationships tend to empower both parties. They offer the possibility of a win-win outcome for both patron and client. When leaders and followers practice affectionate exchange, it opens a wide pathway to healthy empowerment.

But there's a catch. Outside of families and classrooms, few relationships practice the rules of affectionate exchange from the very beginning. Most affectionate exchange tends to grow out of instrumental exchange. It is a transformation that takes time.

When an instrumental relationship begins to morph—that is, when it becomes less utilitarian by taking on some characteristics of affectionate *bunkhun*—leaders are more likely to approve of the face gains of their subordinates. Consider the common tactic of subordinates who try to win the heart of the boss and get the boss to love them. This is a clear attempt to tilt the relationship in the direction of affectionate *bunkhun*. In other words, by introducing mutual affection into the equation, subordinates hope for the tenor of the relationship to become more relational and less instrumental. They do this so they can be more efficient in their efforts to gain face. Leaders do the same thing for the very same reason. They form entourages by developing warm relationships with trusted subordinates so they can use them as tools for accelerated face gain.

Another important variable affecting the empowerment of clients is *the patron's level of virtue*. Noble-hearted leaders are more likely to support the rise of worthy subordinates. Leaders with good moral values can help subordinates to have 'face-eyes'" by doing two things: giving them honor and giving them opportunities. It is possible for subordinates to rise when their superiors reinforce them in these ways.

"Someday he who trails behind must move to the front, and this second wave should be bigger than the first," says a community leader. "A good patron is aware that he's not going to be in that high place forever. We have a saying: 'Above the sky there is more sky.'[10] So no matter how capable we become, others will eventually rise up to become more capable. We may grow 'big,' but those who follow will grow even 'bigger.'"

But leaders who lack virtue are often envious. They look for ways to demote or destroy rising subordinates. If in the end they fail to suppress them, they switch tactics. They may "remind them of their past kindness,"[11] or they may attempt to claim credit for the rise of the subordinate.

The *specific arena* of a client's empowerment is also a pivotal factor. If a subordinate's success is not seen as a threat to his leader's vested interests, the leader may even express congratulations. In fact, some leaders attempt to gain face by "riding on the coattails" of an emerging leader. They will credit themselves for discovering the rising star.

Things are vividly different, however, when a subordinate begins to rise within a leader's domain of influence. The average patron resists the empowerment of any subordinate who attempts to compete with him. He can accuse that client of cutting off the legs of his chair or "comparing himself with his radiance." He can chide him for not recognizing kindness or being ungrateful. These accusations invite a client to feel shame for rising. When leaders give off these threatening signals, rising subordinates often lose courage and back down.

Not always, though. Contests for prominence are highly competitive. Subordinates are in search of pathways to empowerment. It may be bad form for them to crowd the vested interests of their patrons, but it happens nonetheless. A tantalizing hunger for prestige is more than enough to motivate certain aspiring clients to take formidable risks.

Timing is also a huge variable. If, during the prime of a leader's career, a former subordinate happens to win a position that the leader has long coveted, the leader will probably view him as a competitor. But if a patron is near retirement and knows that he had no real chance of reaching the same level as that client, he may respond quite differently. If he likes the client, he may express his support of the promotion. This is when he may attempt to gain face by declaring proudly, "Here is one of 'my people' I've supported from his earliest days!"

Third-party pressure on patrons is another variable that can impact the empowerment of a client. If a client is frustrated that his superior will not let him advance, he may go looking for a more powerful patron to intervene.

Envision patron A and talented client B. Their relationship is poor. B cannot rise. But patron C comes along and helps B to rise, much to A's displeasure. If patrons A and C have a good relationship, A will normally concede to C's attempt to raise B higher.

This is a good reminder to be cautious about analyzing patron-client relationships exclusively as dyads—that is, as one-on-one relationships. Complex outside forces can influence the outcome of a struggle between a patron and a client. Because empowerment takes place in vast webs of *bunkhun*, tertiary relationships exercise considerable influence over the outcome of contests for power.

On the surface, this interesting world of patrons and clients, leaders and followers can look perfectly genteel and orderly. But just out of view is a struggle between two parties with egocentric agendas. They both want the same thing. Each wants to manipulate the rules of exchange to win some personal advantage. Each attempts to increase his social power by nurturing relational affinity and creating relational indebtedness.

Neither party wants to be a victim of excessive manipulation, so both vigilantly monitor the sincerity of the other side. It's common sense, really. Leaders need truly loyal followers more than they need disingenuous suck-ups. Followers, on the other hand, need leaders they can trust and respect. They dislike leaders who feign warmth and affection for the sake of their own selfish designs.

Patrons manipulate relationships so as to control and expand their vested interests. Clients attempt to do the very same thing. It seems that someone is always tinkering with the fragile balance of power.

Prevalent leadership dynamics favor the face gains of patrons and suppress the empowerment of clients. But all players—patrons and clients alike—strain to exploit the rules of exchange in order to acquire greater prestige and enduring power.

14
FACES OF POWER

LEADERS ARE ENCHANTED with power. After all, getting things done is their bottom line. At every level of society, leaders are acutely interested in moving agendas forward and catalyzing change, often in the face of resistance. To be effective they *must* learn to access and use power.[1]

Their quests are restrained by certain boundaries. For example, power *is always shared* between a leader and his followers. This became crystal clear to us as we explored patron-client dynamics. As an agent of change, a leader simply cannot do it alone. Leadership isn't something *he* does; it's a cooperative dance between him and those who rally around him. Because of this, leaders need followers as much as followers need leaders. Good leaders grow to be amazingly shrewd in winning the assistance and cooperation of those they lead.

Also, *societal values strongly influence how leaders access and use power.* No matter how dominant a leader becomes, he cannot and does not singlehandedly dictate how power flows around him. If he wishes to last very long, he must respect boundaries established by convention and social sanctions. All leaders work within the confines of what is socially acceptable, and even outstanding leaders are subject to the whimsical instability that characterizes life for those who wield power.

These two realities—leadership as a shared experience, and the irrepressible force of social sanction—set limits on the attempts of leaders to acquire power. Yet there is still spacious room for the pursuit of power in Thai society.

So how *do* Thai leaders leverage power?

Considering the vast, convoluted array of leaders in thousands of social arenas across the country, the scope of this question feels boundless. But, surprisingly, *there are just a few basic pathways to power.* We will explore these well-worn trails and the kind of leader each trail tends to shape.

To explore this elaborate world of Thai power, we will continue using "face" as a portal. You may be skeptical that the study of face can contribute anything unique to discussions about power. Isn't it enough to ask about power and simply leave it at that?

If we were to make that unfortunate choice, we would forgo many robust insights. Our understanding of power would be monochromatic and dull, lacking the colors of the Thai worldview.

In modern Thai life, face is inextricably entangled with power. You can hardly talk about power without alluding to face. On the other hand, face dynamics continually reveal the flow of power. Thai leaders at every level of society live by rules of face in their pursuit and use of power.

Niels Mulder calls power "the central axis around which public life revolves" (2000, 140). But listen to Thais talk and they'll remind you to pay attention to face as well. "To gain face is to build power," asserts the managing director of a large company. Leaders with "face-eyes" win the acceptance of others and gain access to greater power.

So are face and power synonymous? Not exactly. Face is *like* power, and power is *like* face, but they are not identical. Generally speaking, face is power viewed as *an undefined amount of potential.* Power is more concrete and quantifiable than face. It is characterized by *agency*—by the demonstration of the ability to have one's own way, to create order or bring change. But since an increase in power (almost always) leads to an increase in face, and an increase in face (almost always) leads to an increase in power, we can postulate with confidence that *each potentiates the other.*

In other words, Thai leaders *use face as a resource for their personal empowerment in leadership.* That claim has further implications: they also use face to empower or to squelch the rise of other emerging leaders.

How many distinct sources of power are available to Thai leaders? To explore that question, we must not overlook the incisive research and findings of David William Conner. In his ethnographic fieldwork, Conner explored leadership formation in Thai society. From a pool of potential informants with reputations of being "good leaders," he selected fifteen leaders from five areas of public life—business, government, the military and police, Buddhism, and local communities. In his long interviews he pursued one primary question: "What constitutes a 'good leader' and how does one go about being and developing such a leader?" (1996, 4).

Conner isolated three "leadership foundations" within Thai society: *amnat* (อำนาจ), which he calls "authority;" *itthiphon* (อิทธิพล), which he calls "influence," and *barami* (บารมี), which he calls "personal power."[2] Figure 7 presents the three primary sources of power available to Thai leaders.

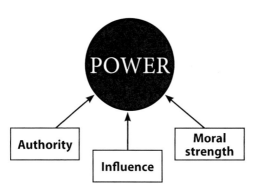

Fig. 7. Sources of power available to Thai leaders.
Content adapted from Conner (1996)

Amnat is power that emanates from a legal or institutional code and is available to a leader because he or she holds an official office, a position of authority. *Itthiphon* is the power to sway others because the leader controls valuable resources that others need. *Barami* is power founded upon the "interpersonal moral goodness" of the leader (Conner 1996, 234, 243). It resides in the perceptions of others, both followers and bystanders, and it is demonstrated by their spontaneous expressions of admiration for the leader and their compliance with him or her (ibid., 268).

It is more precise to speak of Conner's three foundations as *paradigms*—three multivalent approaches to envisioning and exercising power. Each carries unique assumptions about power, and each relies on distinct methods for gaining the cooperation of others.

We are about to build on Conner's seminal discoveries, but we will extend beyond them. Our unique focus will be to compare the facework of leaders as they draw from the differing sources of power in leadership. We want to discover what is going on in terms of face. Does each paradigm have its own unique face dynamics, and if so, what are they? How does each type of leader view his or her own "face-eyes," and how does he or she relate to the "face-eyes" of others? And in each of these three paradigms, exactly how do leaders win the compliance of others?

We will explore those specific questions in three parallel chapters, but first let's shore up our understanding of power in Thai society by unpacking each paradigm.

The *amnat* "authority" paradigm is based on legal or institutional power. It is available to a leader because he or she holds a position of legitimized power. A police chief calls this power "with boundaries."[3] In this paradigm, the leader takes note of the precise confines of his job description and (theoretically) stays within them.

"You represent state power, a power that is greater than yourself. So in a sense, you are using some other capital, not your own," explains a banker.

This kind of power is relatively secure but also relatively transient. It lasts only for as long as a person holds a given position of authority. That's a problem—a *real* problem—for anyone who has grown accustomed to the perks of status. Demotions or retirement affect a leader's store of "face-eyes" considerably. Put into face language, a leader's store of *nata* ("face-eyes"), *kiat* (honor), and *chuesiang* (public acclaim) diminishes considerably when he exits from his position. Note that I did not write that his *barami* decreases. Just note that, and read on.

In Thai society an official title confers honor (*kiat*) and legitimacy to its holder. When a leader assumes this kind of power, it is much like slipping on a mask in traditional Thai theater, something Thais refer to as *sai hua khon*.[4] Classical Thai actors perform scenes from the Ramayana wearing intricate, colorful papier-mâché headpieces. The masks are meaningful for the duration of the drama, but as soon as they come off, actors no longer lay claim to that persona.

This is a brilliant way to envision power that is official but temporal. The *amnat* leader feels powerful, but the power is not really his. It is in the position he temporarily holds. When he steps down from that position, he no longer lays claim to the authority invested in that title.

The *itthiphon* "influence" paradigm comes from a leader's access to and control of certain valuable resources that others need. This kind of power can be rooted in socioeconomic force (money), physical force (ability to gain compliance by physical coercion), or psychological force (the threat of using one or both of the former) (Conner 1996, 231). This is power without clearly established boundaries. In exercising power and selecting options for gaining face, these leaders simply have more freedom than leaders with authority.

Of the three sources of power, this is the easiest to abuse for selfish gain. Why? Leaders in the other two paradigms *must* use their power for the common good or society will question their faithfulness to their duties, whether legal or moral. But leaders in this paradigm face fewer social constraints.

Thais tend to view this type of power as socially unacceptable, or at least questionable. They readily associate it with "dark powers"[5] in society. Even Conner writes, "By definition *itthiphon* is self serving, used for personal gain [rather than] for the benefit of others" (1996, 232).

Public perceptions are powerful. Even when the actions of influential leaders are legitimate (the resources are theirs) and perfectly legal (they have violated no laws), they often remain *morally* suspect. In collectivist Thai society, where the masses love generous leaders and loathe selfish leaders, people easily *assume* that influential leaders acquire power by taking unfair advantage of others. But that perspective is unsophisticated. Influence is not inherently bad. It is merely power generated by a leader's control of resources that others need.

This kind of power is less secure than authority. The leader retains power because he does not "tread water." He must tirelessly expand, solidify, and intensify his influence. "These are natural leaders," says a banker. "These people create and utilize their own power base. Their power is not derivative."

The *barami* "moral strength" paradigm drafts power from the perceptions of others who have observed and benefited from the leader's consistent expression of "interpersonal moral goodness" through "meritorious selfless behavior" over a period of many years (Conner 1996, 241–42, 251).[6] That's a mouthful, but every part of that definition is essential.

Take note that this power resides not in the leader, but *in the hearts of others* who have observed and benefited from the leader's virtue. Followers commonly respond by willfully offering the leader social acceptance, deference, loyalty, faithfulness, love, admiration, gifts, unconditional assistance, cooperation, physical care, protection of his reputation, hearts that seek his counsel, and a desire to associate intimately with him (ibid., 252, 256).

We are already quite familiar with *barami*, so it should not surprise us that these leaders are guided by their moral goodness. They are sincere and trustworthy. They are willing to make sacrifices for the sake of others.[7]

Compared to the other two approaches to leadership, the *barami* paradigm imposes greater restrictions on leaders. Society sets strict legal and ethical boundaries for their use of power. People highly respect them, but their use of power must stay within the bounds not only of the law, but of conventional wisdom and broader moral preferences as well. With remarkable consistency, subordinates of this kind of leader retain their goodwill long after their leader retires. *Barami* is the only dimension of Thai face with this lasting glow.

After soaking in Thai descriptions of leadership for hundreds of hours, one day I stumbled upon a splendid book introducing the "stick," the "carrot," and the "hug" as analogies for three kinds of power (Boulding 1989).[8] These delightful metaphors capture the essence of the kinds of power—*amnat*, *itthiphon,* and *barami*—that Conner observes in Thai society. They will guide us through the next three chapters as we gain a deeper understanding of the values and behaviors of leaders.

For each paradigm, we will explore the same three topics: the emotional investment leaders place in their "face-eyes," common dispositions they often assume toward those with less status, and preferred methods for enriching their stashes of social power. I will paint in broad strokes how leaders *tend* to behave, not how they are sure to behave. But keep in mind that this is a view of Thai leadership sculpted by Thais themselves and based on internal cultural elements rather than Western theory.

As we take a look at the three prototypes of Thai leaders, think of Thai leaders you know or have observed. Try to identify the kinds of power those leaders access from day to day. Here is a chance to hone your skills, to train yourself to recognize a given leader's approach to power so you can adjust to his or her expectations. When all is said and done, we will be better acquainted with the three faces of power in Thai society.

15
THE STICK

AT A TOWN MEETING, a police chief sits in front of a tier of images of the Buddha and photos of Their Majesties the King and Queen of Thailand. That backdrop delivers a subliminal message to the convocation: the chief presides as one who wears a mantle of honor greater than his own position of authority. Also, the presence of an honorary guest, the MP, symbolically dispenses honor to the police chief. Honor flows once again during the meeting whenever the police chief singles out a lower-ranking officer to deliver a report. On and on it goes.

These examples are all about "the stick." *Amnat* (อำนาจ), as we have said, is power that emanates from a legal or institutional code. It is available to leaders because they hold an official rank or an office with a specific title. Authority, we often call it.

To understand this kind of power in the simplest of terms, envision any leader who has a legitimized capacity to hurt you if you don't cooperate with him. This kind of power is at work wherever we find sanctioned hierarchy in society—government, businesses, the police, the military, educational institutions, social clubs, community associations, guilds, and even religious communities. The point is that someone else is telling you what to do and how to do it, and if you don't comply he'll make good and sure that you suffer an uncomfortable, painful, or undesirable loss. To make matters worse, all of this happens with the wide approval of those around you, because they've set up rules, protocol, and laws to deal with people like you.

How does a leader in the *amnat* paradigm tend to view his own "face-eyes"? I asked this question for all three paradigms, and it often triggered fleeting looks of confusion. Many informants paused or asked for clarification. The question itself was difficult to phrase in the Thai language because it delves into tacit cultural knowledge— questions never before posed, let alone discussed or analyzed. It asks cultural informants to attempt to verbalize the value leaders place on their personal stores of "face-eyes."

I am confident, based on my findings, that leaders with authority usually care a great deal about their "face-eyes."[1] In the words of a successful financier, "They feel high and mighty."[2] After all, leaders in this paradigm have the backing of legitimized power, and they are supposed to represent that power with dignity. The secure and pleasant feeling of possessing unquestioned power (in a limited context, of course) is one of the things that fuels intense competition for promotions, awards, levels, decorations, positions, ranks, and titles. And since most pockets of Thai society are exceedingly hierarchical, *amnat* leaders tend to view themselves as being unequivocally superior to others, giving way at times to unhealthy feelings of self-importance. The indisputable honor inherent in positions of authority, especially the highest positions, can sometimes lure incumbent leaders into viewing their "face-eyes" as an all-important locus of their behavior.

There are variables that attenuate this, however. One is personality, or to be more specific, how secure a leader feels in his self-worth. "There is a frog in Thailand called the *ueng ang*[3] that is smaller than some of the other species, but it puffs itself up," says a border patrol policeman. "Some people are like that. Out of their insecurity they have to act big."

It also depends upon the level of virtue in the leader. "If he is a virtuous leader, the higher he rises the more he serves. If he is not a virtuous person, he holds fast to his chair," claims a community leader.

Another variable is the sheer weight or height of an office. Generally speaking, leaders who hold *high* positions tend to be more conscious of their "face-eyes," and they expect others to give proper respect and deference. Lower-level leaders operate with less pomp and circumstance. For example, although the budget manager in a district office wields authority, she probably views her "face-eyes" quite differently from the district officer or the governor. To a great extent it depends upon the number of people under a leader's control.

Because society automatically grants a considerable amount of "face-eyes" to persons in official positions of leadership, it is intuitive to presume that those who desire these positions also covet, to some extent, the "face-eyes" intrinsic to the office. It is likely that leaders with authority have a moderately high attachment to face and a moderately high desire to develop their "face-eyes."

The level of emotional attachment leaders invest in their own stores of face will inevitably affect the way they engage people below them, particularly subordinates. So how *do* leaders with *amnat* tend to treat others?

They have to take into account, at least to some extent, the "face-eyes" of their close subordinates. They show them appropriate honor and deference because they depend upon them.

Remember, *amnat* leaders rise by excelling in the performance of their duties. They need the cooperation of underlings in order to implement policies and programs. "It's very natural," says a banker. "If you're going to depend upon the help of someone else, you must give that person face and honor. Then the work goes more smoothly."

Also, the smart boss treats his subordinates well because he knows they are mouthpieces—they'll be speaking about him to others. He protects their face to win their loyalty so they will help him guard his store of "face-eyes" and expand his public acclaim.

Another reason why subordinates have the attention of this kind of leader is that some of them form his entourage. Society views members of an entourage as extensions of a leader, people who reflect the image of their boss.[4] Whenever you see a leader and his entourage, don't forget the phenomenon of face by association—or shared face—that exists between a leader and members of his inner circle. Close subordinates reflect the leader's repository of "face-eyes." By making close subordinates look good, a leader can make himself look better.

Members of his entourage help him cast desirable impressions into public space. They help him shine.

But the importance of the entourage among *amnat* leaders is somewhat attenuated by dynamics unique to this paradigm. The face of a leader with authority is tied up in the honor of his position, and he is less dependent (theoretically, at least) upon his entourage than the *itthiphon* (or influential) leader, whom we will discuss in the next chapter.

Many leaders with authority coddle their close subordinates, but not all of them. Some pay little attention to the "face-eyes" of people under their authority. One reason for this is that they are busy taking care of *their own* superiors. In this paradigm of power, leaders are always gazing upwards—conspiring to gain the favor of their bosses. They have a laser focus on one thing—bolstering and protecting their own social capital. It is a perspective that views subordinates as tools, as means to an end. "He's not going to view them as people with 'face-eyes,'" says a judge. "He is going to view them as people who are 'his hands, his legs, his arms.' They're supposed to help him get work done, to accomplish things."

A number of variables influence a leader's attitude toward the "face-eyes" of his close subordinates. The most common is that of *utility*—how useful a given subordinate might be. Leaders pay special attention to the face of subordinates who play roles vital to the preservation of their authority and their vested interests. When a subordinate helps his leader to gain "face-eyes," the leader will tend to show increased attention to that subordinate's face.

Another variable is the level of fairness a leader employs. Some are equitable. Others show partiality according to the rules of instrumental *bunkhun*. "It really depends upon the leader's view of himself," says a community leader. "We have an idiomatic saying: 'Big lord, big boss.'[5] Someone infatuated with his own power is not really interested in the 'face-eyes' of his close subordinates."

Leaders who show little honor toward close subordinates operate on the premise that *authority alone* is enough to gain the cooperation of underlings. But let's remember something enormously important about power in this paradigm of leadership. It is impermanent. As long as a leader maintains his position of authority, subordinates will show him respect and endure his self-centered or unreasonable behavior. But this honorific behavior can fade very quickly after he exits from the position.

Many *amnat* leaders manage to gain the compliance of close underlings without treating them especially well. They simply give orders, and they do not hesitate to *abuse* power[6] in order to prove to others that they *possess* power.

But that approach is short-sighted. When leaders attempt to motivate followers on the basis of authority alone, it may not be enough for them to *thrive* in their positions. There is fierce competition for advancement, and leaders need the genuine loyalty of their subordinates. They are smart to tap into the relational glue of *bunkhun* by treating underlings well and creating a warm sense of indebtedness in them.

All in all, *amnat* leaders will tend to treat close subordinates with appropriate honor. "If you don't treat them as important, they won't show deference to *your* face," says a subdistrict leader.

How, then, do *amnat* leaders tend to treat the face of people way down the chain, those far below them? For the most part, common politeness rules the day. But let's be practical. If people are not in their orbs of close relationships they probably don't see their importance, because, like most Thais, they are focused on a coterie of allies, close friends, and family. People in this category are so far removed from leaders' direct exercise of power that they are not even on the radar. "They don't even think about their face," claims a leader in village administration. "They simply give orders."

In a land content with hierarchy and wide power differentials, it is not uncommon for *amnat* leaders to view themselves as superior to those far below. "I'm bigger than you," says a retired air force officer, mimicking leaders with authority. "Your 'face-eyes' have to be smaller than mine."

So if an *amnat* leader doesn't really know you, don't be surprised if he doesn't even see you. If you're a known entity that might be of some use to him, however, he may wonder, "Can I reap some benefit by doing this person a favor?"

As a matter of fact, sometimes an *amnat* leader's interest in a group of less powerful people is an intentional display with a hidden purpose: to demonstrate that he or she has a heart to help others. Why? This can bring a lift in the leader's level of "face-eyes." Distant subordinates might begin to whisper to each other, "Our boss is a good person. We are so far removed, yet he shows an interest in us!" When a leader takes this approach over a significant span of time, that's when Thais will say that he or she is "building *barami*."[7]

When you observe the demeanor of leaders with authority, always keep in mind the pivotal dimension of personal virtue. Thais will tell you that leaders who lack virtue are often "power crazy."[8] They pompously enjoy giving commands and intimidating others. But leaders with good character tend to respect the "face-eyes" of people with less power, whether close or distant. A retired bureaucrat describes this kind of leader as someone with an "elevated heart."[9] "Some leaders reach high positions in society but they maintain a humble perspective that they're simply trustees of the power inherent in their position," explains a high-ranking border patrol policeman. "These are leaders who do not use power to coerce others," adds a district police chief. "They are rather unassuming. They don't use that authority to behave bigger than they really are."

But as you may suspect, a raft of leaders still think that all they have to do is give orders. They emphasize the gap between themselves and others and motivate followers with fear. In their minds, leadership is shored up by *phradet*[10]—that is, legitimate power to harm. "These are the kind of leaders who think, 'If I get that title, I will have power,'" says the owner of a small bakery. "So when they win that coveted position, they view it as a weapon."

What can leaders in this paradigm do to increase their stores of social capital? How do they expand their power?

To gain face, leaders with authority must succeed in carrying out the duties of their office. They must complete projects for the sake of the company or collectivity they serve. To raise their visibility in the eyes of bosses and peers, *they must produce*—carrying through on responsibilities, avoiding favoritism, fostering solidarity, proposing ideas and policies that profit the company or the community, and accomplishing major initiatives.

For this to happen, they must depend upon the productivity of their subordinates. It is difficult to maintain or gain face without the cooperation of a team below them. Leaders must ensure that subordinates succeed in carrying out their assigned duties. If they deliver, the leader looks good. If they fail to accomplish objectives, the leader can lose face.

There is nothing ambiguous about this paradigm's primary pathway for increasing social capital. *Leaders must ascend the rungs of their respective hierarchies.* Promotions bring more than economic lift; they bring a fine boost in "face-eyes." And only superiors have the power to make that happen.

For *amnat* leaders, the secret to professional success is to look *upward* in their hierarchies and attempt to win the hearts of their superiors. Sometimes they can accomplish this through decent hard work. But even when their track records are not very impressive, they can leverage the rules of favoritism. If they suck up to their bosses, one day those bosses may drag them up the ladder. "Stick very close to the boss,"[11] says a university professor. "Be 'tight' with him, and you will see an increase in your 'face-eyes.'"

Leaders with high positions of authority have many avenues for face gain. As we noted in chapter 10, for example, they accept invitations as special guests of honor at public gatherings. On these occasions, leaders can make a show by bringing an entourage in order to enhance their "face-eyes" even further.

Last, but not least, sometimes *amnat* leaders gain face by forming secret liaisons that bring financial gain—things outside their jurisdiction, and perhaps even outside of the law. They use their subordinates and their constituted authority to generate personal profit on the side. As long as these indiscretions remain hidden, members of the public are not disposed to investigate carefully. These schemes can be *very* lucrative, allowing them to gain face by displaying symbols of wealth. This emphasizes that they are people to be reckoned with—people of power.

The present social environment entices many leaders to pursue personal profit over productivity on behalf of the collective. Government employees or *kharatchakan*—literally, "servants in royal affairs"[12]—are particularly vulnerable to this strategy because they are not paid very well. For centuries, common citizens have instinctively granted a measure of "face-eyes" to workers in the king's service. But economic growth in the past century has put tremendous pressure on prominent leaders in this sector. Increased materialism has played a role in fusing the concept of honor with the ability to display wealth. This is a source of great stress for a host of leaders receiving government salaries, whether cabinet members, members of parliament, governors, mayors, district officers, or high-ranking soldiers and policemen. Their pay is inadequate to satisfy soaring societal expectations that they play the role of generous patrons. These are the "lords without shrines" of the modern era, much like the nobles in the nineteenth century (Athajak 2006, 7). They can be particularly vulnerable to overtures from leaders in the *itthiphon* paradigm, whom we will discuss next.

You now have a snapshot of how things work when leaders use "the stick" to gain the cooperation of subordinates and followers. It's just one way to wield power in Thai society, but it plays a prominent role in business, government, and community life.

Nevertheless, this paradigm alone is insufficient to explain how power flows within the bounds of this sovereign nation. Authority is just one constellation in a much larger galaxy of power. Read on. We are about to explore a paradigm of power that is far less predictable and—in many cases—even more potent.

16
THE CARROT

PICTURE A MAN on his donkey. From the tip of a pole he dangles a carrot near the donkey's mouth, but *just* out of reach. You can guess where I'm going with this. Hungry and impelled by hopes of visible reward, the beast willfully pursues the carrot in whatever direction the man chooses. That's a great characterization of how influence works in Thai society.

The *itthiphon* (อิทธิพล) "influence" paradigm draws power from a leader's access to and control of valuable resources that others need. Conner's research reminds us that this kind of power can be rooted in the ability to gain compliance through physical coercion. But the real potency in this paradigm is socioeconomic. The leader has money. He has valuable assets. He has people who owe him something. Whether he controls modest resources or a small fortune, this guy knows how to use what he owns to grow his power over others.

At the heart of this paradigm is a leader's audacious proposition: he is the greatest lion in the lair. That lair is not unbounded. It most certainly has limits, whether geographical, political, ethnic, or financial—to name just a few. But whether it is small or cavernous, it belongs to *him*. And within the confines of that fiefdom he thinks that his public acclaim is second to no one.

It is unfortunate that the phrase "those with influence"[1] in Thai often conjures notions of godfathers, gangsters, hit men, and hooligans from the criminal underworld. That's a perfectly legitimate attribution, but it clouds a more accurate understanding of the extensiveness of this paradigm.

Itthiphon is by far the most pervasive and effective form of power in Thailand today. To wield this kind of power you must accumulate and control coveted resources, things that other people dearly need, or at the very least, greatly desire.

This type of leader will almost inevitably have a robust emotional attachment to his "face-eyes." He may not always be aware of that (and he may even deny it), but his sense of personal honor is tightly tethered to his proven ability to access and distribute wealth, resources, and opportunity. "He believes he has the biggest face," says a university professor, "and he wants no one else to have more influence."

It should not surprise you, then, to learn that *itthiphon* leaders do not respond well to any loss of face—even the slightest loss. "These people—you can't touch their face," says a village official. "You can't disrespect them. Their face is of grave importance."

Influential leaders are interested in protecting their face because it has an impact upon their influence, the basis of their security. If their influence wanes, they lose face. If they gain face, they gain influence. They treat their "face-eyes" as a sacred symbol of their ability to gain the compliance of others through money and threat.

We find ourselves in the swirling cloud of a paradox. On the one hand, these leaders thrive in the safety of *real* capital—economic security—things that give rise to tangible power. They have little time for superficial attempts to look good. Yet on the other hand, if you touch their face, you will learn very quickly that there are few things more sacred and more defended. You will pay.[2]

There are good reasons why influential leaders tend to demonstrate such a robust attachment to face. Foremost among them is that their power is *insecure*. It is self-generated. They cannot rely upon power inherent in a position of authority. They must relentlessly search for fresh deposits of power to replace past expenditures. At the end of the day, no one is going to do that for them. It is their insatiable quest.

Leaders with authority (the stick) find satisfaction in two things: their legitimate power and their personal "face-eyes"—social capital extending beyond titles (education, personal assets, and generosity with others). Leaders with influence, by contrast, create their power base entirely on their own. They do this through acumen, good decisions, smart business practices, or political aptitude. But a huge dimension of this fight for survival is that they must continually improve their position by manipulating the rules of facework to gain more face. They can hardly afford to relax. They must sustain their "place" with acute sensitivity to threats and an expeditious response to every potential loss. Amidst the vagaries of competition for face—replete with sabotage and subterfuge—these leaders are on high alert.

This paradigm of power has ancient roots. In feudal times, every commoner was counted as either a *nai* "master" or a *phrai* "ordinary peasant" (Akin 1975, 95). Princes and nobles (*nai*) were under the command of the king, but due to the expanse of geography and the absence of modern media for communication, "masters" found ample leeway to engage in deeply egocentric competitions for resources.

Modern games of influence mimic that very same egocentricity. *Itthiphon* leaders define and defend the bounds of their personal fiefdoms. Their sense of worth is highly *autogenic*—generated by their own blood, sweat, tears, tenacity, courage to take risks, and personal sacrifice. This is clearly distinct from leaders with authority who can find a considerable portion of their sense of worth (if they so choose) in the legitimate power of their honorable position.

Influential leaders tend to give greater attention to close subordinates than leaders with authority. In the *amnat* paradigm, leaders are bound to subordinates by law or institutional code. In the *itthiphon* paradigm, leaders gain power only to the extent that they and their subordinates are willing to *join together* to generate influence over others.

So how do influential leaders treat their close subordinates? They nurture an irrevocable sense of connection with them because they need their love and steadfast loyalty in order to remain secure and prosperous. If they cannot trust them, they put themselves in jeopardy.

Remember that members of an influential leader's entourage are extensions of the leader himself. They display—or better yet, *objectify*—his personal store of "face-eyes." He benefits if the public perceives them as people who wield power.

To protect social capital, *itthiphon* leaders develop the face of close subordinates and shield them from public losses of face. If someone disrespects or harms a close subordinate, these leaders regard it as a personal affront.

Behind closed doors, these leaders often rule with fear. There is a constant hint of anxiety, something described as "relational warmth with undertones of terror."[3]

In private, influential leaders can be face-threatening and unforgiving toward members of their entourage. They often send messages that they will not welcome failure and they will not tolerate the slightest disloyalty. Certain leaders—I emphasize the word *certain*—are ruthless. Through boorish demeanors, harsh words, and negative emotions they communicate an utter lack of respect for those closest to them. They do this as a warning to other subordinates that—when push comes to shove—they won't even maintain the face of their very own.

"It's called 'threatening a person by cutting a piece of wood,'"[4] says a high-ranking military officer. This curious idiom identifies fear as a weapon. Centuries ago, an executioner would take a swipe at a nearby branch to test the sharpness of his sword before beheading some unfortunate soul.

Sometimes leaders conclude that they can no longer trust a member of their entourage. Whenever they directly attack the face of a subordinate, it often portends the end of that relationship. In the most extreme cases, leaders will show little mercy. "If you screw up badly, there is no forgiveness," asserts a village leader.

Consider an extreme example from the world of dark influence. One day a client fails to show up for his patron's birthday celebration. The patron interprets it as a veiled announcement of intent to compete with his power. Days later, that client is murdered.

"They think, 'If one of mine begins to compare himself to me, I have to take him down!'" says a former military officer, recalling the incident. "This local leader claims he's never ordered anyone to be killed. But all he has to say is, 'You know, it just doesn't seem right for him to go on living,' and a few days later the stooge is murdered."

So *itthiphon* leaders have two primary tactics for controlling their entourages. They woo them with kindness and promises of profit, and they restrain them with displays of power. In other words, these leaders want subordinates to both love them and fear them at the same time.

Can these two goals be compatible? Leaders attempt to build trust by indulging subordinates with benefits. At the very same time, they rule with fear by showing little mercy. Over time, subordinates may grow to fear the leader more and more and trust him less and less. It is no wonder that some clients cheat their patrons and flee to the dens of other patrons.

With few exceptions, this paradigm is driven by *instrumental*, not affectionate, social exchange. "They view others as tools in their hands. Tools in their hands, that's all," says a government employee. Leaders allow subordinates to gain face by sharing social capital and taking a cut of profits. But if any subordinate begins to grow too "big," leaders will find ways to deliver a clear message: "No way. You stay right where you are." These leaders must dominate.

Let's now shift to the attitudes and behavior of *itthiphon* leaders toward distant subordinates or faceless people they meet in the course of daily living. In general, they are relatively indifferent toward people in this category.

This changes quickly if someone gets in their way. These leaders rarely spare the face of people who frustrate them. Unlike leaders with authority, who always have the law looking over their shoulders, these leaders do not need to defer to people if they don't feel like it. I do not mean to imply that they are always rude to strangers. Thai custom dictates that all social players—including those with great influence— must show common courtesy toward strangers. But for the most part, influential leaders pay little attention to people who have no real bearing upon their influence. Distant others simply lack usefulness.

There are exceptions, however. Influential leaders often show interest in capable people that cross their paths. They are always looking to recruit smart and proficient subordinates. Whenever they run into someone new who appears to have influence, they will first evaluate that person's "face-eyes." If it is someone they cannot control—someone with impressive spheres of influence—they must be careful to acknowledge the boundaries of that person's jurisdiction and monitor him carefully. But they will seek to dominate any newcomer who begins to trespass on their vested interests. They will regard him as a competitor, and they will attempt to damage his "face-eyes" and weaken his ability to control others.

Note that the power of many influential leaders tends to be narrow in geographical scope. It is not accepted broadly in other business sectors, districts, or provinces. It is territorial.

When influential leaders enjoy profound local dominance, a wider recognition of their "bigness" often eludes them. This leaves some leaders thirsting for greater public acclaim, so they embark on quests to project a fresh image by showing kindness to the masses. This behavior is very common among leaders who wish to extend their power base by assuming a more visible public role. They attempt to build *barami,* as Thais describe it. I will write more about this tactic later.

What can leaders in this paradigm do to gain "face-eyes?" How do they expand their power?

Leaders with influence lean heavily upon one primary method for gaining face: providing assistance or financial benefits as a means of creating relational debt. They expand spheres of influence by increasing the number of subordinates and clients loyal to them. They must create an ever-widening web of indebtedness.

Let us, therefore, state the obvious. To be accepted in the eyes of others, these leaders must have wealth. They must be relentless in accumulating greater financial assets. Some leaders achieve this goal through exploitation, corruption, and fraud because the attendant gains of face and influence are just too great for them to pass by. Once they secure significant resources, they continue to gain face by putting their wealth on display. They donate money to charities and community projects. They sponsor merit-making festivities at temples. They contribute toward the construction of temples, schools, and hospitals. "To gain greater power, they create a positive image in the community," says the owner of a small business. "They make it look as if they are goodhearted."

An indispensible requirement of this approach is that generosity *must be made known to others*. By broadcasting their good deeds, leaders increase their positive public acclaim. This is why you will see plaques at temples listing the names of major donors and the amounts of their donations. Often this vital information is memorialized by chiseling it into granite or marble and filling the engraved letters with gold leaf. Leaders also donate the costs of shelters at bus stops, or they honor the royal family by paying for elaborate buttresses that span major highways. In most cases, their names will appear in a prominent place for all to see.

"Money buys face," explains a respected author.

Leaders also gain influence by using fear to subjugate others. Politicians sometimes resort to veiled threats as a means of solidifying their support base. In extreme cases—when they feel that someone has disdained their endogenous worth (*saksi*)—they take drastic measures to avenge their losses. If they can successfully avoid indictment after hurting or killing an opponent, others will fear them even more. Thais describe this behavior as "slitting the chicken's throat so the monkey can see."[5]

By no measure do all influential leaders resort to such tactics. But for the ones who do, they are happy when others fear them. "Their 'face-eyes' is based on their ability to show that they have power— power to give life or death, power to let others possess or not to possess," explains a respected community leader.

As we noted earlier, wealthy individuals can gain face by entering politics. They spend decades building riches and influence, but once they are no longer sated by wealth, they often ask, "What else do I want? Do I want wide acclaim?" At that point they attempt to win a legitimate title in society by jumping into politics.

Leaders with influence are often more assiduous and intentional about gaining face than leaders with authority because gains solidify their tenuous power over others. They must be tireless in creating and sustaining their bases of power. They also have a broader selection of options for gaining face than the leader who stays strictly within the *amnat* paradigm.

This pursuit of face often happens within the confines of a power game that is played *downward*. Leaders seek to control those who are "theirs" and use them to expand their influence in ever-increasing measure. Those in the entourage of *itthiphon* leaders look downward for opportunities to expand their personal spheres of influence. Even so they keep looking upward with great intensity and fear: they must avoid displeasing their patron and must seek ways to win his heart.

Leaders' weapons for gaining compliance are twofold: they *create indebtedness* through generosity, and they *reinforce fear* of consequences should clients fail to comply.

That is how leaders use "the carrot" to access and wield power. Day in and day out, these tried and tested methods continue to yield alluring results for thousands and thousands of contemporary Thai leaders. In fact, this approach to leadership is so effective that we can scarcely think of a different way, a fresh alternative for winning the right to lead.

Yet another pathway still remains.

17
THE HUG

AS A YOUNG MAN, a university professor once worked for a large corporation in Bangkok. He had the good fortune of working for a benevolent boss.

"He pushed people up to higher positions, even higher than himself," recalls the professor. "He released them to grow somewhere else, even in other departments. He pushed them up—whoever did well, he always pushed them up. He wasn't interested in himself. All his subordinates loved him and respected him, to the very last person. They never forgot him. They still drop by to visit him. They continue to speak of him, remarking that he is such a good leader. He has *barami*. I have seen it with my own eyes. He was a good example."

The professor's words are disarming. They compel us to stop for a moment to ponder where this approach to power might possibly fit.

When you combine the clout of "the stick" and the draw of "the carrot," you have a range of power that is flat-out formidable. Together they seem so comprehensive in explaining Thai leadership behaviors that one is hard pressed to envision any other realistic way for someone to access and use power. The country is teeming with sticks and carrots.

But a third paradigm is ever on the lips and in the hearts of Thai people. *Barami* (บารมี). This approach drafts power from the perceptions of followers who observe a given leader over a span of time and notice his or her consistent expressions of virtue and meritorious, selfless behavior.

You are now quite familiar with this uniquely Thai word. In earlier chapters I refer to it as both "accumulated goodness" and "moral strength." But alas, the English language is glaringly insufficient for expressing the rich layers of meaning subsumed by this ancient word.

We can trace this concept of power directly back to the throne—to the leadership style of a just, benevolent monarch. But His Majesty King Bhumibol Adulyadej is not the only leader in the country who receives this attribution. Ask around, and you will discover followers in many circles of society who ascribe *barami* to their leaders. As a matter of fact, the word is thrown around so loosely these days that its counterfeit meanings have multiplied in strength, and the moral root of the word is in danger of being clouded by ignorance.

Many, many Thais have told me that *barami* status should not be conferred upon leaders based solely upon their generosity. We must also scrutinize their motives for demonstrating kindness to others.

Some leaders—perhaps most—use authority and wealth for the sake of their own vested interests. Others use the same kinds of resources to pursue whatever is in the best interest of their followers. Leaders in the first group are *mercenary*. They selfishly manipulate followers by leveraging relational debt. Leaders in the second group are *benevolent*. They focus not on personal gain, but on using power for the sake of others. Of these leaders, a few eventually emerge as people truly qualified for the description, "those with *barami*."[1]

There is little doubt that Thai people, for their own good, need to use greater prudence in ascribing *barami* to their leaders. It is in their best interest to reserve high honor only for those who are truly worthy of honor. At the very same time it is absolutely essential to understand that this style of leadership is not meant for kings alone. It is meant for any leader who wishes to embrace a liberating approach to power.

Enter "the hug." This pathway to power is based on affectionate social exchange (refer back to fig. 8). Its genius is rooted in the curious, almost eccentric idea that leaders can hold the interests of followers front and center as the primary focus of leadership. Leaders choose to expend their stores of social capital to help others solve their problems.

That's a refreshing approach, but couldn't it actually put leaders at a disadvantage? Amazingly, the opposite is true. When the leaders saturate their relationships with affection, it can actually boost their capacity to lead. Followers grow to recognize and admire their good will, and they usually respond by pouring out their hearts[2] in love and fierce loyalty.

How do leaders with moral strength tend to view their caches of face? In remarkable unison, most Thais will tell you that these leaders have little interest in "face-eyes." They exhibit a very low attachment to their repositories of face.

"They don't do things for the sake of 'face-eyes,'" claims the owner of a language school. "They have a personal propensity to help others because they enjoy doing so." These leaders are not infatuated with their power, and they do not abuse power because they *do not need to resort to this means of control.* Their followers rally around them in loyal support and gladly cooperate with their instructions and advice.

It is possible for a leader's moral strength to give rise to considerable power and influence. A university professor expresses this ever so clearly: "The leader in this category will love his face[3] the least, but ironically, the very fact that he's not interested in face is something that boosts him up so he has even more 'face-eyes'! He ends up with more face than all the others. It's strange."

Some Thais argue that these leaders know their face is big and they must maintain face in society. What they mean is that they—like everyone else—understand the great value of face. They care about their stores of social capital because they have won them at great cost. Their approach is different, however. They rely upon their goodness to maintain face because that is how they accumulated *barami* in the first place.

But be aware of imposters. Many leaders out there have ulterior motives. They pursue this accolade because they covet its spoils. They are mindful that this form of social capital yields high dividends.

Since it is difficult to guess the intentions of a leader's seemingly selfless generosity, herein lies an opening for those who wish to subvert the honor system. Leaders often become interested in *barami* as a tool to climb surreptitiously to levels of greater power. This lust for wild public acclaim can tempt even those with the best of intentions. Some leaders start out well. They launch their careers with moral strength leading the way. But eventually, even *they* become sidetracked by a growing desire for power itself.

Whenever followers directly benefit from the generosity of an influential leader, it is not uncommon for them to attribute *barami* to him or her. Often, however, *they confuse generosity with moral strength*. By rushing to ascribe this honor to a leader they can easily overlook a distinction of monumental importance: in this paradigm of leadership, acts of patronage must be selfless, uncalculated acts of kindness.

Reality whispers that there are two types of *barami* leaders. One humbly pursues what is best for followers. He is not interested in his "face-eyes." The other is interested in having a reputation of generosity and goodness because he desires to rise in society. To put it simply, some leaders win *barami* passively. Others pursue it actively.

Research reveals that truly virtuous leaders—when compared to those who lead by mere authority or influence—exhibit a patently unique perspective on "face-eyes" as social capital. They are not preoccupied with their stores of capital, and they refrain from the active pursuit of "face-eyes." Their focus is fixed on using their social capital to mobilize others to work together to improve the quality of life for everyone.

The *barami* leader's store of social capital is awarded to him because he, with no thought of personal gain, is fair with others. He demonstrates kindness. He cares more about *being truly honorable* than merely having the appearance of honor. He cares more about doing what is right than reaping the rewards of morally good choices.

So how do leaders with moral strength treat close subordinates? Research findings assert that these leaders have genuine interest in the welfare of others, including all subordinates. Their interest is unfeigned and their good intentions are sincere. They see underlings as important because each person contributes, in part, toward the success of collective efforts. They support subordinates as a means of empowering them to do good works in society.

These leaders tend to be respectful of close subordinates because their approach to power is founded upon mutual respect. They rarely assume a competitive attitude toward leaders directly below. They grant them the right to express opinions. They have no desire to gain face by erasing the "face-eyes" of subordinates. They view members of this group as worthy of honor, and they *give* them honor.

We have already learned that it can be dangerous for leaders to show honor to subordinates. After all, honor, when recognized by others, is a powerful "lifter." In most circles of society there is such stiff competition for face—such fierce battles for limited resources and titles—that leaders do not dare to support the successes of their close subordinates.

Yet leaders with moral strength consistently give honor to their associates. This extraordinary behavior demonstrates a commendable amount of trust in their associates, as well as a sense of security in their own treasures of social capital.

"The more his subordinates grow beyond where he is, the happier he is, because his foundation is goodness," claims a religious leader.

Here are the words of a community leader who appears to have embraced this paradigm of power. "When we give honor to those worthy of honor, we don't need to anticipate what we'll receive in exchange," he says. "Yet the truth is this. He who consistently gives honor to others is likely to receive honor in return. He who consistently tries to take honor away from others consistently loses honor."

Leaders with moral strength accurately weigh the true merit of each person in their inner circle. They intentionally protect the "face-eyes" of close subordinates, showing more deference to their face than leaders in the other two paradigms.

We should not presume, however, that they spare the face of wrongdoers. These leaders have high standards for their entourage and they are stringent in maintaining them. They correct unacceptable behavior, and they teach their subordinates the ways of virtuous leadership. They show no undue favoritism. Those who attempt to ingratiate themselves by "sucking up" often find that this kind of leader is unmoved by their tactics.

In their facework with close subordinates, these leaders introduce dynamics that tend to empower others. They enjoy seeing virtuous and competent people rise within the power structures of society so they can succeed in helping others in ever-expanding ways.

It should not surprise us to learn that these leaders also view distant subordinates, even common people, with interest and a desire to help. "Their method of looking at people differs from that of most Thais," observes a judge.

Barami leaders are appropriate in the ways they "grant honor" and "give face" to all distant subordinates. From their perspective, all subordinates in a hierarchy deserve a chance to benefit and grow based on equitable and ethical standards. Because they think this way, they are able to identify good people under them and they grant promotions based on true merit, not relational indebtedness.

Whenever leaders with moral strength observe someone worthy of praise, they often praise that person. They exercise discernment, however. They maintain their principles. They grant honor based on what is truly honorable, not on the basis of a person's status, fame, or store of "face-eyes." People of humble means are not disqualified. These leaders are at ease granting honor and giving face, even to people with far less status.

Their demeanor invites those below them in the hierarchy to feel as if they are acceptable no matter what their level might be—high or low. In conversations, they have this knack for lowering themselves to the level of each person so they can understand his or her problems. This magnanimous attitude spawns feelings of intimacy that are capable of spanning the considerable power distance between them.

A Thai proverb alludes to the fruit of this style of leadership: "When the sky is adjacent to the earth, the earth supports the sky."[4] A district police chief helps us understand this saying. "If the sky successfully stoops down—in other words, if that leader comes down and spends time with the lowest levels of society," he says, "those common people will ascribe virtuous benevolence and *barami* to him for the rest of their lives, wholeheartedly."

These leaders are diligent in recognizing wrongdoing and disagreeing with it, but they are also merciful. They choose culturally acceptable ways to save the face of wrongdoers from unnecessary loss. They avoid criticizing others in ways that disparage them. In fact, they are inclined to help others redeem their face and function in society as people with "face-eyes."

This behavior generates a potent form of social capital. *Barami* leaders do not choose this pathway with a view toward gaining more face, but that is exactly what awaits them at the end of the path. Their primary social capital—their accumulated goodness—is a *byproduct* of their virtuous leadership.

The words of a judge help us to understand. "*Barami* is not born among those with mere influence," he says. "People like to use this word to praise those with great influence or power, claiming that they're building up *barami*. But you can never accumulate true *barami* intentionally. You can only do that with influence. True accumulated goodness only emerges when someone is a genuinely good person. If someone has moral strength you can see it. It's a personal characteristic that simply surfaces on its own."

Ironically, leaders who exhibit moral strength do not struggle to gain face in society. In fact, they are capable of amassing great amounts of social capital through magnanimity, generosity, and hard work.

Wait a minute! Doesn't that sound just like the influence paradigm?

Yes. Much like influential leaders, leaders with moral strength gain face by giving to others. That's where all similarities end, however. The approach of *barami* leaders is far less teleological. They gain face by selflessly doing good with no intention of gaining face for themselves. Also, whenever they attempt to increase stores of social capital, they prefer methods for gaining face that are above reproach.

Their style of giving is conspicuous as well. They do what they can *within the bounds of the limited resources at their disposal*. They look after others, but only to the degree that their resources will allow. If they command few material resources, they will give from their hearts through things like encouragement and advice. But they will avoid the temptation to over-extend resources or to go into debt in order to play the role of patron—something Thais label with the pejorative phrase, "going beyond their abilities." Leaders with moral strength feel little obligation to meet needs they are incapable of meeting.

For example, a leader in the community may not have much wealth or education, yet she works for the good of the collective. Or a monk may attempt to assist others in the community, yet he will not rely on money or coercion. They get things done through the power of devotion that others feel towards them.

Curiously, leaders with true moral strength have little need to seek fresh gains in face. In chapter 21 I will explain exactly why this is true, but for now we might simply consider how remarkable it is that this leader sustains the cooperation of others without striving to acquire fresh deposits of social capital. It is truly mysterious.

"Because of the moral strength and virtue they have accumulated, they already have people speaking highly of them. Others lift them up with their hearts. They don't need to force anything," says a government worker.

In addition, loyal followers often tenaciously take on the protection of their leader's face. They do this to such an extent that their leader does not need to be as concerned as other leaders about losing face.

Let's take a moment to appreciate how utterly unique *barami* leaders are in the way they gain the cooperation of others. In the other two paradigms, followers have extrinsic reasons for being compliant— namely, respect for the authority of the *amnat* leader, and desire to share in the resources of the *itthiphon* leader. But followers of leaders with moral strength are motivated intrinsically. It is an "inside-out" dynamic, something Thais describe with the adverbial phrase, *doi dusadi,*[5] meaning "with pleasure," or "with admiration." These leaders are not active in competitive face interaction because their power to lead is rooted in the devotion of their followers. It is secure and adequate for further acts of leadership.

"This guy puts gold leaf on the back of the image of the Buddha," claims the managing director of a company. Once again, here is that familiar idiomatic phrase. He is speaking metaphorically, saying that a leader with moral strength does virtuous things out of a pure heart, *whether or not others happen to take notice*. In the world of leadership, Thais hold selfless benevolence in extremely high regard.

Society awards fresh grants of face to *barami* leaders on the basis of one weighty stipulation: that they continue to express morally good hearts by giving kind and selfless assistance to those in need. This approach is unrealistic for many leaders in Thai society. It is far too restrictive, squelching their attempts to accomplish personal goals and ascend the hierarchies of power. Yet leaders with moral strength find creative ways to lead and succeed without straying from the principles of virtue.

These leaders seem arrestingly different from other leaders. They do not focus on personal profit as a compensation for their actions. Their face-gaining behaviors are motivated by a desire to help communities accomplish collective goals for the purpose of improving the quality of life for all.

This approach to face gain is winsome in the eyes of followers. They respond with true devotion and an inside-out motivation to comply and meet the needs of the leader. They grant him or her generous amounts of face in increasing measure. This lasting gratitude is the secret of a *barami* leader's staying power.

That is the power of "the hug" in Thai society. It baffles the mind yet beckons us to believe there is something more—something supremely valuable that transcends the daily push and shove of banal competitions for money and power.

18
THE GREAT OVERLAP

JOIN ME POOLSIDE at the prestigious Bangkok Polo Club, sitting with a highly successful retired banker. The ambience is calming.

"Goodness by itself doesn't mean shit," he says, "yet everybody pays it lip service." Quietly I wonder if I am with a man so jaded and cynical that he scoffs at virtue altogether. He then goes on to state his dramatic claim: "There is no leader whose sole power comes from *barami*."

"There is *barami* everywhere," he continues. "The leader with authority has *barami* because he has legitimate power. The leader with influence has *barami* because he has money to induce others. But no one has *barami* all by itself. He doesn't have a halo, you know! *Barami* must be founded upon *something*!"

His words are disquieting, to say the least, but they are a blessing in disguise. He points us to an immensely valuable discovery.

Before we unpack the meaning of his words, let's review in macro what we have learned. There are three major approaches to the use of power in Thailand: *amnat, itthiphon,* and *barami*. When we place the facework of leaders from these three paradigms side by side, the disparities become clear. Table 1 is a concise comparison across paradigms. You can use it as a reference tool to help you discern the behaviors and expectations of leaders you know. Take a minute to scan laterally across each category.

Table 1. Facework in leadership across paradigms

Facework category	Authority / *Amnat*	Influence / *Itthiphon*	Accumulated goodness / *Barami*
Source of power	authority of law or institutional code	access to and control of needed resources	leader's interpersonal moral strength and goodness
Stability of power	relatively secure; limited to incumbency	insecure; difficult to sustain	secure; lasting
Face attachment	considerable	profound	relatively low
Face maintenance	high amount of face maintenance	extremely high amount of face maintenance	minimal amount of face maintenance
Stance toward face gain	active	highly proactive	passive
Diversity of face-gaining tactics	moderately diverse	highly diverse	simple
Strategies for gaining face	perform duties well; win the heart of the boss	create indebtedness; threaten, flaunt power	virtuous/fair decisions; selfless assistance
Attitudes toward close subordinates	interest due to utility; bias toward grovelers; face is shared in tasks	interest in loyalty and utility; attitude differs from public to private	genuine interest, respect; not threatened; desire to honor the honorable
Treatment of close subordinates	deference; show honor appropriately; preferential treatment	*in public*: bolster, protect; *in private*: reward loyalty, punish failure	honor the honorable; protect their face; rebuke wrongdoing
Attitudes toward distant subordinates	indifference; sense of superiority	indifference; elevated sense of superiority; distant others not useful	genuine interest, respect; humble demeanor; desire to help
Treatment of distant subordinates	indifference; proper courtesy; little deference for the powerless	selfish disinterest; little respect; no deference for the powerless	protect their face, give honor to all levels; correct wrongdoing
Goal of facework	productivity in duties	profit; selfish interests	empowerment of others

Notice how the values, attitudes, and behaviors of each leader are shaped by the contours of the particular paradigm. Each leader uses face as social capital but he or she spends that capital differently. The leader with authority uses face for the sake of productivity and a chance to climb the hierarchy. The leader with influence uses face for the sake of personal profit and increased control over others. The leader with moral strength uses face for the sake of implementing justice and empowering others.

When we take paradigms of power and suspend them motionless like specimens in a laboratory, it's easy to see stark differences. But if you're familiar with the realities of Thai leadership, you know that things are not as clean-cut as they have been sounding. The combined whole of leadership behaviors forms a vast universe with many nuanced expressions of power, and they are enormously difficult to untangle.

To gain a modicum of clarity we must recognize that *these three paradigms of power continuously overlap and interact.* On any day in the kingdom there are millions of points of confluence. I'm not merely saying that leaders from different streams of power interface with each other, although they do. My real point is that most leaders must harness more than one type of power to get their jobs done.

A powerful phenomenon surfaces at points of confluence: synergy. *Leaders quickly learn that they advance faster when they access and make use of more than one paradigm of power.* They blend paradigms by embracing other approaches to power and adding them to their primary power game. By tapping into this fruitful strategy, they benefit far more than if they attempted to gain face only within the bounds of their primary paradigm. One plus one does not always equal two, at least not in circles of power in Thai society.

The more we are aware of face dynamics in arenas of power, the more it can boost our understanding of Thai leaders we encounter in daily living. But as we launch into this fluid world of leadership where paradigms collide, we must be careful lest we misunderstand and misapply what we have learned.

For example, if you have a strongly egalitarian background or a bias toward servant leadership, you might be tempted to conclude that *barami* is the only worthy paradigm. Not only is that perspective unrealistic, it is also flatly invalid. It ignores the firmly ensconced structures of power in Thai society.

For society to function effectively, all three approaches to leadership are needed. Despite our perception that leaders seem prone to manipulate the privileges of power for selfish gain, each paradigm is potentially beneficial to society. We should avoid demonizing or glamorizing any one of them.

We also should avoid naiveté by reminding ourselves that these are prototypes. They are conceptual models gleaned from good ethnographic work, but they still are *theoretical* categories. They are much cleaner on paper than they are in real life—in the actual behavior of leaders.

Why? Well, things are just messy.

It is confusing that most leaders function simultaneously in more than one paradigm. They have a primary source of power, but they switch and blend styles depending on circumstances, roles, and specific objectives in leadership tasks. This habit of blending can blur the lines of our perception.

Also, our understanding is muddied by the way that followers throw around ascriptions of *barami* so loosely. It is difficult to identify the true presence or absence of this coveted form of social capital. To be fair-handed we must judge a leader's motives for being kind and generous. This is an attempt to weigh the invisible—a delicate and difficult task. Whenever we question the motives of a leader, our curiosity can lure us down paths plagued with pitfalls. Sometimes we are too cynical. We judge a leader unjustly. At other times we are too naive. We are duped by a leader's slick, smooth-tongued efforts to subvert fair rules for gaining honor.

There is something even more baffling, however. Although there are three *ways of envisioning* power, there are just two *games* of power: the authority game and the influence game.

The authority game is played in the context of authoritative power structures and socially legitimate hierarchies. It comes to life because of sanctioned positions of authority in such realms as education, government service, political office, corporate structures, and community associations. A leader's exercise of power in these hierarchies must remain within clearly established boundaries.

Leaders who wish to succeed in this game must focus their attention, for the most part, *upward*. Of course, they must attend to subordinates because leaders look good when their teams accomplish projects. Sometimes they must look laterally as well, especially when they're members of an entourage. They try to get to know, outsmart, and outperform other leaders who share their level in the hierarchy.

But most importantly, leaders in this game must look upward. Empowerment is measured by their ability to ascend hierarchies by winning the hearts of their bosses, ostensibly through productivity, honesty, and fairness in the exercise of their duties.

The influence game is played differently. It takes place in self-generated hierarchies that are not socially sanctioned. Its players are business owners, politicians, entertainers, professional athletes, wealthy citizens, and yes, members of the mafia.

Players in this game have more freedom in the exercise of power, but their power itself is not guaranteed in any way. It is summarily dependent upon their ability to create and sustain dependency in others by providing for them—at a cost, of course—a steady supply of resources that remain under their control.

Overtly, the game is played *downward*. These leaders seek to draw new people into a net, luring them into frames of influence and control. Their subordinates glance upward so as to please the boss in every way, but their primary job is to focus downward with a view toward expanding their boss's influence. For all players in this game, empowerment is measured by their ability to gain control of resources to be used to indebt others and induce them to comply.

Let's fade back to the scene with the banker sitting poolside. "No one has *barami* all by itself," he says. "*Barami* must be founded upon *something*!"

I have grown to understand his words. His argument is simple. The power I have been calling accumulated goodness or moral strength is not generated in a vacuum. It is dependent on the other two bases of power.

The *amnat* and *itthiphon* paradigms emerge directly from the country's two major power games. But *barami* is unique. It lacks its own arena for displaying its peculiar approach to power. To be precise, *the only way* barami *can emerge is from within one of the two games of power*. It has no guaranteed place in either game, and it is—by far—the least practiced and the most shunned of three approaches to power.

What I call "the great overlap" is this: leaders in both power games accelerate face gain by *blending* paradigms. This is exceedingly common.

"People want what they don't have," says a wealthy businessman. "Influential leaders lack legitimacy. Once they make it, they want to appear respectable. Positional leaders lack longevity."

The secret to climbing faster is to perfect the art of blending paradigms. Leaders find themselves limited by the bounds of their respective games, so they attempt to transcend those limitations by embracing more than one approach for gaining power. This strategy is highly beneficial for leaders who want to multiply opportunities for face gain. Leaders, in other words, are not prisoners of their primary game. They use creative options to accelerate their own rise. They work the angles of both power games to their personal advantage.

A leader blends paradigms when he adds the dynamics of another paradigm to his repertoire of leadership behaviors. Such a move, if successful, lends considerable synergy to his efforts to gain face, money, and power in his primary game.

Let's first look at how leaders in the authority game blend paradigms. Theoretically, success in the authority game is measured by an individual's performance and productivity for the sake of a given collectivity. Superiors are supposed to promote underlings based on true merit earned through the successful fulfillment of their duties.

A classic case of blending in this game, however, is the phenomenon of the *amnat-itthiphon* blend. In this blend, leaders with authority will attempt to foster instrumental *bunkhun* with their superiors and subordinates by practicing relational indebtedness, a hallmark of the *itthiphon* paradigm.

To gain the cooperation of their superiors, for example, they will grovel, flatter attentively, and perform favors above and beyond the call of duty. To increase control over certain subordinates, they will treat them preferentially and then expect strict compliance and special favors. They initiate relational indebtedness as a strategy for escalating their efforts to build social capital and wield power. These tactics go beyond the pure confines of the authority game, and they promise a sweet payback for the aspiring *amnat* leader.

An ancient example of this blending can be found in what one scholar, William J. Siffin (1966, 25), calls an "eat the state"[1] mentality. In past centuries, he notes, members of the administrative staffs of monarchs governed the citizens of the kingdom, but at the same time they used their authority to make unfair personal profit off of them.

Another researcher, probing power structures and the patronage system in a rural village in Ayutthaya, finds that leaders increase their power by using their formal authority as the foundation for sustaining patronage relationships and acquiring economic benefits (Natthawuth 1995).

Yet another researcher argues that personalism and paternalism are still "normative" behaviors in contemporary Thai administration (Johnson 2006, 44, 130).[2] He observes that leaders, after attaining a formal position of authority, will feel entitled to give up former trustworthy, equitable behavior in favor of self-interest and efforts to ensure "that their close friends and associates are the beneficiaries of any incoming material goods" (ibid., 12–13, 202–10).

Practical examples of this blend abound. For example, if a superior unjustly holds down a rising subordinate who is worthy of promotion, that underling needs help. He will search for a third party with sufficient influence, someone who will pressure his superior to desist in unjustly holding him down. In this case, both the superior and the subordinate are applying the principles of *itthiphon* within the authority game.

Another example is when a government official refuses to perform his duty until a citizen pays "tea money" (a bribe). Truthfully, he is obligated by law to grant any worthy request. But he stalls to give the message that he expects personal profit in reciprocation for the exercise of his duties.

Government employees who are able to build up financial resources can also open businesses on the side. This enables them to boost their income and influence without ever leaving the authority game.

Leaders in corporations and businesses use this same blend when they build valuable personal influence in the organization. Their relational tactics reach beyond the bounds of power inherent in titles and job descriptions.

Positional leaders blend paradigms because the framework of the authority game is simply too restrictive for leaders who wish to experience frequent, significant gains in "face-eyes." It is true that winning a promotion brings an increase in prestige. But the higher these leaders climb, the fewer the positions above them and the stiffer the competition for those positions. Promotions often require time—a *lot* of time—to evolve. Sometimes they never come. A pathway out of this inertia is to access opportunities to gain face in society outside of and unrelated to their direct job descriptions. This allows them to continue to rise.

Government employees find this particularly attractive. They are often poorly paid in comparison to jobs in the private sector. If they want to increase their level of "face-eyes" they must find ways to generate significant income outside of their salary. They do this by blending the *amnat* and *itthiphon* paradigms. If they are successful, they gain an edge over their peers. This is exactly why two men with the same rank or title may possess very, very different amounts of face.

Another blend in the authority game is the *amnat-barami* blend, when a positional leader attempts to build *barami*.

In his research, Natthawuth (1995) found that *amnat* leaders tend to use patronage relationships and entourages as a means of gaining a reputation of *barami*. Most leaders who earn widespread *barami* in society tend to grow it within the confines of government service. When they perform their duties in a fair and compassionate manner, or when they please large sectors of their constituencies by using authority to bring assistance and progress, they gain a reputation of evenhandedness and kindness. This can stir whispers that they "have *barami*."

However, even leaders in businesses can adopt the *barami* paradigm. They have the power to give orders and the power to hire and fire, but they, too, can gain reputations of being bighearted and impartial. If those reputations remain consistent over the course of many years, followers will often ascribe accumulated goodness to them.

Leaders who rarely blend paradigms might assume that authority alone should be enough to gain the cooperation of subordinates. Why bother creating a sense of loving indebtedness? There are a couple of good reasons.

Cooperation based on job descriptions alone may not be enough to drive the level of performance that *amnat* leaders need to thrive in positions of authority. Competitions for coveted promotions are fierce. Leaders need subordinates who will comply wholeheartedly, not grudgingly. To secure that kind of assistance, leaders can blend toward *barami* by going the extra mile, treating subordinates with a kindness that goes above and beyond convention or job description. They can be gracious when they don't have to be. They can avoid using power selfishly, even though it's within their reach to do so. When subordinates judge this kind of gracious leadership to be sincere, often they reciprocate by working harder and cooperating wholeheartedly.

There is another reason for introducing the *barami* paradigm into the authority game: leaders can open the door to lasting honor. In the pure game of authority, as long as leaders retain positions of authority, subordinates must be respectful. But this adulation often fades when leaders exit their positions and leave their titles behind.

There is one grand exception to this rule. Followers will often feel a lasting loyalty toward leaders who empower worthy candidates by treating all subordinates with respect, kindness, and impartiality.

Both blends—the *amnat-itthiphon* blend and the *amnat-barami* blend—are based on the same proposition: if you meet the needs of others, they will follow you. The unqualified difference, however, is the way each blend achieves that task.

One offers benefits with strings attached. Followers comply because of pressure from the outside. If they fail to comply with the wishes of the leader, they will be harmed, shamed, or disenfranchised.

The other blend uses resources to benefit others without scheming, guile, or ulterior motives. Followers have an *inside-out* motivation to comply. They genuinely respect their patron and wish to do almost anything to please him, knowing that he can be trusted not to take advantage of them.

When leaders with authority rise in hierarchies, it is often because they have pursued one of these two "blends" in paradigm.

Let's flip it around now and talk about paradigm blends in the influence game.

In contrast to the authority game, the influence game shows fewer blends. This is because leaders in the influence game already have access to a wide array of face-gaining tactics.

Blending still occurs, however. The most common form is that big players in the influence game love to grow broad reputations of being generous. This is the *itthiphon-barami* blend.

"Some patrons have so much money they don't know what to do with it all," muses a former air force officer, "so they spend it on their entourage for the sake of their own *barami*."

It is not uncommon for leaders in the game of influence to exhibit some of the superficial characteristics of *barami*. Their power is anchored in money and other formidable resources. When they play the role of grand patron, it is not difficult for them to cast convincing impressions that they have many loyal followers. But very often, this is not "pure *barami*."[3] It is contrived for the purpose of selfish gain.

This blend can also be detected when influential leaders attempt to gain wider public reputations of being "good" by using their wealth to broadcast and choreograph grand demonstrations of generosity toward society. This highly visible patronage can lure others—especially those who benefit directly—to ascribe accumulated goodness to them.

The *itthiphon-amnat* blend is subtler. Leaders in the influence game lack the legitimacy of ranks and titles, and they covet what they do not have. They welcome awards—especially royal decorations—and they seek for opportunities to sit on boards of prestigious institutions and other community organizations. These ways of gaining face are ancillary to their primary game, but very precious indeed.

To play either power game you need not use only a stick or a carrot. You can accelerate face gain and optimize your rise to power by blending paradigms. In fact, if you want to stay competitive—if you want the full arsenal of options for advancement—you *must* harness the synergy of wielding multiple kinds of power.

That is great advice for leaders, but it may not be enough to avoid the back of the pack. If you want to surge to the front, you must learn to leverage yourself against leaders in the adjacent power game. You must master the art of symbiotic relationships, a topic we will consider next.

19

CLIMBING THE LATTICE

CONSIDER THE CASE of old friends, drinking buddies. One has authority. The other has influence. They live by the code, "Hey, if I can help you in any way, let me know." Each leader has risen to power in his respective realm. Each can use his particular kind of power to help lighten burdens for the other.

Leaders welcome these liaisons as opportunities for gaining face and climbing the rungs of power. Relationships are robust because they are *symbiotic*—leaders in each game have something that leaders in the other game sorely need. Without ever leaving their primary games of power, leaders can leverage relationships across platforms to augment their reservoirs of face. In fact, to excel in circles of influence and power, leaders must forge these alliances.

This interplay between opposing games is as fascinating as it is common. Leaders agree to unspoken covenants of mutual ingratiation: "Scratch my back, and I'll scratch yours." Take, for instance, a governor and a very wealthy man in his province. Both men have "face-eyes," but for different reasons. The governor's face is planted upon his legitimate authority and the honor of his very high position. The tycoon's face is buoyed by his wealth, his connections, and his influence. He has less legitimate power than the governor, but in some local contexts he may exercise more tangible power. Still, each leader has something to provide to accelerate the other leader's quest for face. It is a symbiotic relationship that helps each party to gain greater prominence.

It is easier to conceive of this interplay as a dyadic exchange—that is, one to one. In reality, things are much more complicated. Affinities grow within sophisticated *webs* of relationships. Complex alliances and diverse camps of loyalty dot the landscape. Sometimes leaders are relationally indebted to whole lairs of cronies, and those collateral relationships intensify pressure on indebted leaders to reciprocate and make good on their debts. But for the sake of clarity, we will keep our illustrations simple.

A leader in either game can initiate a cycle of reciprocity by finding ways to obligate a leader in the opposite game. It seems intuitive that the more powerful of the two parties would initiate this cycle of mutual dependence. But even when there is significant asymmetry in power, *either party* can initiate obligation. The lesser party simply must find something in his pool of resources that the greater party needs or wants.

When mutuality is established, leaders rarely—almost never—verbalize obligations. A tacit understanding instinctively guides them. By making the contract neither verbal nor written, the amount of obligation is almost impossible to quantify. It becomes difficult to determine when debts are fully repaid, or who is more indebted to whom. As we noted in a previous chapter, this practice of mutual ingratiation helps to sustain relational stability and longevity. It lays a foundation that is highly beneficial to both parties in their respective attempts to acquire power and greater "face-eyes."

Examples of reciprocal obligation are legion. Many of them smack of unethical or even illegal behaviors, but I want to be categorically clear that this chapter is not an exposé on corruption. My intent is to paint in broad strokes how symbiotic relationships form a trellis that leaders can climb with a view toward gaining face.

Let's start with the phenomenon of *amnat* helping *itthiphon*—when government workers use their authority to aid a friend in the influence game.

Here we have a leader in the influence game. He has money and sway in the community, but despite his wealth, he lacks legitimacy. He desires honor. He attempts to attract this valuable dimension of face by donating to community projects sponsored by local government officials. He is invited to serve as chair of community planning committees. At major seasonal celebrations he makes sure he is present and seen with top officials from the province. All of these tactics pay off because he actively cultivates friends in the authority game.

We have already learned that influential leaders invite special guests of honor to their large dinner parties. These esteemed guests from the authority game are there to gain face themselves, no doubt, but a major function of their presence is to enhance the "face-eyes" of the host. "Attendees will say, 'Oh, this host is so distinguished. He must have a lot of face if he's able to get such high-ranking authorities to attend,'" explains a border patrol policeman.

Policemen often play the role of patron in communities. Imagine two stores in a town. Over the years one store has donated often and generously to special projects at the police station. The other has not. When the second store experiences a theft, local police are less responsive than if it had been the first store.

"Or let's say a businessman, a person with 'face-eyes' in the community, breaks the law," says a lower-ranking policeman. "When we go to arrest him, he says, 'Can we just not do anything about this?' He then offers us some benefit, some material gift—money or gold. See, we police have the ability to grant kindness or administer punishment."

Here's another influential leader who wants to initiate a potentially lucrative business venture, but governmental bureaucracy is slowing him down. Worse yet, one of his local competitors may beat him to the punch. Lacking the right kind of power to move things along, this influential leader needs friends in the authority game. He sets up the local district officer by ingratiating him in numerous ways. He then asks for a favor, and this friend with legitimate authority pulls strings to see that the project is approved.

Consider the influential leader who owns a string of bars and wants to open a new one. He needs the favor of local police because he knows that if cops park their motorbikes in front of a bar to check identification cards, customers will stay away. So the owner delivers a monthly payment to the police, something he calls "buying convenience."[1]

Or suppose that fierce bidding is underway to win a municipal construction contract. When the contract is finally awarded, there is one winner and many losers. One of the losers begins to threaten the winner in some way. The winner then asks his friends in uniform to mediate by paying a visit to the threatening party. Voilà! The winning party gains protection. Of course, quiet payment is made for such services.

Here is an example from the logging industry. Because laws limit the amount of teakwood that can be harvested from the forests of the kingdom, Thai loggers practice a sleight of hand called "wood wrapped in a sarong." They sneak wood from trees cut in Thailand across the river into Burma and then fabricate papers certifying that the wood is being imported. Leaders in the authority game wink at this illegal scheme—for a price, of course.

The bottom line is that those with wealth and influence must rely on the power of leaders with authority in order to get their way. "If those with money and gold do not have the backing of political power," says a judge, "there's no way they can maintain their 'face-eyes.' At every level—whether national, provincial, or local—people with prestige must have *some* interaction with the political process. If they don't, their 'face-eyes' will not be around for very long."

Assistance also flows the opposite direction—when *itthiphon* helps *amnat*. Leaders in the authority game need the help of friends in the influence game.

Consider a leader with rank in government. She has authority and the honor of her title, but her salary is pitifully insufficient for generating the trappings of someone with "face-eyes." Her economic worries are compounded by widespread public expectations that she should embrace the role of patron with generosity and flair. If she doesn't have the money, she'd better know how to find it. This is where her friends in games of influence can help her. She gets to know the "right" people. She pulls a favor or two. She begins to receive "gifts" from time to time. When she wants to open a business on the side, she accepts veiled offers of capital. This is how friends in the other power game can enhance her efforts to gain face.

Let's return to a familiar example. A leader with authority attends a public gathering at the invitation of a wealthy man. When the master of ceremonies introduces him as a special guest of honor, he receives a loud round of applause and a chance to say a few words. This boosts his public recognition. That may sound like an insignificant amount of face gain, but do not discount the cumulative effect of this practice. When the same scene plays itself over and over again at parties and ceremonies in that locale, certain prominent leaders with authority can gain valuable public acclaim that amplifies their honor. They begin looking bigger-than-life.

When influential leaders want to make connections with leaders in the authority game, they look for gaps to enter. Certain leaders with great wealth and influence are capable of attracting people with very high positions of honor, perhaps members of the nobility, generals, or cabinet ministers. Sometimes leaders with authority are reluctant to accept assistance from influential figures. They know that somewhere down the road they will be asked to reciprocate, perhaps in ways that will violate personal values. They must learn to decline assistance graciously, so as not to offend prominent patrons.

But many authority figures are vulnerable to the overtures of influential leaders. A leading antecedent—one that we've reviewed several times—is that salaries of leaders in the authority game are insufficient for playing the role of a generous patron.

Stories abound regarding colossal corruption and abuse of power in society due to the clout of those with great wealth and influence. A well-documented example is the notorious godfather from a southeastern province who was loved by the local police because he paid them so handsomely. The police became his cronies. This man of dark influence cared for "his" policemen to the point that he took revenge on anyone who threatened or harmed them.

Dominant players in influence games work tirelessly to curry favor with local authorities. They take them out to lavish dinners, make generous donations to favored projects, or even lend them personal financial assistance. Let's say a leader with authority wants to buy a car, but he's a little short on funds. His friend adds a sum of money to make up the difference. Perhaps the leader wants to host a house-warming ceremony, a dinner party, or some other gathering. Once again, his influential buddy gives him a million baht to pay for it. He may also help his children gain entrance into private schools, and he may not even hesitate to assist him with the heavy costs of tuition. The possibilities are endless.

"This influential guy now has leverage over him," observes a community leader. The *itthiphon* leader gains assurance that he will have help in higher places. Should he ever come into problems with the law, he simply "makes a withdrawal on the *bunkhun*" he has accrued.

Politicians function simultaneously in both games to such an extent that it's difficult to decipher their primary game. Most seem to rely heavily on influence. Members of parliament are often the patrons of policemen. In fact, sometimes they have more clout in helping a police officer to rise in rank than the man's superior officers. It is with strings attached, of course. An MP might say to a powerful policeman, "Help me garner votes for the next election." The policeman uses his clout in the district to boost the representative's electoral base. "In return he can help pull us upward," says one policeman.

Eventually, some leaders swap one primary power game for the other. Leaping high off momentum in one game, they bound with bold-faced esprit into the adjacent game. It is not surprising to see this among leaders with substantial wealth and commanding influence. It is as though they are no longer sated by a life of affluence and localized honor, so they run for political office as a way of extending the reach of their conglomerated power.

Stop for a second and think. When Thai leaders make this leap, what aspects of face are they pursuing? They are cutting a wider swath of *chuesiang*, or public acclaim, to be sure. But there are greater treasures to be seized. Remember, they pursue what they lack. They have substantial wealth, but they desire *kiat* and *barami*—legitimate honor and a reputation of possessing accumulated goodness.

There are countless ways to build a reputation of *barami* while remaining in the influence game, yet the siren of political office calls with bewitching sweetness. Why? This most precious social capital—the crown of all face gain—can be garnered more efficiently from within the authority game, where your documented duty is to improve the lives of those in the collective below.

Prominent members of the police and military like to switch games from *amnat* to *itthiphon* by bounding into politics. This gives them a freer hand to play games of influence on much grander scales. Many former prime ministers have done this after amassing power through careers in the authority game.

In a country where cultivating strategic relationships is a well-practiced art, symbiotic alliances are everywhere. This interplay between the two major games of power has been going on for a long, long time.

Power and money—or, authority and influence—have been bed partners for centuries. Leaders in one power game often need the help of leaders in the other game. And when they venture out to look for that connection, they often find willing exchange partners.

These two streams of power form a latticework that leaders climb to accrue a coveted form of social power—face. The more face you have, the better you can lead. The more *kinds* of face you have, the more you can soar. But it takes *two* streams of power to form that trellis.

To visualize this point, imagine Jackie Chan performing a climbing stunt in one of his films. Before him looms a traditional Thai house on high stilts. With effort, he can shimmy up one lone stilt. But give him two stilts just a meter part, and he'll fly upward with incredible agility.

That is how leaders leverage two games of power to multiply returns in their efforts to gain face and secure lasting dominance. Leaders use webs of interrelatedness to enhance their capacities to lead.[2]

This symbiosis has an undeniable dark side. Influence often corrupts justice, a hallmark of true authority. Authority often engorges influence, empowering it to subvert honorable rules of gain. That's what happens when the desire for "face-eyes" rules the day. The more noble aspects of face fade into the background.

"We see many examples of people who sell illegal goods," says a community leader. "But then they give some money to society and people accept them. It makes these leaders think, 'You can sin, and then you simply make merit.'"

Her words leave us dreaming of a more preferable path, a noble path—one that is exemplary in its use of power, one that is honorable in the midst of rapacious competition. We now turn to that path.

PART 3
REIMAGINING FACE

20
NOBLE FACE

SUPPOSE WE WERE TO DREAM—to shift our attention from the way things *are* to the way they possibly *could* be. How might we reimagine facework between leaders and their followers in such a way that both sides win?

"Man is an animal suspended in webs of significance he himself has spun," writes a renowned anthropologist (Geertz 1973, 5). Thai leaders attempt to fabricate that sense of worth through their pursuit of "face-eyes" as social capital and a lasting radiance.

Their quests for greatness provoke us to consider some legitimate questions of great import. Are leaders sometimes ensnared in their own webs? Do they like to spin webs that entangle their followers? Do they tend to disinherit followers by withholding the kind of empowering leadership they deserve? We are asking, in short, "Could the common facework of leaders use a facelift?"

Leaders who have achieved dominance by scaling the "webs" of significance are likely to answer a categorical "no" to this question. They simply have too much at stake.

But if we were to pose the question before an audience of the disempowered, they might do more than answer a simple "yes." They are weary of hackneyed and callow patterns of social exchange that continue to enrich the powerful and enslave the masses. They desire leaders who take great satisfaction in seeing the truly worthy rise within power structures and go on to a lifetime of helping others to solve their problems. They long for their leaders to practice noble facework.

This represents a cry for leaders with true moral strength. But alas, *barami*—like every other valuable commodity on the face of this globe—has its counterfeits. Many Thais fall prey to bogus imitations, in part, because they disagree about the wellspring of this coveted resource.

Is it sacral power? If so, it is shrouded in mystery. It appears and disappears subject to the inscrutable whims of astrology or karma.

Is it a quality fit only for a monarch? Then why do Thais attribute it freely to leaders with no hint of royal descent?

Is it mere generosity? If so, why do followers resent the charity of some leaders yet deeply cherish other expressions of kindness?

As a social researcher, I note the diversity in popular understandings of *barami*. But qualitative interviews with modern Thais reveal one indispensible criterion of this form of social capital. The gold standard of *barami* is virtue.

Social scientists get very nervous about words like "virtue." To date, most scholars researching and writing about face are mute about its moral dimensions. In their attempts to be fair and dispassionate they refrain from assigning moral value to human behavior. In particular, postmodern scholarship has stigmatized attempts to prescribe clear moral boundaries for social conduct. It endorses subjectivism and moral relativism to such an extent that words like "right," "wrong," "good," or "evil" seem passé.

But my own commitment to impartiality compels me to state that *finely nuanced moral codes wield profound influence over social interaction in Thailand*. Thais inevitably, frequently, and effortlessly offer morally charged judgments about face behaviors.

If we listen long enough, we begin to understand that judgments of face are inherently moral. It is difficult, if not impossible, to attempt to weigh another person's claims to worth without referencing some standard of good.

Members of Thai society use diverse criteria to determine the presence or absence of "face-eyes": good looks, wealth, status, titles, awards, competence, skill, intellect, fame, or power. But when they evaluate the social capital of leaders—especially their *barami*—they commonly raise questions of legitimacy.

Rarely do they openly challenge a leader's reputation of accumulated goodness, for obvious reasons. It can be dangerous to touch the face of someone up the hierarchy.

It is also bad form to do so. For generations, Thai conceptions of karma have invoked a popular belief that people with high status have more intrinsic virtue than commoners. "The Buddhist world view emphasizes achievement within a framework of hierarchical differences in moral status," writes one scholar. "Each individual might be conceived to be a 'balance' of his religious merits and demerits accumulated through his various actions in this and previous lifetimes" (Kirsch 1975, 180, 189). Jasper Ingersoll writes, "Villagers are keenly aware of the important consequences of merit in the life of the individual, in respect to his possessions, his status in society, his inclinations to make more merit, and his prestige" (1975, 234).

The wealthy are often viewed as possessing greater virtue than the poor (Hanks 1975, 198). "It is easily assumed that those of greatly superior status are also purer in character," writes another scholar (Zehner 1991, 160).

Yet we know by experience that not all people with power are virtuous. Many leaders attain power and status through non-meritorious means. They *appear* good due to their positions of honor, but they are not virtuous.

This leads Thais to question the legitimacy of leaders. "He may be wealthy," they say, "but did he gain his wealth by taking advantage of others? She may be famous, but does she use that fame to help others? He may hold an honorable title, but is his life truly honorable?" Their questions point beyond wealth, beauty, skill, or hegemony. Collectively, they stake a claim: *to possess legitimate "face-eyes," you must be a noble person.* Aristotle's (1123b 35) famous saying, "Honor is the reward for virtue," becomes, for Thailand, "Face is the reward for virtue."

Kings of the present Chakri dynasty have adhered to a "moral code for kings," also referred to as the *thammarat*, that descends from teachings of the Buddha. The code cites ten kingly perfections: 1) charity, 2) moral rectitude, 3) forbearance, 4) sacrifice, 5) honesty, 6) compassion, 7) self-restriction, 8) non-anger, 9) restraint from harmful behavior, and 10) rightful conduct.[1] His Majesty King Bhumibol Adulyadej has set the bar for moral leadership in modern times. When we study his reign, "the 'composite' picture of a 'preferred' leader which emerges is that of a good, honest, well-intentioned and loyal person, who works hard to . . . inculcate in the society, especially the young generations, some of the traditional values, such as discipline, compassion, and moderation" (Sukhumbhand 2003, 306).

To explore this tradition of virtue in leadership, I asked dozens of Thais a question: "Who, in your opinion, is a public leader with virtue?"[2] Respondents frequently cited certain familiar names, so from a master list I contacted prominent leaders to request a forty-five-minute interview on the topic of virtue. Not all, of course, were free to assist me. But I was fortunate to interview some very impressive leaders: a member of His Majesty's Royal Privy Council, former prime ministers, the head of a political party, a great grandson of King Chulalongkorn, three high-profile abbots, a popular teaching nun, and eight community leaders with shining reputations.

Although seventeen individuals can hardly speak for the whole mix of leaders in Thai society, these eminent leaders offered intriguing insights. I listened for points of *consensus* about virtue in leadership, and here is what I found.

Virtuous leaders really do exist. They appear in every level of society. They are honest, holding to the truth. They are sincere, avoiding duplicity. They emphasize inner goodness rather than outward appearance. They do good for the sake of good itself, not as a show. They are other-centered, not self-centered. They avoid problems by separating personal relationships from the duties they are bound to perform. They can be trusted to be fair. They nurture subordinates and take joy in their successes. They do not cheat, swindle, or exploit others. They genuinely care about what benefits the collective—solving problems and improving the lives of others. Immersed in a society infatuated with superficial trappings of "face-eyes," they do not abuse their advantageous positions for the sake of personal face gain.

When we study the *face behaviors* of leaders, can we tell the difference between someone who is virtuous and someone who is not? According to seventeen seasoned leaders, the answer is yes.

Virtuous leaders view their stores of prestige in a manner starkly different from leaders who lack virtue. They exhibit *low levels of attachment to their "face-eyes."* They are not altogether indifferent about their social capital, however. "It is a good thing for these leaders to be conscious of their 'face-eyes' as something they must maintain," says a politician, "because it makes them cautious, knowing that if they do not hold firmly to what is right, what is good, what is virtuous, their social capital will disappear."

Noble leaders are aware of the power of goodness and its sufficiency for leadership. They are *satisfied with prestige built on good works.* For them, social capital is merely a by-product of doing what is right. "Face-eyes" is not a prize to be won. It is an echo of response generated by the practice of goodness. "The highest good is to be able to release your good works," says a respected nun. "These leaders resist the need to feel better than others. They aren't drunk on their own goodness."

Virtuous leaders *hold lightly to their prestige.* They are aware of the praise, affirmation, approval, and acclaim that others give to them, but they are not emotionally attached to those things. They are far more concerned about solving problems and meeting the needs in the collective than they are about their own prestige.

For the sake of contrast, let's note that leaders who lack virtue have a strong emotional attachment to their "face-eyes." They carry themselves in a lofty manner.

One leader recalls a government official he once observed. "When subordinates entered the room, they crawled!" he says. "That leader felt proud. He growled impolitely, like, 'What do you want now? Why are you bothering me?' Those who lack virtue always want to flaunt their power.[3] They act as if they are higher than others."

"They use people as servants, as tools," claims a former prime minister. "They're likely to think about 'I, me, and myself.' They lose their bearings in pride—'I think I'm excellent, I think I know everything.' Given time, they will look down on everybody. They will find fault in others all the time. But they themselves are infallible."

"This behavior is fragile. It's not stable," argues a nun. "We don't suffer because we have prestige. We suffer because we're emotionally attached to 'face-eyes.' We don't suffer because we have public acclaim. We suffer because we are addicted to the idea that we must have the acceptance of others."

Tanin Kraivixien argues that contemporary Thais seek power and wealth because of values parents are fostering in their children. One traditional blessing widely recited in homes shuns themes of virtue in favor of status and money:

> My child, may you be determined to excel in study so that afterwards you will become "big," the lord and boss over others, having fortuitous authority, merit, and great power, having only wealth and contentment, so that you will become a benefactor to your father, mother, siblings, children and grandchildren.[4] (Tanin 2005, 25)

"If a person is without virtue, he'll do everything for the sake of his own 'face-eyes,'" says another leader. "Asian culture has conditioned us to say, 'In life, "face-eyes" is everything. To lose face is worse than losing your life. Better to die than to lose face.'"

The behavior of noble leaders is remarkably different. They treat subordinates with respect and honor them appropriately. They train them to do good works for the sake of doing good, not for the sake of increased "face-eyes." They promote people with righteous values over those who lack virtue.

Virtuous leaders focus on the intrinsic worth of others, not on discrepancies in power. They exude a gracious demeanor that reduces the feeling of distance between them and others. Thais describe this behavior as *mai thue nuea thue tua*,[5] meaning not acting aloof or priggish, not acting as if you are better than others. Leaders with this endearing posture are approachable and unassuming with respect to their status in the hierarchy. Followers rate them high in authenticity, empathy, and relational competency.

Why? They speak from their hearts. They show genuine interest in the joys and sorrows of others. They are gracious in the ways they speak with people from both high and low levels of society. This conduct emits a tangible egalitarian tone that is exceptional in a society that is profoundly hierarchical. It creates a public image that is enormously winsome.

This humble behavior *does nothing to dismantle the entrenched hierarchy.* These leaders simply forego their rights to be treated with the fanfare, pomp, and circumstance that other leaders of their ranking (and even below) might demand. In fact, it is precisely *because* their behavior takes place in the context of confirmed power distance that they become so admired by those below them.

Virtuous leaders empower others—not indiscriminately, but willingly and purposefully. They honor subordinates who are worthy of honor. They are satisfied to see subordinates grow in goodness. They are pleased when good people ascend from the hierarchy below. They are not threatened by the progress of worthy protégés, because they remember that, inevitably, their own time must pass.

If all this is sounding strangely familiar, that's because you're already well acquainted with the *barami* leader. Whether you ask Thais about leaders with undeniable virtue or leaders with undeniable *barami*, they paint the same profile. That's because virtue is the indispensible foundation of every person who leads with genuine accumulated goodness.

Actually, that claim is not bold enough. In fact, *virtue lingers as the scrupulous judge of all who use face as social capital*, not just those who lead with moral strength.

In a country where nine out of every ten citizens is an avowed Buddhist, we might wonder what the Lord Buddha taught about the five forms of social capital. If the Buddha were to mingle with Thais today, how would he respond to contemporary manifestations of face? If he were to stroll the lanes of Bangkok, attend a wedding feast in a Northeastern village, read a Thai newspaper, or observe politicians in the throes of heated competition, would he address the topic of "face-eyes?" We will never know, but nine esteemed Buddhists did not hesitate to offer their opinions.

When I asked these prominent leaders what the Buddha taught regarding face as social capital, few had ever been asked such curious questions. Yet in rousing consensus, they argued that Buddhist teachings are highly relevant to this topic.

Let's begin with *barami*, or moral strength—the pièce de résistance of Thai face that has been the focus of this chapter. Teachings of the Buddha imply that this form of capital cannot be manufactured by acquiring wealth or power alone. It is the fruit of a virtuous life. Virtue can guide leaders to a lifestyle of selflessly using their power for the benefit of others.

"Although the Buddha was not at all interested in *barami*, he definitely possessed it, and he correctly understood what it was," says a former prime minister. "I think that a person with great *barami* is a person who has not strived for *barami*."

To attempt to gain a reputation of having moral strength by grasping for it is like trying to take hold of thin air. As one politician expresses it: "It does not belong to us." *Barami* simply arrives on its own to anoint leaders who live a righteous life of service to others.

Kiat, or honor, is the aspect of face often tied to rank, position, title, or status. The Buddha taught that a leader's honor should be founded entirely upon goodness.

Leaders, the media, and the masses regularly grant forms of honor that have little to do with virtue. In public ceremonies, virtue fades into the background as leaders pontificate, palaver, and puff each other up, strutting all the while to the dazzle of lights, sound, and high visibility. But Buddhist teaching exhort that true honor is based on virtue, not wealth, status, rank, talent, fame, or hegemony.

No one should actively seek to gain honor as though it were plunder or loot. It is not a trophy to be coveted and won. It is merely one of the byproducts of a commendable life. The way to pursue honor, therefore, is to pursue virtue with no thought of compensation. With time, others will recognize your honorable ways.

A respected nun is not so sure about that last remark. She contends that a wicked society is incapable of recognizing what is honorable. "In this world we will always have true value and counterfeit value, but most people in today's world are interested in counterfeit value," she says. "Whenever a society concedes honor to the wealthy and the powerful—overlooking those who do what is right—that society becomes fragile and very dangerous."

What might the Buddha have to say about *chuesiang*, or public acclaim? He would discount the value of fame, exposing it as cheap and hollow. He would teach, instead, that true public acclaim is the outgrowth of being gracious, equitable, and generous, time and time again.

Leaders with true virtue never seek public acclaim. They understand that it's merely an echo—something that shadows the leader who loves what is right and seeks to meet the needs of others.

What about *nata*, or superficial prestige, the most common term for possessing face in Thai society? The Buddha cared very little about outward appearances. On the contrary, he taught the necessity of nurturing an inner commitment to goodness itself—a heart that harbors right teaching.[6]

In other words, Buddhist teachings are in vivid contrast to a pronounced preoccupation with *external* things that is so prevalent in contemporary Thai culture. Members of society are driven to accumulate outward symbols of "face-eyes" so as to create a superficial image that "looks good." The Buddha would refuse to be drawn into the collusion of silly competitions for face.

"He is completely detached! No worldly possessions! As far as I'm concerned, there is no such thing as 'face-eyes' in Buddhism," argues a former prime minister. "The two are antithetical."

A nun sounds the same note. "The Buddha, on his way to enlightenment, removed himself from everything having to do with 'face-eyes,'" she asserts. "He wasn't enlightened in a palace. He left behind all grasping for 'face-eyes,' all attachment to the praise of others. That's how he encountered who he really was."

"A true Buddhist does not make merit to gain prestige," she continues. "A true Buddhist scrapes sinful cravings from his heart. We often claim to be Buddhists, yet we fail to behave as we should. Attachment to 'face-eyes' is addiction that ultimately dishevels our pathway to *nirvana*."

The Buddha removed himself completely from all things having to do with "face-eyes." He taught detachment from all desires and affections. This implies that *a virtuous person will judge "face-eyes" as something marginal and unimportant* when compared to other things. True value resides in being good and doing what is right.

What might the Buddha teach about endogenous worth? *Saksi* is an inner goodness that savors whatever is noble and righteous.

A popular connotation of *saksi* is the idea of having "power born of status." It is based on a theory of aristocratic superiority, something that has been won by a heap of good deeds in past lives.

In the opinion of one Buddhist leader, this belief induces many leaders to be highly sensitive about and defensive of their inherent worth. "The Buddha taught that there is only the present," she argues. "To point to one's past goodness and say, 'Look at the present status I've earned!' is not honorable."

A respected politician agrees. "If it's like, 'Hey, *who* made me lose *saksi?*', that's not good. If I begin to think, 'I'm *big*! I've got *saksi*! I always have to be right!' That is certainly not justified."

A venerable abbot presses the issue even more. "The highest possible honor is to gain victory over wickedness.[7] Being able to defeat greed, defeat anger, and defeat foolish understanding—that is the person who has *saksi*, has honor."

"To lose is godlike; to win is devilish,"[8] he continues. "In an argument with your wife, who should be the first to quiet down? But instead you'll argue until the walls fall in, just so you can prove that you're 'the biggest' in the house."

The lesson for leaders is this: if you think you must always win, in the end you will succumb to your sinful cravings. The only way to defeat cravings is to be willing, with discretion, to defer in humility to others.

In other words, Buddhist teachings urge leaders to respond with composure to insulting words by detaching themselves from the praise and disapproval of others. Yet in the heat of competitions for power, that standard is easily shoved aside. It seems too otherworldly to be of any earthly good.

One illustrious leader, a former prime minister, invites leaders to reconsider their assumptions. Here are his rare and disarming words:

Fools, the arrogant—those who are infatuated with themselves—will consider their own status to be very high. Those in this category will be sensitive about their *saksi*. But leaders who are virtuous and sincere have very little of this kind of *saksi* left. They're no longer interested in it. In the end, when they are completely detached, the idea of accumulating *saksi* will be exceedingly scarce.

According to nine exemplary Buddhist leaders, the Buddha never modeled the hypersensitive ego-orientation embraced by so many Thais (Suntaree 1990, 133–35). This assertion stands as a significant critique. Thais often defend their *saksi* with fiery anger, claiming, "Thai people are like this." It would be fair (but unwise) to respond gently, "Yes, but virtuous people are not."

The views of seventeen highly admired Thai leaders introduce a shocking moral discussion into public conversations about face as social capital. They unanimously link face to virtuous character, not to exceptional skill, performance, appearance, rank, or status. They argue fearlessly for the value of "noble face."

These lofty ideals have profound implications for the facework of leaders in thousands of localized contexts across the country. "Whether or not we lose face is not important, as long as we hold to what is right and righteous," says a member of the king's circle of sixteen privy councilors.

That stunning claim probably seems ridiculous and impractical to most leaders entrenched in competitions for face, but it points to a primal truth. All facework and all notions of face have an inescapable moral dimension. In the end, leaders cannot escape the standard of virtue.

Leaders with virtue demonstrate a refreshing perspective on face. They hold this award of confidence with a light grasp. They never need to pursue it as an outright goal, because they know that to love what is good and to live in goodness is much more precious.

That is how they practice noble face. It is simply a matter of learning to value what is preeminently valuable.

But—ironically—because virtuous leaders defy many of the cardinal rules of powerbrokers, priceless social capital eventually comes looking for them. True face is the reward of virtue.

21
LASTING FACE

JUST ONE KIND of Thai social capital outlasts them all. This elusive treasure—*barami*—mesmerizes leaders because of its incomparable staying power. When it comes to offering security and longevity in leadership, moral strength has no peers. No other form of face offers such high honor and lasting radiance.

Why does *barami* endure so well? Emic research reveals that the *barami* pathway to power is fully indigenous and inherently *empowering for followers*. This finding should prick the ears of anyone genuinely interested in developing leaders who are good for Thai society. But this leadership style is also provocatively *empowering for leaders*. Actually, Thais have known this for so long that it's scarcely a secret. They know well that *if* they can tap into this source of power it will vest them with a prodigious ability to generate and sustain fresh supplies of power for leadership tasks. So to say that the *barami* approach empowers leaders barely deserves press.

What deserves our attention is this question: *why* is this pathway so empowering? I have yet to read a sensible answer based on the merits of social theory, so I will offer one here.[1]

Peter Blau, an authority on power and social exchange, makes a conspicuous assertion. "Exchange processes," he writes, "lead to the emergence of bonds of intrinsic attraction and social integration, on the one hand, and of unilateral services and social differentiation on the other" (2005, 328). In other words, *social exchange performs two basic functions* in every society, including Thai society: it establishes bonds of relationship, and it establishes superordination over others.

This is immediately relevant to the Thai context. Patron-client interaction between Thai leaders and followers is an example, par excellence, of social exchange. Blau helps us to envision two inescapable dimensions that form the "playing field" of leadership.

Think math for a second. Visualize an X-axis, running horizontally and measuring solidarity in relationship, the *level of affinity* a leader shares with his followers. Then visualize a Y-axis, running vertically and representing *disparity in power* between the leader and his followers. These two axes run perpendicular to each other (see fig. 8).

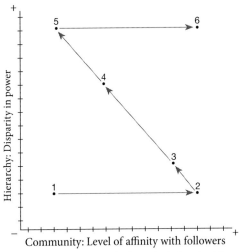

Fig. 8. Community and Hierarchy in Leadership

Social exchange functions in Thai society to create unique expressions of *community* (X-axis) and *hierarchy* (Y-axis).[2] On the axis of community, social actors pursue "fellowship-face," or the desire to be included. On the axis of hierarchy, they pursue "competence-face," or the desire for others to admire and respect their special abilities (Lim 1994, 211).

Now let's plot the leader's rise to power on this graph. Social exchange between a potential leader and a potential follower always begins with establishing a good relationship (point 1 shifts to 2). Forces of attraction first create "social integration and solidarity"—that is, mutual approval, relationship, and a sense of belonging together (Blau 2005, 267). Exchange partners are drawn together in mutual attraction by the thought, "I like you because you and I are alike."

Both parties have extrinsic motivations. They pursue the relationship for what they can extract from it. But with time, intrinsic motivations can develop—a mutual, affectionate pursuit of the relationship itself. This represents progress on the continuum of *relatedness*. If a leader is ever to win the loyalty of followers, he must first establish this sense of closeness (point 2). There are no exceptions.

But the story does not end there. Continued social exchange in relationships *inevitably* gives rise to differentiations in power. Blau's second point is that all social exchange inevitably elevates certain members of a group over others. This happens because of competition for limited resources as well as natural inequalities between social actors, such as differences in capability and opportunity. This differentiation is often created when an act of assistance or generosity is not or cannot be fully reciprocated by one of the exchange partners, in this case, the follower. When this occurs, the follower responds with respect for the leader's superior qualities and, in cases of greater and greater power distance, even compliance. This represents an increase in power distance between the two parties, based upon universalistic standards (point 3).[3]

The leader is moving up the vertical continuum. The follower agrees to this shift in their relationship because of the leader's excellence in some area. The one with lesser power now says to the one with greater power, "I like you because in some way (talent, looks, smarts, competencies, wealth, charisma) you are *unlike* me, and I'm okay with that." Take note that, at this early stage, the distinction of the emerging leader over a follower does not threaten the sense of solidarity they share.

So far we have contemplated two shifts. The first is from *initial attraction* to *approval*, creating solidarity. The second is from *approval* to *respect*, which elevates some social actors over others, creating disparity and distinction.

In terms of healthy leadership formation, so far all is quite good. Every leader, to attain access to legitimate power, must have two things: (1) the cohesion of social approval, or solidarity with followers, which fosters voluntary compliance and lends legitimacy and stability to leadership, and (2) respect or distinction, which yields power (Blau 2005, 200–202; Parsons 1967, 289; Weber 1962, 20).

Up to this point (point 3), our imaginary leader has both increased power and approval. But the scenario is about to be dramatically altered by an inescapable paradox. "The dilemma of leadership," writes Blau, "is that the attainment of power and the attainment of social approval make somewhat incompatible demands on a person" (2005, 203). What he means is that leaders who wish to establish distinction or dominance must be willing to trade some of their approval for increased power. They communicate the following message: "To get ahead, I must compete with you—I must have *my* best interests in mind, even if it is at your expense."

The leader, therefore, experiences "intrapersonal conflict" between his "desire to gain social approval and support and his desire to gain instrumental advantage" (ibid., 114). Blau is stating that the relational dynamics that create respect, distinction, advancement, or growth in power are *counterproductive* and even *antithetical* to the dynamics that nurture and sustain approval, solidarity, or a sense of connectedness and belonging. To put it simply, significant progress on one axis *begins to strain any gains the leader has won on the other axis.*

This is an absolutely vital point: the leader's successful efforts to gain distinction put him at risk of losing the approval and affection of his followers. In fact, as he catapults into greater and greater power, followers begin to feel alienated (point 4). And that's bad.

Remember that valuable bond, that sense of commonality he fostered earlier on? Well, now his progress triggers a growing sense of relational distance. Subordinates and followers begin thinking, "Maybe you aren't the same as we are. Maybe you aren't part of our group. Maybe you no longer care about what's best for us."

Over the passage of time, especially if leaders are perceived as having benefited personally by taking advantage of followers, approval can disintegrate quickly into disapproval and resentment—the stuff of passive-aggressive resistance, opposition, or even mutiny (point 5).

Is there no logical way to fix the problem? Can't the leader just work to rebuild that affinity?

Yes, but not without some undesirable consequences. Blau reminds us that when leaders seek approval by reemphasizing solidarity with their followers, that affiliative behavior slows their ability to take advantage of opportunities for advancement. Furthermore, in strongly hierarchical societies, if leaders practice too much approachable and self-effacing behavior, sometimes it causes followers to raise the unspoken question, "Do you really have power?" In other words, for the leader, social exchange is always "an intermediate case between pure calculation of advantage and pure expression of love" (Blau 2005, 112).

This is the dilemma of leaders who grow prominent due to *itthiphon*, or influence. Their good reputations are largely constrained within their entourages and others who receive direct benefits from them. Those on the dole of their generosity speak of them in positive terms. They ascribe *barami*. But there is a problem. These leaders have a heinous reputation among the people they exploit. The rules of the game dictate that they must continue to gain advantage over others in society—exploiting them—or their power will begin to wane. Their "generosity" attempts to parallel the generosity of leaders with accumulated goodness, but often their magnanimous charades are less than convincing. Influence attempts to shadow *barami*, but it does a poor job of doing so.

Our momentary dip into social theory equips us splendidly to make greater sense of the Thai leadership scene. Leaders rise by taking part in one (or both) of two power games: the game of authority or the game of influence. Leaders with authority assume that advancement up hierarchies will bring greater legitimacy. Leaders with influence assume that increased dominance must eventually give way to a measure of legitimacy. But *ascendancy in either game does not, in and of itself, maintain or cultivate the affection and genuine approval of others*. In fact, it strains that approval.

In the good old days before the leader gained significant power, followers felt a strong relational connection with him—a sense of closeness and reciprocal goodwill. But his sharp ascendancy (point 5) leaves them entertaining a legion of doubts: "Now that he's powerful, does he still have our best interests in mind? Is he using power for selfish gain? Are we just being used? Does he even see us?"

Contemporary Thai followers can hardly be blamed for this lack of trust. They share a long history of unequal and exploitative patron-client exchange dating back to feudal days.[4] This lack of trust is a problem. How can leaders attain legitimacy?

It is at this point that many leaders in both power games get it wrong. They fail to understand that legitimacy is not an automatic byproduct of preeminence. Legitimacy is granted when leaders use their repositories of social power *for the good of others*—for the good of the collectivity, for the sake of the client. This is the pathway of *barami*.

It is not that leaders in the two games are disqualified from the *barami* path. It is just that they may not even see it. Their thirst for power often blinds them to the need for genuine solidarity with followers.

We know that true *barami* leaders view face and power from a perspective that is refreshingly distinct. They *expend* their resources for the sake of the collectivity. This attitude enables them to look downward in hierarchies to honor the honorable and empower clients *for their own sake*. Followers respond with deepest respect and affection (point 6).

This approach actualizes a stunning form of referent power, the ability of a leader to cultivate the respect and admiration of followers in such a way that they wish to be like him (Hughes, Ginnett, and Curphy 1996, 125).[5] When leaders embrace this paradigm of power over an extended period of time, something called the "Pygmalion effect" pervades the leadership process.

> Somewhat paradoxically, then, followers feel stronger and more powerful yet at the very same time they willingly subordinate themselves to the charismatic leader. Charismatic leaders are able

to make their followers feel more powerful without any diminution or threat to their own status. (Ibid., 293)

Is this really true? What about the rules of social exchange, the ones that dictate that affiliative behavior will work against a leader's efforts to establish superiority and dominance? Here we have a grand exception to the rule. Ironically, *when followers grow to believe that their leader has their best interests in mind, his attempts to draw close to them do not diminish his superordinate status.* In fact, on the basis of deeply entrenched Thai values, when a lofty leader's affiliative behavior is judged to be sincere, it can actually *boost* his status and increase his repository of face. Followers voluntarily give back incredible amounts of social capital: approval, loyalty, compliance, and fondness for the leader—a loud echo of affection and willing submission.

Social theory sheds light on this mystery as well. It teaches us that every time a follower obeys a leader, that act of compliance serves to diminish the power distance between the two, if ever so slightly. To increase that distance once again—to regain dominance—the leader must experience fresh gains in face.

Leaders without *barami* are subject to the cold rules of instrumental exchange. With every show of respect and obedience, subordinates make a partial payment against their indebtedness. This is why leaders must be tireless in seeking to replace social capital that has been consumed in leadership tasks.

Leaders with *barami* transcend these dynamics for one very simple reason. Followers are convinced that leaders have their best interests in mind, so they view their leaders' directives as words of *advice* rather than executive *orders.*

That shift in perspective is highly significant. To appreciate it, we must distinguish between the fruit of advice and the fruit of commands.

Indeed, giving advice and giving orders have opposite consequences; advising another creates obligations, while ordering him to do something uses them up . . . by enabling him to discharge his obligations through his compliance. (Blau 2005, 131)

As you can see, social exchange theory contends that a *barami* leader's directives further obligate his followers to him because followers receive those words as advice meant for their benefit (ibid., 141). That is why *barami* leaders can gain the cooperation of followers without draining their own power. It is also why their decisive leadership generates so much fresh power.

But there is more. Because a *barami* leader's power is relatively secure, *he can afford to use less of it than he is entitled to use.* By his soft, humble demeanor, by not insisting on the deference due his rank, he actually increases his legitimate authority over others, which "obviates the need for making excessive demands that undermine power" (ibid., 136). This behavior forms an ever-growing cycle of plenitude—one of the rewards of transformational leadership (Burns 1979). It eludes "power-wielders," but it is the inheritance of leaders with *barami.*

On the Thai landscape, the interaction between a *barami* leader and his followers represents two disparate sides successfully sharing the same "social-influence process" (Hughes, Ginnett, and Curphy 1996, 17). It represents win-win collaboration between a leader and his followers (Kelly 1992).

Christine Firer Hinze (1992, 279) calls this a "power-to" model in contrast with a "power-over" model. A power-over model assumes that efficacy "is achieved in spite of or against others." A power-to model assumes that efficacy is "achieved because of and with others."

Amnat leaders use face to climb hierarchies by successfully performing their duties. *Itthiphon* leaders use face for personal profit as a means for attaining greater wealth and influence. Both approaches are essential for society to function. Either is capable of producing positive models for leadership. Whether you are a *nai amphoe* (district officer) or a business entrepreneur, you have the potential to be honest and bighearted, contributing to the needs of society in positive ways. But neither paradigm of power is *inherently empowering to underlings.* In fact, leaders in both camps commonly use the rules of face exchange to squelch the rise of leaders emerging from below.

Barami leaders, by contrast, use face to accomplish collective goals by helping people solve their problems. In short, they use face to empower others. They win cooperation by relying on the purest and most positive form of reciprocity: the loving indebtedness of affectionate *bunkhun*. The hug. Followers deeply love and respect them for their consistent, altruistic kindness—kindness for the sake of the other. Their desire to cooperate is natural and free of coercion. Words of praise for the patron-leader flow freely and continually from the inside out because they know that their leader's assistance is tangible and sincere, not feigned or fabricated for selfish purposes.

Who begins this cycle of plenitude? The leader. *Any* leader in either major game of power can make a simple decision that will change everything. He or she can put self-centeredness aside and elect to use social capital for the primary purpose of bettering the lives of others. It's that simple, that exacting, and that profound. It begins with the leader.

Let's return to an important finding. *Thais believe that honor flows from above.* It trickles down hierarchies like water down a cascade. A person at any locus in a hierarchy can behave honorably and catch the admiration of those around her, but that egalitarian affirmation—even if it is a groundswell—is not enough to send her up the hierarchies of power. She must be recognized and affirmed by someone higher, someone with the power to "give face away" and the integrity to show honor to whom honor is due.

Now, look up and around you with eyes wide open. A natural pattern of empowerment surfaces in Thai social circles, big and small. It is everywhere. It happens whenever a person with a substantial store of "face-eyes" gives honor or gives face to a person in the hierarchy below. This model of empowerment works because it is driven by the status and character of the leader who dispenses the honor downward.

Often it takes place publicly, where it *heightens* the recipient's honor (*kiat*) and *broadens* his recognition in the eyes of a wider audience (*chuesiang*). It also happens in smaller circles of leadership—for example, in the context of a leader and his entourage—whenever the leader chooses to honor or promote an underling. Sometimes those choices to empower are founded on true merit and morally commendable behavior. But let's be honest. At other times—perhaps too often—leaders are merely shifting sycophantic underlings like pawns on a chessboard.

It is often within the power of leaders to give face away, but it seldom seems to happen for the right reasons. Leaders have freedom to honor the honorable and promote the truly deserving, but that particular approach tends to be exceptionally scarce. Instead, leaders discriminate and deliberate. They hesitate, and often they withhold.

Why? For many leaders, it is dangerous to empower subordinates. Leaders compete intensely for limited resources and a limited number of titled positions. If they freely extend opportunities to those below, in the end it can threaten their own status and command of resources. Certainly, careless empowerment biases things in favor of the power-hungry in their hell-bent rise to dominance and exploitation. It is not in the best interests of society.

But there's another reason why healthy empowerment is rare. As patterns of instrumental *bunkhun* show, leaders themselves have so much to gain when they make their acts of goodness toward underlings conditional on some kind of payback. We have documented that leaders use subordinates in this way to increase their own stores of "face-eyes." The sad outcome of this behavior is that it often subverts the honor system by overlooking leadership candidates with true merit and goodness in favor of candidates who are more useful to the selfish purposes of their bosses—candidates who may be less qualified, manipulative, and perhaps even unethical.

Blau (2005, 7) states the following claim: "Unreciprocated exchange leads to the differentiation of power." He argues, in other words, that the beneficence of Thai patrons often creates a widening power gap between the giver and the receiver *because the receiver cannot fully reciprocate.* The receiver then feels a growing weight of relational debt. This, by design, retains or widens power distances between leaders and subordinates. It weights things in favor of the incumbent leader so that he is not easily replaced or surpassed by someone from below, someone who may be more competent and less self-serving than he is. This kind of empowerment too easily torpedoes the progress of the most deserving. It is not in the best interests of society.

The delicate issue at hand is for leaders in Thai society to find avenues to empower the *worthy*—those who are both capable and morally good. For this to happen, one specific prototype is preferable: a leader who, as an intentional lifestyle, nurtures and trains commendable leaders. Now *that* would be in the best interests of society.

The *barami* leader is precisely that kind of leader. He possesses power, but he sees it as a mantle of responsibility, not as a coveted prize or a weapon to be used for selfish gain. He possesses a great amount of "face-eyes," but he is not preoccupied with that status. He wants to use his assets to help others.

Leaders with genuine accumulated goodness can be trusted to use power in fair and beneficial ways. These leaders do not hoard their social capital. They are delighted to give face to whom face is due. Under their care, people rise in hierarchies for the right reasons. Leaders identify subordinates with virtuous character who are truly competent and hard working—people who can give members of society the expertise and guidance they deserve from their leaders. When people with moral strength rise to fill positions of power, members of society enjoy an increased ability to shed the shackles of injustice and bloom in healthy ways. And because the masses tend to trust the integrity of *barami* leaders, they tend to respect their protégés as well.

In this imperfect, power-hungry world, this kind of leader seems too good to be true, yet Thais contend that he is alive and well. A sobering sidebar, however, is that he appears to be in *very* short supply. He is a rarity on the landscape of Thai leadership. Power systems seem prone to promote the power-hungry over the virtuous.

Because Thai leaders are so active in competing for face and pursuing power, the goal of empowering others is lost, quite frankly. But *barami* leaders are different. They take great pleasure in sharing power with emerging leaders who are both competent and virtuous.

To have true *barami* is to achieve legitimate superiority. It is to be secure in society's most defining courts of honor. Leaders can nurture warm relationships with followers without unduly diminishing their power to lead. They also can ascend to great heights without alienating followers.

In collectivist Thai society, that is a brilliant feat. Followers yearn to feel warm relational interdependence with their leaders. At the same time, most of them accept their profound dependence upon the power of their leaders. Only *barami* bridges both dimensions with aplomb.

According to social exchange theory, *barami* is the most empowering of the three paths to power in Thai society. This disarming approach is both indigenous and healthy for society. It opens the door to the holy grail of leadership in every culture—legitimacy. Followers *willingly* award their leader with both superordinancy and solidarity. Herein lies the secret of lasting face.

22
THE OPEN PALM

ONE FINAL METAPHOR brings our creative exploration of healthy Thai leadership to a befitting end. Picture an empty hand. That image of an open palm is pleasant enough, but it bids us to stretch our thinking well outside the box of conventional wisdom.

We have learned that face as social capital is inextricably entwined with leadership processes at every level of Thai society.[1] That is precisely the reason we have invested so much time into understanding Thai face: its anatomy, its context of clientelism, its relationship to power, and its profoundly moral dimensions.

A lucid argument has surfaced from fresh ethnographic data, and it is this. *When leaders perceive their honor to be founded upon virtue rather than wealth, hegemony, or any other form of excellence, face becomes a potent resource for empowering desirable new leaders.*

In Thai leadership circles far and wide, this selfless approach is very much the road less traveled. It is risky because it is less competitive. At times, virtuous leaders simply cannot keep pace with the beguiling maneuvers of the power-hungry.

Yet in the end, if virtuous leaders patiently stick to paths they have charted, people who know them well begin to ascribe *barami* to them. That accolade, if it is confirmed by broad consensus, makes their endogenous worth (*saksi*) incontestable. It often awards them with everything else as well: "face-eyes" (*nata*), public acclaim (*chuesiang*), and honor (*kiat*) of the highest order.

Ironically, *the leader who pursues face the least ends up with the most face of all.* Read that sentence again and ponder its orphic meaning. If this counterintuitive assertion is true, then why do *barami* leaders seem so scarce?

One patent reason is that the general public does not rush to ascribe moral strength to leaders. Before anyone becomes a legitimate candidate for this coveted label, he or she must demonstrate selfless generosity and integrity over a long span of time. Thankfully, this prerequisite exposes and eliminates many candidates who are self-absorbed and self-serving.

The scarcity of this kind of leader is also due to a faulty assumption. To envision *barami*, the Thai people appropriately look upward to the throne. They revel in the goodness of His Majesty King Bhumibol Adulyadej. They affirm his generous and sacrificial use of resources for the sake of bettering the lives of citizens. He is their ultimate model of an acceptable leader.

But the behavior of many leaders below the throne suggests that they revere the model in theory only. Alan Johnson says it well: "Inherent in prototypical models is a dark side; they are valued precisely because they are not practiced" (2006, 309). Leaders seem to have concluded that to become great based upon goodness alone is utterly impractical. Their egotism has conditioned many Thais to believe that true *barami* is a glowing ascription to be reserved for the highest echelons of prestigious stock, rather than a selfless lifestyle that is open to any leader who might choose it.

The problem is exacerbated by a lack of virtue among followers as well. In evaluating their leaders, too many expect too little. And because they themselves lack virtue, they are content to shove virtue aside. Followers are guilty of affirming their self-obsessed leaders purely because they receive personal benefits by associating with them.

This is grievously shortsighted. Generosity itself is not virtuous. Selfless, underived kindness for the sake of others is. The difference lies in the silent motives of each leader.

There is another incisive reason why the Thai populace often looks upward in anticipation of *barami* leaders, but to no avail. To qualify, leaders must have hearts that are not selfish, hearts that want the best for others. They must grow in character to the point that, in the end, they love virtue above all things, and that approach seems to be the exception rather than the rule.

But true *barami* is a lifestyle, not a trophy. It is not meant to be the exception in leadership patterns. It is meant to be—with no apologies or equivocation—the ultimate standard. Those with true *barami* are not defined by their economic successes or their political dominance. They are defined by their habit of loving truth and choosing to use power in a righteous manner.

Seventeen highly esteemed virtuous leaders have leveled a gentle but scathing critique of the face-oriented values of most Thais. They have claimed in remarkable unison that virtuous leaders should be content to build face upon goodness alone, that they should never pursue face as a prize to be won, and that they should always treat others—even the most humble—with respect.

This behavior seems almost otherworldly. It is a far cry from the thirst for "face-eyes" that prevails in all levels of society, and not just among leaders.

Buddhist teachings challenge popular values right on down the line. They teach that virtuous people should not attach themselves emotionally to their "face-eyes." They teach that honor should never be a goal in and of itself—that goodness has its own honor. They teach that public acclaim is merely the fruit of morally commendable behavior. They teach that accumulated goodness is the byproduct of a selfless lifestyle of helping others, and it cannot be "built" by money or power alone. They teach that endogenous worth is founded upon inner goodness, and it is not easily ruffled or defensive when threatened or attacked by others.

Any one of these teachings profoundly challenges the values and behaviors of many professing Buddhists in Thai society. How can this be?

One scholar suggests an answer. "Unaware that our culture has subverted our faith," he writes, "we lose a place from which to judge our own culture" (Volf 1996, 53). In other words, Thais—like people of every culture—cling to salient cultural values as utterly sacred treasures, even when some of those values impugn the straightforward teachings of their most exalted moral teachers. Another scholar explains it like this: "Our cultural palaces are our prisons" (Lingenfelter 1998, 20). They engender feelings of familiarity and safety, but sometimes they keep us from exploring what is truly noble and praiseworthy.

Is there a remedy? Perhaps, but it's easier said than done. "Religion must be de-ethnicized so that ethnicity can be desacralized" (Volf 1996, 49). In other words, the Thai faithful must separate their religious teachings from their "Thai-ness" long enough to discern the sacred from the profane. Without this measure of scrutiny, many of the devout will continue to lurch and flounder in facework that spurns virtue and dares to give approval to immoral actions. And leaders, with their thirst for power, are some of the chief transgressors.

One of the intractable dilemmas of leadership "is how to remedy powerlessness without succumbing to power seeking" (Shuster 1987, 12). This problem confronts not only leaders, but followers as well. Conventional wisdom effectively reinforces the disempowerment of the marginalized and the dispossessed. In contemporary Thai society, for example, prevalent interpretations of teachings about karma do exactly that. Members of society exhibit a surprising acceptance of exploitation due to a popular belief that the powerful must have done something glorious to merit such ascendancy, and the oppressed must have done something heinous to deserve such woe. This scripted ideology is distasteful, to say the least.

But sadly, empowerment of the dispossessed often fixes nothing. If their hearts are as selfish as the hearts of their oppressors, then when the tables are turned and they gain power, they only christen a new round of oppression. In other words, "one party appears more virtuous only because, being weaker, it has less opportunity to be cruel" (Volf 1996, 103). We do not have to look far to see evidence of this disheartening cycle in the political gridlock of recent years.

A haunting sense of powerlessness seems to linger unexplained in the psyches of many Thais. One demonstration of this craving, this fragility, is a prevailing over-sensitivity that many Thais feel about their endogenous worth. "They cannot tolerate any violation of the 'ego' self," writes a foremost psychosocial researcher (Suntaree 1990, 133).

Ironically, *even powerful leaders can demonstrate this hyper-defensiveness*. In the throes of actively wielding great power, many leaders are extremely thin-skinned about perceived threats to their personal honor. This greatly complicates their decision-making. Here is an eerily accurate description of what takes place:

> The importance of his personal goal outweighs the importance of all rational considerations . . . More painful yet, the personal goal at issue is not as much a specific achievement as the desire to remedy felt deficiencies or a sense of threat by attaining some sort of impregnable perfection. Hence any failure, however minor, becomes intolerable. (Shuster 1987, 159–60)

Especially for leaders, the temptation to protect face and seek power is palpable. To give face to a leader is to potentialize his path to wielding greater and greater power. It effectively places power in the palm of his hand. And when leaders gain control of something immensely precious, they exhibit an instinct that is common to the rest of us. They clench it with tightly grasping hands.

Is there a better way to lead? Yes, but not without first correcting colossal confusion about one aspect of face as social capital.

For centuries Thais have been leading with the assumption that it is best to force the compliance of followers by indebting them. This feudalistic approach works. In fact, if it weren't so effective, it wouldn't be so wildly popular. But it is perilously blind to an insight so fundamental that we would all do very well to give it some attention, and here it is. *We are blatantly confused about who is indebted to whom.*

One delicate secret will easily right the ship. We need to understand that *face is not a possession*. It is on loan.

Strong linguistic evidence suggests that Thais view face as a personal possession. Think about it. "Wealthy people *have* 'face-eyes,'" they say. "The governor *has* honor. That actress *has* public acclaim. The privy councilor *has* accumulated goodness." And, of course, "We all *have* endogenous worth."

These innocent expressions are brilliant examples of how common parlance can be woefully misleading. Excluding the sentence about endogenous worth, these sentences do not speak truth. Why? Most forms of face are not personal possessions. They are on loan.

Every form of face granted in public space is always on loan. It can always be rescinded. No one is exempt from this rule. For all of us— you, me, our leaders, *everyone*—face is never a possession.

To strengthen this claim, I turn to one of the masters of social theory on power, Talcott Parsons. He observes how dollars do "double-duty" in a credit banking system. Deposits of cash into a bank represent loans that the bank must repay to depositors on demand. But the bank is not merely a caretaker of money. It reinvests that capital for profit by loaning it to companies or individuals so long as they repay the bank, along with interest, at the term of the loan. "This means that *the same dollars* are functioning double as circulating media, so that the bank loans outstanding constitute a net addition to the quantity of the circulating medium" (Parsons 1967, 379).

This illustration of credit through banking is fertile for conceptualizing how face empowers a leader. Face functions as social capital in leadership much like credit banking, where dollars do "double duty." If we conceive of the leader as banker, his loyal followers as depositors, and his newly indebted contacts as borrowers, we can visualize how face functions in leadership.

Followers who grant face to a leader always retain the right to rescind it based upon his character, behavior, and productivity. Initial loans of face give him a valuable mandate of trust, but followers want him to use face to generate fresh social capital that circulates back to benefit *them.* The leader's personal gains in face represent "interest," an increase in the total value of the investment. As long as a leader doesn't "blow it" by soundly losing face, he has opportunities to accrue "interest" on the trust granted to him. By being self-controlled and dignified in public, by showing empathy to common people, and especially by playing the role of a benevolent patron who returns good things to his supporters, a leader communicates to followers that he and they are conjoined and their investment retains value.

If a leader loses face badly, it is akin to the release of information suggesting that his ability to protect their investments is somehow suspect. This causes certain followers to make withdrawals of their respect and acceptance. If a leader's mistake or moral violation is profound, the resulting hysteria among followers and the public at large is much like a "run" on a bank in which depositors panic and withdraw their money en masse. Those who are invested in him cancel their investments, and those who owe him favors—seeing that he is going down—renege on their commitments to him. At that point the leader's store of social capital is nakedly insolvent.

What does all this mean? Face is a treasure, to be sure, but it is *never* an outright gift or a possession. It is always on loan and subject to stipulations that leaders must honor. Leaders would do well to remember that face does not belong to them. They are merely stewards who must prove themselves faithful and worthy of trust and respect.

Leaders have a sacred vow to keep. They should lead with an open palm, not a grasping hand. This defies many assumptions about power, but then again, so do the examples of some of the most revered leaders in history.

When Thai leaders glance toward the example of the Buddha, they see an approach to power so curiously different that it borders on irrelevancy. The Buddha stepped out of his place in structures of power to live a simple life of detachment from all cravings. This lofty example of moral goodness communicates a subtle but precious message. Power, in itself, is empty.

One of the lies we so readily embrace is that in order to become great we must be grand. But true greatness is built upon *goodness*. Goodness shuns the grasping hand, and it certainly is wary of the fist.

When self is transformed by virtue, a whole new remedial power is unleashed into leadership through the agency of face. Leaders do not cling to power defensively. Rather, they are salutary in their relationships with followers. They want to serve, assist, nurture, restore, provide for, and create health in followers. And they take great delight in empowering worthy people.

That approach to leadership goes far beyond the parameters of common facework. It engenders a fresh creativity that reimagines face as social capital.

Perhaps it is only when a leader undergoes a dethroning or a decentering of the self that he can understand: *the power that face affords does not belong to him.* It is to be used for the good of others.

Face and leadership intersect at this crossroad. One important lesson is that leaders should not attempt to "take by force what can only be freely given" (Shuster 1987, 169). They must earn the right to lead by winning the hearts of followers. But there is another lesson equally poignant. Covetous hands rarely know the pleasure of sharing good things with others. That is why it is inadvisable and dangerous for leaders to be in love with their stores of face. Face should always rest in an open palm.

Virtue enables leaders to avoid the grasping hand. Only then can they approach facework like an embrace. A hug, after all, is a mutually satisfying proposition.

When guided by goodness, facework meets some of the deepest needs of the human heart. It addresses hierarchy by imparting a feeling that each party is respectable. It addresses community by infusing a feeling that both belong. This mutual celebration of alterity and solidarity can transcend the dangers of asymmetry in power to give each faceworker a sense of true worth—a warm feeling that he or she really matters.

That is the way of *barami*. A leader with resources needs just one thing to walk that footpath: a virtuous heart that wants to encourage and embolden others. And somewhere down that trail, he or she will inevitably discover that true "face-eyes"—lasting face—is a byproduct of a more serious and worthy task: giving face away.

NOTES

INTRODUCTION

1. To explore how cultural capital and social capital differ, consult Pierre Bourdieu's seminal article, "Forms of Capital" (1986, 241–58). Bourdieu classifies embodied assets such as knowledge and character as cultural capital. Social capital consists of relational wealth—connections and social obligations that can be leveraged for profit. Both kinds of capital differ from economic capital, and both are extremely valuable for effective leadership.

2. For a scholarly treatment of the content of this book, see my PhD dissertation entitled "Face Dynamics, Social Power and Virtue Among Thai Leaders: A Cultural Analysis" (Fuller School of Intercultural Studies, Pasadena, CA, 2008).

3. Frank Henderson Stewart (1994, 21–22) argues that the sense of being worthy of honor is "a true personal quality" that leads each of us to claim honor as a right.

1 FACE IS EVERYWHERE

1. A *wai* is a prayer-like gesture used by Thais as a standard greeting. They perform it by pressing their palms together in front of their bodies with fingers gracefully pointing upward. If they hold their hands fast against their faces, it is a show of great honor toward the person they are greeting.

2. A *prarachathan* jacket is a jacket with mandarin collar often worn by men to formal public events.

2 ALL THAT GLITTERS

1. "Have face, have eyes": มีหน้ามีตา, *mi na mi ta*. The Thai word *nata*, "face-eyes," is similar to the Chinese *mienmu*, the Korean *myenmok*, and the Japanese

menboku, all of which are based on the Chinese characters *mien* (face) and *mu* (eyes) (Ho, Fu, and Ng 2004, 67; Ervin-Tripp, Nakamura, and Guo 1995, 57–58).

2. "The dead are selling the living": คนตายขายคนเป็น, *khon tai khai khon pen*.

3. "Broken face," embarrass oneself: หน้าแตก, *na taek*.

4. "You sold my face," you embarrassed me: ทำฉันขายหน้า, *tham chan khai na*.

5. Would you like to "have face, have eyes"?: คุณอยากมีหน้ามีตาไหม, *khun yak mi na mi ta mai*?

6. "Hi-so" is slang that has entered the Thai language from the English words "high society." It alludes to the extraordinarily wealthy who keep a high profile and spend money frivolously.

3 A CASCADE OF WATER

1. Two derivatives of this word, *kiatiyot*, เกียรติยศ, and *kiatisak*, เกียรติศักดิ์, also refer to honor. *Yot*, by itself, means rank or title, and *sak*, status or inherent dignity.

2. Virtue: ความดีมีคุณธรรม, *khwam di mi khunnatham*.

3. "Honor eats deeply to the center of your being," honor is deeply rooted in character: เกียรติกินลึกถึงแก่น, *kiat kin luek thueng kaen*.

4 A DRIFTING FRAGRANCE

1. Place gold leaf on the back of a Buddha image: ปิดทองหลังพระ, *pit thong lang phra*.

5 A LARGE TREE GIVING SHADE

1. For those who want to dig deeper, I recommend a handful of researchers who address the meaning of *barami*: Maha Chakri Sirindhorn (1981), Likhit (1993), Conner (1996), Suntaree (1999), Johnson (2002).

2. In Thai these ten perfections are called ทศบารมี, *thotsabarami*. They are, in order: renunciation: เนกขัมมะ, *nekkhamma*; energy: วิริยะ, *wiriya*; loving-kindness: เมตตา, *metta*; resolution: อธิษฐาน, *athitthan*; wisdom: ปัญญา, *panya*; morality: ศีล, *sin*; forbearance: ขันติ, *khanti*; equanimity: อุเบกขา, *ubekka*; truthfulness: สัจจะ, *satcha*; and liberality: ทาน, *than* (Maha Chakri Sirindhorn 1981, ง; Johnson 2002, 18).

3. Show deference, spare someone's face: ไว้หน้าคนอื่น, *wai na khon uen*.

6 A PLACE TO STAND

1. Have a place to stand: มีจุดยืน, *mi chut yuen*.

2. You can kill a real man, but he won't let you despise his worth: ลูกผู้ชายฆ่าได้แต่หยามไม่ได้, *luk phu chai kha dai, tae yam mai dai*.

3. Resident locus of a person: จุดประจำตัว, *chut pracham tua*.

7 THE ANATOMY OF THAI FACE

1. A show of respect: แสดงความนับถือ, *sadaeng khwam napthue*; true acceptance and respect: ยอมรับและนับถือด้วยใจจริง, *yom rap lae napthue duai chai ching.*

2. Respect someone's face and "eyes": นับหน้าถือตา, *nap na thue ta.*

8 NOTHING GOLD CAN STAY

1. Lose silver, lose gold, but never allow yourself to lose face: เสียเงิน เสียทอง แต่ อย่าให้เสียหน้าเลย, *sia ngoen sia thong tae ya sia na loei.*

2. Lose face: เสียหน้าเสียตา, *sia na sia ta*.

3. "Sell one's face," embarrass oneself or one's group: ขายหน้า, *khai na.*

4. Four-legged creatures stumble; even sages make mistakes: สี่ตีนยังรู้พลาด นัก ปราชญ์ยังรู้พลั้ง, *si tin yang ru phlat, nak prat yang ru phlang.*

5. Break someone's face, show someone up: หักหน้า, *hak na.*

6. Redeem face: กู้หน้า, *ku na*; restore face: รักษาหน้าให้กลับมา, *raksa na hai klap ma*; retrieve face: เอาหน้ากลับคืนมา, *ao na klap khuen ma.*

7. Pound someone's face, attack someone: ตอกหน้า, *tok na*; rip someone's face humiliate someone: ฉีกหน้า, *chik na.*

8. Desire for revenge: แค้น, *khaen.*

9. Stubbornly insist that the rabbit has but one leg: ยืนกรานกระต่ายขาเดียว, *yuen kran kratai kha diao.* This enigmatic saying is said to have originated from the story of a monk whose relatives brought a roasted rabbit to the temple as a food offering. A temple boy, seeing how delicious it looked, pulled off a leg to sample, and it tasted so good that he pulled off another, and another. When the monk came by, he saw the one-legged rabbit and asked what had happened to the other three legs. The temple boy insisted that this particular rabbit had ever had only one leg.

10. Loss of inner power: เสียพลัง, *sia phalang.*

11. Make excuses: แก้ตัว, *kae tua.*

12. Embrace everything good, but push evil onto others: เอาดีใส่ตัว ชั่วใส่คนอื่น, *ao di sai tua chua sai khon uen.*

13. Phrase from Frost, *New Hampshire*, 84.

9 GUARDING YOUR TROVE

1. Preserve one's face: รักษาหน้า, *raksa na.*

2. Protect others' face: ไว้หน้าคนอื่น, *wai na khon uen.*

3. Comport oneself: วางตัว, *wang tua.*

4. Gold wrapped in rags: ผ้าขี้ริ้วห่อทอง, *pha khirio ho thong.*

5. "Went beyond one's abilities": ทำอะไรเกินตัว, *tham arai koen tua.*

6. The base of the steps is never dry: หัวกระไดไม่แห้ง, *hua kradai mai haeng.* Traditional wooden houses were built on stilts, and it was customary for villagers

to wash their feet at the base of the stairway before climbing to consult a leader. In other words, for generations Thai leaders have dealt with steady flows of needy clients.

7. "Their people," followers, friends: พรรคพวก, *phak phuak*.

10 LET THE GAMES BEGIN

1. Promote one's face: เสนอหน้า, *sanoe na*; grab face: เอาหน้า, *ao na*; want face: อยากได้หน้า, *yak dai na*.

2. Brownnoser: เสือก, *sueak*.

3. Be the lord and master of others: เป็นเจ้าคนนายคน, *pen chao khon nai khon*.

4. Be big: เป็นใหญ่เป็นโต, *pen yai pen to*. The word "big" surfaces often in conversations about Thai leaders. Common connotations of this phrase are: to be the boss, to be on top, to have power and authority, to be a big shot.

5. "Life and death" behavior, seriously: เอาเป็นเอาตาย, *ao pen ao tai*.

6. Vie for prominence: ชิงดีชิงเด่น, *ching di ching den*.

7. Foster father: พ่อเลี้ยง, *pho liang*.

8. Making curry paste and dissolving it in the river: ตำน้ำพริกละลายแม่น้ำ, *tam namphrik lalai maenam*.

9. Bring honor to the ceremony: ไปเป็นเกียรติในพิธี, *pai pen kiat nai phithi*.

10. Create an image: สร้างภาพลักษณ์, *sang phap lak*.

11. Advertise oneself: โฆษณาตัวเอง, *khosana tua eng*.

12. "Like a big face," desire prominence: ชอบหน้าใหญ่, *chop na yai*.

13. Show one's face: ไปออกหน้า, *pai ok na*.

14. "Cut the chair" out from under someone, impede: เลื่อยเก้าอี้, *lueai kao-i*.

15. "Suck up to," deceitful flattery: ประจบสอพลอ, *prachop sop lo*. "Lick shins and legs," flatter: เลียแข้งเลียขา, *lia khaeng lia kha*.

16. Do good, but don't become prominent or you will be in danger. No one wants to perceive you as more prominent than he is: จงทำดีแต่อย่าเด่น จะเป็นภัย ใครเขา ไม่อยากเห็น เจ้าเด่นเกิน, *Chong tham di tae ya den, cha pen phai. Khrai khao mai yak hen chao den koen*.

11 WHAT GOES AROUND COMES AROUND

1. Loving indebtedness expressed through grateful behavior: กตัญญูกตเวที, *katanyu katawethi*.

2. "Display water from the heart," show kindness: แสดงน้ำใจ, *sadaeng namchai*.

3. Benefactor, patron: ผู้มีพระคุณ, *phu mi phrakhun*.

4. Big people: ผู้ใหญ่, *phuyai*; little people: ผู้น้อย, *phunoi*.

5. "Father king," king: พ่อขุน, *pho khun*.

6. Patronage system: ระบบอุปถัมภ์, *rabop uppatham*.

7. Princes: เจ้า, *chao*; nobles: ขุนนาง, *khunnang*; commoners: ไพร่, *phrai*; slaves, ทาส, *that*.

8. The sky and the earth will punish you. The earth will swallow you up: ฟ้าดินจะลงโทษ แผ่นดินจะกลืนกิน, *fa din cha long thot, phaendin cha kluen kin*.

9. Love gratitude, recognize kindness: รักกตัญญู รู้คุณ, *rak katanyu, ru khun*.

10. Feel loving indebtedness: รู้สึกกตัญญู, *rusuek katanyu*.

11. Feel mutual generosity: มีน้ำใจต่อกัน, *mi namchai to kan*.

12. Be willing to die in place of someone: แม้แต่ตาย ก็ยอมตายแทนได้, *mae tae tai ko yom tai than dai*.

13. Know *bunkhun*: รู้บุญคุณ, *ru bunkhun*.

14. Ungrateful: เนรคุณ, *nerakhun*; without loving indebtedness: อกตัญญู, *akatanyu*.

12 WARM FUZZIES AND FEARFUL HEARTS

1. "Build arms and legs," build influence over subordinates for personal profit: สร้างแขนสร้างขาของตัวเอง, *sang khaen sang kha khong tua eng*.

2. Genuine *bunkhun*: บุญคุณแท้, *bunkhun thae*; righteous *bunkhun*: บุญคุณที่ชอบ, *bunkhun thi chop*.

3. Indebtedness to *bunkhun* can never be eaten away," indebtedness lasts forever: หนี้บุญคุณกินไม่หมด, *ni bunkhun kin mai mot*.

4. Flee a tiger and meet a crocodile: หนีเสือ ปะจรเข้, *ni suea pa chorake*.

5. Power: พระเดช. *phradet*.

6. Kindness: พระคุณ, *phrakhun*.

13 UNEASY ALLIES

1. Depend on someone's kindness: คนที่พึ่งใบบุญ, *khon thi phueng bai bun*.

2. A child not taught by his father and mother: เด็กพ่อแม่ไม่สั่งสอน, *dek pho mae mai sang son*.

3. The value of a child depends on whose child s/he is: ค่าของคนขึ้นอยู่กับเด็กของใคร, *kha khong khon khuen yu kap dek khong khrai*.

4. Show respect to the teacher: ไหว้ครู, *wai khru*.

5. Nurture so as to preclude growth: เลี้ยงไม่ให้โต, *liang mai hai to*.

6. Match someone's radiance: ทาบรัศมี, *thap rassami*.

7. A student scheming to do away with his/her teacher: ศิษย์คิดล้างครู, *sit khit lang khru*.

8. A society that grovels, literally, "licks": สังคมเลีย, *sangkhom lia*.

9. A child who does better than his father or mother: อภิชาตบุตร, *aphichatbut*.

10. Above the sky there is more sky: เหนือฟ้ายังมีฟ้า, *nuea fa yang mi fa*.

11. Remind someone of one's past kindness: ทวงบุญคุณ, *thuang bunkhun*.

14 FACES OF POWER

1. The Thai language has many words for power. The most common are: *sak* (ศักดิ์), *kamlang* (กำลัง), *raeng* (แรง), *phalang* (พลัง), *det* (เดช), *itthi* (อิทธิ), *anuphap* (อานุภาพ), *sakda* (ศักดา), and *amnat* (อำนาจ).

2. We have glossed *barami* as "accumulated goodness" and "moral strength."

3. Have boundaries: มีหลักเกณฑ์, *mi lakken.*

4. Put on a khon mask: ใส่หัวโขน, *sai hua khon.*

5. Dark powers: อำนาจมืด, *amnat muet.*

6. Thirayuth Boonmi (1999, 270) argues for a connotation of *barami* that is linked to sacral power, something not necessarily linked to virtue: "*Barami* is like something sacred that has the characteristic of spreading outward so as to be able to control [both] people in society and the things that surround the one who possesses *barami.*" I acknowledge his differing viewpoint, but based on ethnographic research of contemporary perceptions of *barami*, I argue for a strong link to virtue.

7. My research corroborates Conner's findings regarding *barami*. For more reading on *barami*, consult H. R. H. Princess Maha Chakri Sirindhorn (1981), Suntaree Komin (1999), Thirayuth Boonmi (1999), Likhit Dhiravegen (1993), and Alan Johnson (2002).

8. I am indebted to Boulding for the titles of my next three chapters.

15 THE STICK

1. Johnson (2006, 13, 222) claims that Thai leaders, when they attain a position of authority, often undergo an "ontological change." They assume the attitude that "those under you have the role of helping you with what you are doing, but not vice versa."

2. High and mighty: ยิ่งใหญ่, *ying yai.*

3. Bullfrog: อึ่งอ่าง, *ueng-ang.*

4. Reflection of the boss: ตัวสะท้อนเจ้านาย, *tua sathon chao nai.*

5. Big lord, big boss: เจ้าใหญ่นายโต, *chao yai nai to.*

6. Abuse power: ใช้อำนาจ, *chai amnat.* Compare note 3, ch. 20, p. 237.

7. Build *barami*: สร้างบารมี, *sang barami.*

8. Power crazy: บ้าอำนาจ, *ba amnat.*

9. Elevated heart: จิตใจสูง, *chitchai sung.*

10. Legitimate power to harm: พระเดช, *phradet.*

11. Stick close to the boss: ติดสอยห้อยตามเจ้านาย, *tit soi hoi tam chao nai.*

12. Government employee, civil servant: ข้าราชการ, *kha ratchakan.*

16 THE CARROT

1. Those with influence: ผู้มีอิทธิพล, *phu mi itthiphon.*

2. Let's be clear. Not every *itthiphon* leader you encounter is ready to snuff out your life at the slightest miscue. Leaders in this paradigm represent a continuum, with those who are only mildly egocentric on one side and those who'll not tolerate the slightest sign of disrespect on the other.

3. Relational warmth with undertones of terror: อบอุ่นแฝงไปด้วยความน่ากลัว, *op un faeng pai duai khwam naklua.*

4. Threaten someone by cutting a piece of wood: ตัดไม้ข่มนาม, *tat mai khom nam.*

5. Slitting the chicken's throat so the monkey can see: เชือดไก่ให้ลิงดู, *chuet kai hai ling du.*

17 THE HUG

1. Those with *barami*: ผู้มีบารมี, *phu mi barami.*

2. Pour out one's heart: เทหัวใจ, *the huachai.*

3. Love (one's) face: รักหน้า, *rak na.*

4. When the sky is adjacent to the earth, the earth supports the sky: ฟ้าจดดิน แล้วดินก็จะส่งเสริมฟ้า, *fa chot din lae din ko cha songsoem fa.*

5. With pleasure: โดยดุษฎี, *doi dusadi.*

18 THE GREAT OVERLAP

1. Make unfair personal profit from a government position, literally, "eat the state": กินเมือง, *kin mueang.*

2. Johnson forges his argument by citing many scholars, including Norman Jacobs (1971, 79–89), John L. S. Girling (1981, 147), Herbert J. Rubin (1979, 1980), William J. Siffin (1966, 150–68), Chai-anan Samudavanija (1987a, 1987b), James N. Mosel (1959), and Harvey Demaine (1986).

3. Pure *barami*: บารมีบริสุทธิ์, *barami borisut.*

19 CLIMBING THE LATTICE

1. "Buy convenience": ซื้อความสะดวก, *sue khwam saduak.*

2. My descriptions of how leaders employ synergy and symbiosis to gain face and power deepen our understanding of Lucien Hank's (1975, 202–4) depiction of entourages and "circles" in Thai society.

20 NOBLE FACE

1. Maha Chakri Sirindhorn 1981, 141–43. The *totsaphit ratchatham,* ทศพิธราช ธรรม, in Thai are 1) ทาน, *than* (charity); 2) ศีล, *sin* (moral rectitude); 3) ขันติ, *khanti* (forbearance); 4) บริจาค, *borichak* (sacrifice); 5) อาชชวะ, *atchawa* (honesty); 6) มัททวะ, *matthawa* (compassion); 7) ตบะ, *taba* (self-restriction); 8) อักโกธะ, *akkotha* non-anger); 9) อวิหิงสา, *awihingsa* (restraint from harmful behavior); and 10) อวิโรธนะ, *awirotchana* (rightful conduct). These form a guideline for ruling justly.

2. I consistently used the same word for virtue: ความดีมีคุณธรรม, *khwam di mi khunatham.*

3. Flaunt power: ใช้อำนาจ, *chai amnat.* Compare note 4, ch. 15, p. 236.

4. Here is the saying in Thai, though the exact wording varies: ลูกเอ๋ย ขอให้ลูกตั้ง อกตั้งใจเรียนให้ดีนะ ต่อไปจะได้เป็นใหญ่เป็นโต เป็นเจ้าคนนายคน มีอำนาจวาสนา มีบุญหนักศักดิ์ใหญ่ มีแต่ ความมั่งมีศรีสุข แล้วลูกจะได้มาเป็นที่พึ่งพาของพ่อแม่พี่น้องและลูกหลานของเราต่อไป.

5. Not act as if you are better than others: ไม่ถือเนื้อถือตัว, *mai thue nuea thue tua.*

6. A heart that harbors right teaching: มีธรรมะในใจ, *mi thamma nai chai.*

7. The highest possible honor is to gain victory over wickedness: เกียรติของมนุษย์ ที่สุดคือ ชนะความชั่วร้ายได้, *kiat khong manut thi sut khoe chana khwam chua rai dai.*

8. To lose is godlike; to win is devilish: แพ้เป็นพระ ชนะเป็นมาร, *phae pen phra chana pen man.*

21 LASTING FACE

1. H. R. H. Maha Chakri Sirindhorn (1981), David William Conner (1996), Suntaree Komin (1999), and Alan R. Johnson (2002, 2006) shed light on the notion of *barami* leadership, but none of these scholars explains at any length why it is so empowering.

2. Mary Douglas (1973), an anthropologist, calls these two dimensions "group" and "grid."

3. "Universalistic standards give rise to differentiation of social status, since attributes or performances that are universally valued give prestige and power to those who have them" (Blau 2005, 267).

4. See Griswold and Prasert (1975), Akin (1975), Hanks (1962, 1975), Kemp (1984) and others.

5. R. P. French and Bertram Raven (1959, 263) first introduced "referent power" into academic discourses on power. Johnson (2006, 181) perceives referent power in Thai society whenever Thai followers value "non-exploitative relationships characterized by positive and warm feelings of reciprocation and gratitude."

22 THE OPEN PALM

1. Herbert P. Phillips (1965), Akin Rabibhadana (1975), Alexander B. Griswold and Prasert na Nagara (1975), Lucien M. Hanks (1962, 1975), David William Conner (1996), Suntaree Komin (1999), Alan R. Johnson (2002, 2006, 2007) and others contribute to our understanding of Thai leadership issues, yet there is no more than a fleeting mention of face or face values in any of those writings. Suntaree Komin (1990), Leela Bilmes (2001), Chaiyun Ukosakul (1994), Margaret Ukosakul (1999, 2003), and Christopher L. Flanders (2005) offer fresh understandings of critical themes regarding Thai face, but their insights are tangential, at best, to the topic of Thai leadership.

REFERENCES CITED

Akin Rabibhadana. 1975. "Clientship and Class Structure in the Early Bangkok Period." In *Change and Persistence in Thai Society: Essays in Honor of Lauriston Sharp*, edited by G. W. Skinner and A. Thomas Kirsch, 93–124. Ithaca, NY: Cornell University Press.

Aristotle. 1934. *The Nicomachean Ethics*. Translated by H. Racham, *Loeb Classical Library, 73*. Cambridge, MA: Harvard University Press. Original edition, Harvard University Press, 1926.

Athajak Satyanurak. 2006. *Rahat Mai Thi Mong Mai Hen Khong Wattanatham Boriphok Niyom: Prawatsat Khwam Rusuek Rueang Kiatiyot Nai Sangkhom Ratchakan Thi 4–7* (Invisible Code: History of Mentality Concerning "Honor" During the Reigns of Kings Rama IV–VII). Paper originally presented at the Fifth Annual Anthropological Conference, Culture of Consumption: Consuming Culture. Bangkok: The Princess Maha Chakri Sirindhorn Anthropology Centre.

Ayal, Eliezer B. 1962. "Value System and Economic Development in Japan and Thailand." *Journal of Social Issues* 19: 35–51.

Bilmes, Leela. 2001. "Sociolinguistic Aspects of Thai Politeness." PhD diss., University of California, Berkeley.

Blau, Peter M. 2005. *Exchange and Power in Social Life*. New Brunswick, NJ: Transaction Publishers.

Boulding, Kenneth Ewart. 1989. *Three Faces of Power*. Newbury Park, CA: Sage Publications.

Bourdieu, Pierre. 1986. "The Forms of Capital." In *Handbook of Theory and Research for the Sociology of Education*, edited by J. Richardson, 241–58. New York: Greenwood.

Chai Podhisita. 1998. "Buddhism and Thai World View." In *Traditional and Changing Thai World View*, edited by A. Pongsapich, 31–62. Bangkok: Chulalongkorn University Press.

Chai-anan Samudavanija. 1987a. "The Bureaucracy." In *Government and Politics in Thailand*, edited by S. Xuto, 75–109. Singapore: Oxford University Press.

———. 1987b. "Political History." In *Government and Politics in Thailand*, edited by S. Xuto, 1–40. Singapore: Oxford University Press.

Chaiyun Ukosakul. 1994. "A Study of the Patterns of Detachment in Interpersonal Relationships in a Local Thai Church." PhD diss., Trinity Evangelical Divinity School, Deerfield, IL.

Conner, David William. 1996. "Personal Power, Authority, and Influence: Cultural Foundations for Leadership and Leadership Formation in Northeast Thailand and Implications for Adult Leadership Training." PhD diss., Northern Illinois University.

Demaine, Harvey. 1986. "Kanphatthana: Thai Views of Development." In *Context, Meaning and Power in Southeast Asia*, edited by M. Hobart and R. H. Taylor, 93–114. Ithaca, NY: Cornell University Southeast Asia Program.

Dictionary of the Royal Institute. 2003. (*Phochananukrom Chabap Rachabunditiyasathan 2542*). 1st ed. Bangkok: Nanmee Books Publishing Company.

Douglas, Mary. 1973. *Natural Symbols: Explorations in Cosmology*. London: Barrie and Jenkins.

Eisenstadt, S. N., and L. Roniger. 1984. *Patrons, Clients and Friends: Interpersonal Relationships and the Structure of Trust in Society*. Cambridge, UK: Cambridge University Press.

Embree, John F. 1969. "Thailand—A Loosely Structured Social System." In *Loosely Structured Social Systems: Thailand in Comparative Perspective*, edited by H.-D. Evers, 3–15. New Haven, CT: Yale University Southeast Asia Studies.

Ervin-Tripp, Susan, Kei Nakamura, and Jiansheng Guo. 1995. "Shifting Face From Asia to Europe." In *Essays in Semantics and Pragmatics*, edited by M. Shibatani and S. Thompson, 43–71. Amsterdam/Philadelphia: John Benjamins Publishing Company.

Evers, Hans-Dieter. 1969. "Models of Social Systems: Loosely and Tightly Structured." In *Loosely Structured Social Systems: Thailand in Comparative Perspective*, edited by H.-D. Evers, 115–27. New Haven, CT: Yale University Southeast Asian Studies.

Flanders, Christopher L. 2005. "About Face: Reorienting Thai Face for Soteriology and Mission." PhD diss., Fuller Theological Seminary, Pasadena, CA.

French, John R. P., and Bertram Raven. 1959. The Bases of Social Power. In *Studies in Social Power*, edited by D. Cartright, 150–167. Ann Arbor, MI: University of Michigan Press.

Frost, Robert. 1923. *New Hampshire: A Poem with Notes and Grace Notes.* New York: Henry Holt and Co.

Geertz, Clifford. 1973. *The Interpretation of Cultures.* New York: Basic Books.

Girling, John L. S. 1981. *Thailand: Society and Politics.* Ithaca, NY: Cornell University Press.

Goode, William J. 1978. *The Celebration of Heroes: Prestige As A Control System.* Berkeley, CA: University of California Press.

Griswold, Alexander B., and Prasert na Nagara. 1975. "On Kingship and Society at Sukhodaya." In *Change and Persistence in Thai Society: Essays in Honor of Lauriston Sharp,* edited by G. W. Skinner and A. Thomas Kirsch, 29–92. Ithaca, NY: Cornell University Press.

Haas, Mary R. 1964. *Thai-English Student's Dictionary.* Stanford, CA: Stanford University Press.

Hanks, Lucien M. 1962. "Merit and Power in the Thai Social Order." *American Anthropologist* 64: 1247–61.

———. 1975. "The Thai Social Order as Entourage and Circle." In *Change and Persistence in Thai Society: Essays in Honor of Lauriston Sharp,* edited by G. W. Skinner and A. Thomas Kirsch, 197–218. Ithaca, NY: Cornell University Press.

Hinze, Christine Firer. 1992. "Power in Christian Ethics: Resources and Frontiers for Scholarly Exploration." *Annual of the Society of Christian Ethics* 12 (1): 277–90.

Ho, David Yau-Fai. 1994. "Face Dynamics: From Conceptualization to Measurement." In *The Challenge of Facework: Cross-Cultural and Interpersonal Issues,* edited by S. Ting-Toomey 269–86. Albany, NY: State University of New York Press.

Ho, David Yau-Fai, Wai Fu, and S. M. Ng. 2004. "Guilt, Shame and Embarrassment: Revelations of Face and Self." *Culture and Psychology* 10 (1): 64–84.

Holmes, Henry, and Suchada Tangtongtavy. 1997. *Working with the Thais: A Guide to Managing in Thailand.* Bangkok: White Lotus Press.

Hu, Hsien Chin. 1944. "The Chinese Concepts of 'Face'." *American Anthropologist,* 46 (1): 45–64.

Hughes, Richard L., Robert C. Ginnett, and Gordon J. Curphy. 1996. *Leadership: Enhancing the Lessons of Experience.* 2nd ed. Chicago: Irwin.

Ingersoll, Jasper. 1975. "Merit and Identity in Village Thailand." In *Change and Persistence in Thai Society,* edited by G. W. Skinner and A. Thomas Kirsch, 219–51. Ithaca, NY: Cornell University Press.

Jacobs, Norman. 1971. *Modernization without Development: Thailand as an Asian Case Study.* New York: Praeger Publishers.

Johnson, Alan. R. 2002. "The Language of Leadership in Thailand." Master's thesis, Azusa Pacific University, Azusa, CA.

―――. 2006. "Leadership in a Bangkok Slum: An Ethnography of Thai Urban Poor in the Lang Wat Pathum Wanaram Community." PhD diss., Oxford Centre for Mission Studies, University of Wales, Oxford.

―――. 2007. "An Anthropological Approach to the Study of Leadership: Lessons Learned on Improving Leadership Practice." *Transformation* 24 (3/4): 213–21.

Kelly, Robert. 1992. *The Power of Followership: How to Create Leaders People Want to Follow and Followers Who Lead Themselves*. New York: Doubleday Publishing.

Kemp, Jeremy H. 1984. "The Manipulation of Personal Relations: From Kinship to Patron-Clientage." In *Strategies and Structures in Thai Society*, edited by H. ten Brummelhuis and J. H. Kemp, 55–69. Amsterdam: Anthropological-Sociological Centre, University of Amsterdam.

Keyes, Charles F. 1987. *Thailand: Buddhist Kingdom as Modern Nation-State*. Boulder, CO: Westview Press.

Kirsch, A. Thomas. 1969. "Loose Structure: Theory or Description." In *Loosely Structured Social Systems: Thailand in Comparative Perspective*, edited by H.-D. Evers, 39–60. New Haven, CT: Yale University Southeast Asian Studies.

―――. 1975. "Economy, Polity and Religion in Thailand." In *Change and Persistence in Thai Society: Essays in Honor of Lauriston Sharp*, edited by G. W. Skinner and A. Thomas Kirsch, 172–96. Ithaca, NY: Cornell University Press.

Likhit Dhiravegen. 1993. *Barami Kap Kan Mueang Thai* (*Barami* and Thai Politics). *Watachakkanmueang* 1 (4): 11.

Lim, Tae-Seop. 1994. "Facework and Interpersonal Relationships." In *The Challenge of Facework: Cross-Cultural and Interpersonal Issues*, edited by S. Ting-Toomey, 209–29. Albany, NY: State University of New York Press.

Lin, Y. T. 1939. *My Country and My People*. New York: The John Day Company.

Lingenfelter, Sherwood G. 1998. *Transforming Culture: A Challenge for Christian Mission*. 2nd ed. Grand Rapids, MI: Baker Books.

Maha Chakri Sirindhorn, Princess. 1981. *Thotsabarami Nai Phutasatsanatherawat* (Dasaparami in Theravada Buddhism). Master thesis, Chulalongkorn University, Bangkok.

Markus, Hazel Rose, and Shinobu Kitayama. 1991. "Culture and the Self: Implications for Cognition, Emotion, and Motivation." *American Psychological Association* 98 (2): 224–53.

―――. 1994. "The Cultural Construction of Self and Emotion: Implications for Social Behavior." In *Emotion and Culture: Empirical Studies of Mutual*

Influence, edited by S. Kitayama and Hazel Rose Markus, 89–130. Washington, D.C.: American Psychological Association.

Mosel, James N. 1959. "Thai Administrative Behavior." In *Toward the Comparative Study of Public Administration*, edited by W. J. Siffin, 278–331. Bloomington, IN: Indiana University Press.

Mulder, Niels. 2000. *Inside Thai Society: Religion - Everyday Life - Change*. Chiang Mai, Thailand: Silkworm Books.

Natthawuth Jinagool. 1995. *Khrong Sang Amnat Lae Rabop Uppatham Nai Chonnabot Thai: Sueksa Koroni Ban Ta Amphoe Bang Ban Changwat Phra Nakhon Si Ayutthaya* (Power Structure and Patronage System: A Case Study in Ta Village Bangban District Phra Nakhon Si Ayutthaya Province). Master's thesis, Chulalongkorn University, Bangkok.

Parsons, Talcott. 1967. *Sociological Theory and Modern Society*. New York: The Free Press.

Persons, Larry S. 2008. "Face Dynamics, Social Power and Virtue among Thai Leaders: A Cultural Analysis." PhD diss., Fuller Theological Seminary, Pasadena, CA.

Phillips, Herbert P. 1965. *Thai Peasant Personality: The Patterning of Interpersonal Behaviour in the Village of Bang Chan*. Berkeley, CA: University of California Press.

———. 1969. "The Scope and Limits of the 'Loose Structure' Concept." In *Loosely Structured Social Systems: Thailand in Comparative Perspective*, edited by H.-D. Evers, 25–38. New Haven, CT: Yale University Southeast Asian Studies.

Rubin, Herbert J. 1979. "Will and Awe: Illustrations of Thai Villager Dependency upon Officials." In *Modern Thai Politics: From Village to Nation*, edited by C. D. Neher, 219–49. Cambridge, MA: Schenkman Publishing.

———. 1980. "Rules, Regulations, and the Rural Thai Bureaucracy." *Journal of Southeast Asian Studies* 11 (1): 50–73.

Shuster, Marguerite. 1987. *Power, Pathology, Paradox: The Dynamics of Evil and Good*. Grand Rapids, MI: Academie Books.

Siffin, William J. 1966. *The Thai Bureaucracy: Institutional Change and Development*. Honolulu, HI: East-West Center Press University of Hawaii.

Simmel, Georg. 1906. "The Sociology of Secrecy and of Secret Societies." *American Journal of Sociology* 11: 441–98.

Snit Smuckarn. 1975. *"Rueang Na Khong Khon Thai: Wikhro Tam Naeokhwamkhit Thang Manusiyawithayaphasasat"* (Concerning the Face of Thai People: Analysis According to the Anthropological Linguistics Approach). *Thai Journal of Development Administration* 15 (4): 492–505.

Stewart, Frank Henderson. 1994. *Honor*. Chicago: University of Chicago Press.

Sukhumbhand Paribatra, 2003. "Some Reflections on the Thai Monarchy." In *Southeast Asian Affairs,* 291–309. Singapore: Institute of Southeast Asian Studies.

Suntaree Komin. 1990. *Psychology of the Thai People: Values and Behavioral Patterns.* Bangkok: National Institute of Development Administration (NIDA).

————. 1999. "The Thai Concept of Effective Leadership." In *Management and Cultural Values: The Indigenization of Organizations in Asia*, edited by D. S. Henry, S. R. Kao, and Bernhard Wilpert, 265–86. New Dehli: Sage Publications.

Tanin Kraivixien. 2005. *Khunatham Lae Chariyatham Khong Phu Borihan (*The Virtue and Ethics of a Manager). Bangkok: Office of the Thai Bar for the Training and Study of Law (Under Royal Patronage).

Thirayuth Boonmi. 1999. *Saksi-Nata.* In *Kham: Rong Roi Khwam Khit Khwam Chuea Thai (Words: Vestiges of Thai Thought and Belief)*, edited by Suwanna Satha-Anand and N. Bunyanet, 265–78. Bangkok: Chulalongkorn University Press.

Ukosakul, Margaret. 1999. "Conceptual Metaphors Motivating the Use of Thai 'Face'." Master's thesis., Payap University, Chiang Mai, Thailand.

————. 2003. "Conceptual Metaphors Motivating the Use of Thai 'Face'." In *Cognitive Linguistics and Non-Indo-European Languages*, edited by E. H. Casad and G. B. Palmer, 275–303. Berlin: Mouton de Gruyter.

Ukosakul, Chaiyun. *See* Chaiyun Ukosakul.

Volf, Miroslav. 1996. *Exclusion and Embrace: A Theological Exploration of Identity, Otherness, and Reconciliation.* Nashville, TN: Abingdon Press.

Wales, H. G. Quaritch. 1934. *Ancient Siamese Government and Administration.* London: Bernard Quartich.

Weber, Max. 1962. *Basic Concepts in Sociology.* Translated by H. P. Secher. New York: Citadel Press.

Wurmser, Leon. 1994. *The Mask of Shame.* Northvale, NJ: J. Aronson.

Zehner, Edward. 1991. "Merit, Man and Ministry: Traditional Thai Hierarchies in a Contemporary Church." *Social Compass* 38 (2): 155–75.

INDEX